A DEATH IN THE RAINFOREST

ALSO BY DON KULICK

A Grammar and Dictionary of Tayap: The Life and Death of a Papuan Language (with Angela Terrill)

Loneliness and Its Opposite: Sex, Disability, and the Ethics of Engagement (with Jens Rydström)

Fat: The Anthropology of an Obsession (edited with Anne Meneley)

Language and Sexuality (with Deborah Cameron)

Travesti: Sex, Gender, and Culture among Brazilian Transgendered Prostitutes

Language Shift and Cultural Reproduction: Socialization, Self, and Syncretism in a Papua New Guinean Village

A DEATH IN THE RAINFOREST

How a Language and a Way of Life
Came to an End in Papua New Guinea

DON KULICK

ALGONQUIN BOOKS OF CHAPEL HILL 2019

Published by
ALGONQUIN BOOKS OF CHAPEL HILL
Post Office Box 2225
Chapel Hill, North Carolina 27515-2225

a division of
WORKMAN PUBLISHING
225 Varick Street
New York, New York 10014

Library of Congress Cataloging-in-Publication Data

Names: Kulick, Don, author.
Title: A death in the rainforest : how a language and a way of life came
    to an end in Papua New Guinea / by Don Kulick.
Description: First edition. | Chapel Hill, North Carolina : Algonquin
    Books of Chapel Hill, 2019.
Identifiers: LCCN 2018047044 | ISBN 9781616209049 (hardcover :
    alk. paper)
Subjects: LCSH: Ethnology—Papua New Guinea—Gapun. | Language
    and culture—Papua New Guinea—Gapun. | Taiap language. |
    Linguistic change—Papua New Guinea—Gapun. | Social change—
    Papua New Guinea—Gapun.
Classification: LCC GN671.N5 K845 2019 | DDC 305.8009957/5—dc23
LC record available at https://lccn.loc.gov/2018047044

10 9 8 7 6 5 4 3 2 1
First Edition

CONTENTS

FOREWORD

FOR OVER THIRTY years I visited a small village deep inside the rainforest of Papua New Guinea—a country that lies not in Africa, as people often believe, but in the Pacific Ocean, just north of Australia—to discover how a language dies. The village I came to know during the course of those years is called Gapun. The people who live there all used to speak a unique language that they call Tayap. For all we know, Tayap may be as old as Greek, Chinese, or Latin. But the coming decades will see Tayap die: currently, the language has fewer than fifty active speakers. Soon, all that will be heard of Tayap ever again are the recordings that I have made over the years. They will linger on like ectoplasm, long after the speakers are gone and the language is forgotten.

I first went to Gapun as a graduate student in anthropology in the mid-1980s, and I spent over a year living there then. I wrote a book about what I discovered. It is a good book, a solid study still well worth reading. But it is an academic book, aimed at professional anthropologists and linguists, and university students. Its eye-numbing title, *Language Shift and Cultural Reproduction*—which I attribute to an unhappy combination of eager youthful ambition to appear scholarly, and terrible editorial advice—says it all.

This time I am writing from hindsight. A different kind of book: one that tells a story about what has happened in Gapun in the years since I first visited, and about how the Tayap language is fizzling inexorably to its end.

But this book also tells the story of my work in the village, and why that, too, has come to an end.

Both endings are bound up with violence. On the one hand, there is the material and symbolic violence that the coming of white men to Papua New Guinea has wrought on the people there, their cultures, and their languages. On the other hand, there are local acts of violence, perpetrated by villagers themselves and their neighbors, that harm the villagers, and that have harmed or threatened to harm me too. All these forms of violence course like subterranean flows of magma that occasionally gush up and burst through the surface of the stories I tell here. Those stories are about what it is like to live in a difficult-to-get-to village of two hundred people, carved out like a cleft in a swamp in the middle of a tropical rainforest. They are stories about what the people who live in that village eat for breakfast and how they sleep. They are stories about how villagers discipline their children, how they joke with one another, and how they swear at one another. They are stories about how villagers romance one another, how they worship, how they argue, how they die—and also how they made sense of a white anthropologist who appeared one day out of nowhere, saying he was interested in their language and asking their leave to stick around for a while.

A "while" that ended up extending over three decades.

Can one speak for another? Since I wrote my first book about Gapun twenty-five years ago, a sometimes rancorous discussion has erupted both inside the academy and outside it, about the legitimacy of writing about a group of people to whom one as a researcher does not, oneself, belong. Long gone are the magisterial days of departed anthropologists like Margaret Mead, whose attitude about the people she worked with was neatly summed up in an article she published in 1939 in the professional journal *American Anthropologist*. Mead wrote in response to one of her colleague's claims that for anthropological work to be believable, anthropologists needed to learn the languages spoken by the people among whom they did fieldwork.

Margaret Mead thought that earnest counsel like that was nonsense. She waved it away like an irritating housefly. All the fuss about learning native languages was intimidating to anthropology students and just plain wrongheaded. It wasn't necessary.

To do their job, Mead insisted, anthropologists don't need to "know" a language. They just need to "use" a language. And to "use" a language requires only three things.

First of all, you need to be able to ask questions in order to "get an answer with the smallest amount of dickering." (What you were supposed to make of those answers if you didn't speak the language in which they were delivered was not something that Mead seemingly bothered herself about.)

The second thing Mead thought that an anthropologist needed to use a language for is to establish rapport ("Especially in the houses of strangers, where one wishes the maximum non-interference with one's note taking and photography").

The final thing you need to use a language to do—this is my

favorite—is to give instructions. Invoking an era when natives knew their place and didn't dare mess with bossy anthropologists, Mead offered this crisp advice: "If the ethnologist cannot give quick and accurate instructions to his native servants, informants and assistants, cannot tell them to find the short lens for the Leica, its position accurately described, to put the tripod down-sun from the place where the ceremony is to take place, to get a fresh razor blade and the potassium permanganate crystals and bring them quickly in case of snake bite [wouldn't you love to know how she barked that in Samoan?], to boil and filter the water which is to be used for mixing a developer,—he will waste an enormous amount of time and energy doing mechanical tasks which he could have delegated if his tongue had been just a little bit better schooled." [1]

Since Mead's time (she died in 1978), and partly in response to the imperious hubris with which she and other anthropologists of her era presented the people they wrote about, scholars—as well as some of the women and men who provided anthropologists with the material about which they wrote—have raised the thorny issue of "speaking for" others. Can one do it? Should one?

I am a white American/European middle-class male professor writing about largely moneyless (which is not the same as "poor") black villagers who live in a backwater swamp in a faraway Oceanic country. The immense differences between me and the people whose lives I describe here mean that all the triggers are present from the outset. The ground is strewn with easily visible mines.

Like most card-carrying anthropologists, however, I remain committed to the spirit of Margaret Mead's conviction that we

---

1. Margaret Mead, "Native Languages as Field-Work Tools," *American Anthropologist* 41, no. 2 (April–June 1939): 189–205.

not only can, but we should—indeed, we have a responsibility to—engage with and represent people who are very unlike ourselves. If anthropology as a way of approaching the world has a single message, it is that we learn from difference. Difference enriches. It disquiets, it expands, it amplifies, it transforms. Engaging with difference respectfully always necessarily entails risks: political and epistemological risks (you might get it all wrong), representational risks (how do you describe people—including their idiosyncrasies or shortcomings—in a dignified manner without being patronizing, hagiographic, or sentimental?), and personal risks (encounters with difference are frequently transformative in unpredictable and sometimes even undesired ways. Plus, you incur responsibilities and long-term, often unrequitable debts).

Those are all serious risks. They need to be acknowledged, embraced, and constantly kept in mind. But considering the alternative of not engaging with difference—of ignoring it, refusing it, shying away from it, or denying it—the question is whether the higher risk is not taking those risks at all.

Besides, rather than "speak for" the villagers I write about, this book "engages with" them. The book is about what it is like to work as an anthropologist in a Papua New Guinean rainforest, living among a group of people who continually reminded me, regardless of whatever views I or anyone else may entertain about the matter, that I was not so different from them at all. My white skin and white privilege, for the villagers, were not primarily a symbol of difference. On the contrary, the fact that I appeared among them at all was a sign that I in reality was one of them, and throughout my stays with them, they drew me inexorably into their circuits of exchange, responsibility, and accountability.

This book is one way I have attempted to extend that exchange, fulfill that responsibility, and make myself accountable. My hope is that the story I tell here provides not just an explanation but also a *sense* of how it is that the particular fate I describe has befallen the Tayap language and Gapun: to these specific people, at this specific time, in this specific place.

I also hope that the book conveys something of the curiosity and delight—as well as of the frustration, anxiety, and, occasionally, the sheer terror—that I experienced during my stays in the village during the years I kept returning. When anthropologists write about their work, they tend to accentuate the positive and airbrush out the most difficult aspects of living for a long time with people whom they have, in effect, gate-crashed on and set up shop among.

This book is different.

1: THE AIR WE BREATHE

"ALL YOU HAVE to do is fill in this form and the company will come in and start taking your air," the fat wannabe-corrupt politician explained to the villagers. He was sitting on the floor of a men's house: a large open-air structure on stilts, made out of bark and thatched with sago palm leaves.

The wannabe-corrupt politician, who was visiting from a neighboring village, was a balding man in his midforties. He had run several times for a seat in the provincial parliament, but he always lost to someone else who came to the area right before the election and promised to give people more money and outboard motors than Mr. Wannabe had thought to promise them. The victor proceeded to engorge his own bank account from the access he gained, by winning the election, to government and NGO money earmarked for development—and was never heard from again.

Mr. Wannabe's ambition was to be a politician like that, and he was convinced that one day, he would succeed. In the meantime, he buttered up the corrupt politicians who did win a seat in the provincial elections, and he set his sights on more local forms of expropriation. His ample paunch testified to years of successfully coaxing money out of villagers for schemes he'd convinced them would bring change. The only change they ever saw was that they had less money after his visits than they had before he came. That the promised changes somehow never materialized was always blamed on someone else: a corrupt politician lied, somebody stole the money, a sorcerer bewitched it and made it disappear.

Sitting in the men's house, scratching his back against a corner post, Mr. Wannabe was sweating profusely. This wasn't because he was nervous. He had been in this men's house many times before and he knew how to sweet-talk the villagers. He was sweating because he was fat and the late afternoon sun was hot. He was also sweating because his mouth was stuffed full of betel nut, which stimulates, like caffeine, and it makes you perspire. It also turns your mouth scarlet red and your teeth rust-black.

The villagers who had come to the meeting didn't say much. They just listened as the man—Onjani (whom they called Big Belly behind his back) told them why he had come.

The twenty or so village men scattered throughout the men's house sat like Big Belly, cross-legged on the floor. They grouped themselves in small half-circle clusters, and they were also chewing betel nut, occasionally leaning forward to bend over at the waist and eject a well-aimed stream of blood-colored spittle through the cracks in the bark floor. Women sat spread out on the porches of houses within hearing distance. They were chewing betel nut, too, listening to the talk in the men's house with one ear and keeping the other tuned in to the cutting comments that their neighbors muttered below their breath as Onjani spoke.

"I'm here to make awareness," Onjani announced, speaking in Tok Pisin, the national language of Papua New Guinea—and using a new word, *ewenes*, that he had picked up in one of the NGO-, or church-, or government-sponsored courses that he constantly let it be known he attended in the faraway provincial capital, which only a few villagers had ever visited. He had just come back from the capital, he said. And there, he had participated in a three-day course on something else new, something called carbon trade.

Onjani told the villagers that they ought to know that carbon trade had become a big thing in "the countries" (*ol kantri*)—by which he meant every place in the world outside Papua New Guinea. The countries, he said, were running out of air. The factories that covered practically every inch of ground there had used up all the air. There were no more trees. And trees, Onjani reminded everybody, make air. Without trees, there would be no air. People in the countries were finding it increasingly hard to breathe.

Papua New Guinea, on the other hand, was full of trees. Onjani leaned forward over his crossed legs and dribbled red spit through a crack in the floor. He wiped his mouth with the back of his hand, spreading a crimson stain across his chin. He swept his arm outwards, gesturing towards the rainforest that surrounded everyone. "Look around you," he said. "All you see are trees. Papua New Guinea is full of trees. We have an overflow (*obaplo*) of air."

Perceiving this abundance, the countries had sent their emissaries to Papua New Guinea in search of air. The Papua New Guinean government took pity on the countries, Onjani told the villagers, and it had cut a deal. A government-approved company would transport massive gas tanks into the rainforest and pump them full of air. The full tanks would then be shipped to the countries, where the air they contained would be bottled and sold in stores. This, he explained, was carbon trade.

"There you get air according to how much you can pay." Onjani smiled, letting the villagers glimpse his superior knowledge of how things work in the countries. "If you don't have a lot of money, you can't get a lot of air, and you'll get short-winded in a hurry."

The reason why any of this was of concern to villagers who lived in a backwater swamp was because the pristine rainforest that was their ancestral land was a prime candidate for the air-extracting gas tanks. This was an opportunity, Onjani kept repeating—the villagers' moment had arrived. Carbon trade would earn them mountains of money. Onjani didn't know exactly how many thousand million kina (Papua New Guinea's currency) they would receive, but it was sure to be a substantial amount. Plus, the company would bring development into the village. It would need to cut down a lot of trees (the gas tanks, after all, were big and they needed space), and the villagers would be prohibited from hunting game or making gardens on their land. But they wouldn't need to hunt or grow food anymore—the company would give them untold amounts of money, plus a highway and an airstrip. It would build them houses made of corrugated iron and cement, and trade stores, and a tourist center. It would build them a university.

All the villagers needed to do was to sign the form that Onjani had unfolded from his net bag and laid out on the floor in front of him. The form was typewritten in English, a language that no villager commands. The fine print specified that 100 percent of the income from the carbon-trade deal would go to a company called Pacific Carbon Trade Limited. The company was owned by Onjani and three other men from his village. Those small details were not mentioned by Big Belly at any point during the meeting. He just exhorted the villagers to sign if they wanted to change.

And how they wanted to change! If there is a single topic besides sorcery that occupies the villagers' conversations and their minds, it is change. They desperately want to change. But villagers don't just want to change—they want to change *into* something else. They want to change, I gradually discovered, from black people (like Australian aborigines, most Papua New Guineans have black skin) into white people.

I AM A white person. I was born and raised in the United States, but I moved to Sweden when I was nineteen years old and have lived there since then. I was a twenty-four-year-old doctoral student when I first arrived in Papua New Guinea in 1985, eager, wide-eyed, and comically inexperienced. I knew very little about Papua New Guinea and I knew absolutely nothing about life in a tropical rainforest. But I traveled halfway around the globe to Papua New Guinea because I had decided that I wanted to study how a language dies.

Papua New Guinea has more languages than any other country in the world. In an area the size of the state of California, and with just over eight million people, there are almost one thousand separate languages—nota bene, separate *languages*, not just separate dialects or variants—most of them still undocumented and many of them spoken by groups of five hundred people or fewer.

I had been directed to the village by an Australian linguist named Don Laycock. Laycock was an expansive, hard-drinking man of modest hygienic inclination. In the early 1970s, he had traveled the entire lower Sepik region of northern Papua New Guinea by dugout canoe, gathering word lists from speakers of the many languages spoken throughout that area in order to map them and try to classify them.

From two men he met in a village near the mouth of the mighty Sepik River, Laycock learned that deep in the rainforest lay a single village where a small group of people spoke a language that appeared to be unrelated to any other. The village was called Gapun. Laycock never visited Gapun himself; it was too hard to get to. In fact, before my own trip, only about ten white people had ever visited the village. A few Australian patrol officers and a couple of German missionaries passed through Gapun in the 1930s and in the decades following the Second World War. All of them remarked on how difficult it was to get to the village, and few of them ever went back. The other white people who made it to Gapun consisted mostly of a few Catholic priests who, starting in the late 1940s, also usually made the journey only once. They typically came to the village, said a quick Mass, baptized a few babies, and left, never to return. Only one sturdy old nun based in the Catholic mission station at Marienberg—an eight-hour journey by canoe—persisted in coming, and for decades she arrived in the village once or twice a year on medical patrol. She would stay for one night, setting up a little clinic from which she dispensed chloroquine pills for malaria, squeezed boils, and gave antibiotic injections to anyone who looked in need of one.

When I visited the Australian National University in Canberra on my way to Papua New Guinea and knocked on professor Laycock's office door seeking advice about where I might do my doctoral research on language death, he suggested that I go to Gapun. He didn't know anything about the village or what might be happening there, he said, but he remembered hearing that the language was minuscule. "It's so small that something has to be happening to it," he reasoned. "Why don't you go and see what."

I followed that advice and found my way to Gapun. The first time I went, in 1985, I stayed for a month, to see whether I could manage to live there for longer.

Of course the Gapun villagers were perplexed that a strange white man should arrive out of nowhere one afternoon and announce in broken Tok Pisin—the language that the villagers are switching to—that he wanted to live with them and write a book about their language. The only books they had ever encountered were the Bible and the notebooks that Australian patrol officers used to carry with them before Papua New Guinea gained independence in 1975. One villager had heard a story about the existence of mysterious objects called comic books. All those books, the villagers were convinced, had magical power to bring forth the money, airplanes, outboard motors, and other cargo that white people had but Papua New Guineans like themselves didn't.

That a young white man now suddenly appeared to them talking about a book was intriguing; it was promising. But why in the world had I come to them? Why had I come to Gapun and not some other village?

The villagers pondered this question among themselves and quickly arrived at a conclusion. A few weeks after I arrived, they shared their conclusion with me, revealing the *real* reason for my coming. I was a dead villager, they informed me, returned to Gapun to lead them down the "road" to change.

The moment they chose to impart this information was far from ideal: It was at night in the middle of a violent thunderstorm. Rain was spattering down hard on the thatch of the house where I was sitting on the floor together with an unknown number of people. The only light available was the orange glow of the hand-rolled-newspaper cigarettes the villagers all smoke, which bobbed around in the blackness like disembodied eyes. Occasionally, lightning struck, momentarily freezing everyone into a bloodless bluish tableau. The whole scene had me on edge; it brought to mind the climax of any number of cheap and gruesome horror films that I had watched late at night growing up. And now, during just such a scene, which always ended with a piercing shriek, I found myself in the thick of a tropical rainforest, in the middle of the night, with no way of getting out, surrounded by people whose grandparents had cut off other people's heads as trophies, being told knowingly that I was dead.

I had to stifle a piercing shriek.

Despite being told that I was a ghost, though, and despite almost everything else about the village—the omnipresent mud; the clouds of mosquitos (the villagers have names for eight different species); the scabies-riddled, hairless, blue-skinned village dogs that I occasionally observed cooling themselves by bathing in the shallow wells from which villagers fetched the water they used for drinking and cooking; and the local food, which consists almost entirely of a kind of glutinous starch that, prepared in the way villagers like it best, is pink and has the consistency of thick mucus—I decided at the end of the month that I would come back to Gapun.

The language situation was just as intriguing as Don Laycock had suggested it might be. As far as I was able to tell, no child under ten seemed to speak the village's indigenous language, Tayap. They all seemed to understand it, but none of the children ever spoke it. Instead, all their speech was in the national language, Tok Pisin. I realized that this was a key moment unlike any other that had been described by researchers who studied language death. Those other studies tended to focus on the last speakers of dying languages—they examined languages that were in their terminal stages, documenting them right before they gave up the ghost and were gone forever. In Gapun, I would be able to look at the beginning of the process of shift. Villagers were raising the first generation of kids who, for some reason—for the first time in the language's history—suddenly were not learning Tayap as their first language.

Even more compelling was the villagers' explanation for this sudden tip. When I asked them why their children weren't speaking Tayap, mothers and fathers all insisted that they wanted their children to speak it—and that they were raising their children exactly like their parents had raised them. What had changed, though, those parents told me, was the kids themselves. The children no longer wanted to learn Tayap. They were too bigheaded, adults told me, meaning that their kids were too willful and stubborn to speak the language. A mystery congealed: *The Case of the Bigheaded Babies.*

I also decided to return to Gapun because I liked the just over a hundred people who lived there—I found them hospitable, intriguing, and funny. When they weren't making me anxious with tales of me being dead, they made me laugh.

Besides, it was clear that the villagers wanted me to return. By the end of my initial monthlong stay, they promised to build me a house, where, they assured me, I would be able to store my belongings without having to worry about things disappearing into the palms of thoughtless children or covetous visitors. And right before I left, the old, knowledgeable men—referred to as "big men" (*ol bikman* in Tok Pisin; *munjenum suman* in Tayap)—dressed me up in feathers and boars' tusks, and they instructed me to drink bespelled water they poured onto a taro leaf. The magic water, they explained, would loosen my tongue and make me speak Tayap, which I had died too young to acquire the last time around.

On the same occasion, the men announced that they were bestowing on me a Tayap name. It wasn't the one I'd had in my previous incarnation. Then I had been called Kunji, and I'd passed away when I was only a few months old. The new name the big men decided to confer on reincarnated me was an august one—it was the name of one of the village's founding ancestors.

The name was Saraki. I liked it. Its sinuous beginning, interrupted by the sudden guttural stop that glided down the slope of a careening, excited vowel reminded me of something that J.R.R. Tolkien might have dreamed up for a not entirely benevolent elf.

So the following year, I went back to Gapun. I spent fifteen months there, living in a large and accommodating house on stilts that the villagers built for me. I finished my PhD dissertation and wrote a book about what I had discovered about Tayap and why the language was dying.

Since then, I have returned five times, and all told, I have spent nearly three years living in Gapun.[1]

The villagers always thought of me as a ghost. I was a pretty useless and recalcitrant ghost because, despite all my years of coming and going, I never revealed the secrets about the road to

---

1. My visits to the village were as follows: 1985 (one month), 1986–1987 (fifteen months), 1991 (two months), 2006 (six weeks), 2009 (nine months), 2010 (one month), and 2014 (two and a half months).

change that the villagers were all certain I possessed. That didn't stop them from carefully observing my behavior, though, and weighing my words, in the hope that I might slip up one day and let the cat out of the bag. They believe that when they find the "road" that I had access to—or when they die, whichever comes first—their black skin will crack open like a crab's shell and they will step out soft and white and rich. Because with white skin will come immediate access to all the money and all the goods that white people have.

After "Big Belly" Onjani was fed and left Gapun later to return home to his own village, two hours away by foot, the villagers quietly debated what he had said. The women were derisive. "What will happen to us when the company comes and takes all our air?" they wanted to know. Onjani's declaration that Papua New Guinea had an overflow of air didn't reassure them. "What will happen to the pigs in the rainforest when all our air is gone?" they asked. "What will happen to our sago palms? Our banana gardens, our taro, our tobacco?" "What air will our children breathe?"

The men granted that those perhaps were not nontrivial concerns, but they were more conciliatory. A thousand million kina was an awful lot of money. A highway and an airstrip too. A university even. They knew that Onjani was a conniving blowhard who had cheated them out of money many times before, but they didn't want to dismiss his proposal out of hand. It was true that none of the men could understand the form he'd given them, saying that he would return the following week to collect it with all the villagers' signatures. But it *was* a form. It had been typed on a machine and printed out. It looked official. They asked me to read it and explain it to them. I translated the words on the paper and told them that Onjani was trying to cheat them again. They responded the way they always did whenever I tried to talk them out of a con: they ignored me.

By the time of Onjani's visit to Gapun's men's house, in mid-2009, I had lived in the village for long enough to accept that my views on matters like carbon trade mattered very little. While the villagers respected that I had more firsthand experience of the countries than any of them did, the fact that I didn't actually seem to be doing much to open the road to the kind of change they all awaited seemed to prime them to disregard my objections to schemes like Onjani's. As far as I was ever able to tell, they thought I was ignorant about the sought-after "road." When I first started visiting Gapun, my ignorance was attributed to my youth, to the fact that the big men in my country hadn't yet revealed all the relevant secrets to me.

I think that during my later visits, the villagers just concluded I was thick.

Or that I was being slyly obstructionist. In either case, they had slotted me firmly into their already well-established understandings of the world around them, and my protestations that much of what they believed about life in the countries was not quite accurate were gently dismissed and subsequently forgotten. My insistence that most people in the countries actually had to work to receive money, that there were poor people there, or that white people sometimes actually walked (as opposed to being driven everywhere in chauffeured cars) was always met with blank stares.

On the other hand, my stories about things like subways were enthusiastically embraced and recounted to anyone who would listen: Villagers smiled knowingly when I talked about underground tunnels; they already knew all about them. Tunnels that ran beneath local graveyards were how dead Papua New Guineans traveled to Rome and turned white. My descriptions of big cars zipping through tunnels deep underground confirmed things the villagers already had figured out themselves—things they had made sense of by parsing rumors spread by people from other villages who claimed to know, by carefully sifting through stories told by the odd priest who spent a night in the village once every few years—and by trying to make sense of the drawings and photographs in the few old Australian schoolbooks from the primary school that existed for just over a decade in a neighboring village.

Such was the enduring tenor of my relationship with the villagers: I listened to everything they said, recording much of it and transcribing it word for word into big, lined notebooks.

That relationship wasn't exactly reciprocal. To me, they listened more selectively.

2: A VILLAGE IN THE SWAMP

WHEN DON LAYCOCK suggested that I go to Gapun, I couldn't locate the village on any map, but it wasn't as though I had to find it by setting off into the rainforest in a pith helmet, bearing a compass and a topographical chart.

Gapun was (and remains) very much off the beaten path, and it can take up to three days to get there from Wewak, the capital of the East Sepik Province where the village is located, or from the town of Madang, the capital of the neighboring province of the same name. But many people who live within about a thirty mile radius of the village know approximately where it is, and a few who own outboard motors can lead you at least as far as the massive mangrove lagoon just off the mouth of the Sepik River, which you have to pass through to get to Gapun. Once inside the lagoon, things get tricky because then you have to know where to look between the closely packed mangrove trees for the opening to a shallow, winding creek that cuts into the rainforest. After about a half-hour canoe ride up that creek, you reach the end of line. You disembark from the canoe, gird your loins, and proceed to make your way through a swamp for another hour.

To find Gapun the first time, I traveled to Wewak. In Australia, I had been given the name of an Aussie man in Wewak who was married to a Papua New Guinean woman. That man kindly arranged for his brother-in-law to take me as far as a Sepik River village called Taway, where I was able to hire an outboard-motor-driven canoe that would take me to Gapun. The two men I hired to guide me to Gapun knew their way to the village because they had a distant relative who had married a Gapun woman. They had gone to Gapun once to visit him.

We left Taway just after sunrise and arrived in Gapun in the late afternoon. By the time we got to the village, I was exhausted from the grueling trek through the swamp and in a kind of stuporous daze from hunger and disorientation. My two guides parked me in the open-air men's house and sent a child to find their relative.

At that point, I had been in Papua New Guinea for only about two weeks, and my command of Tok Pisin was minimal. All I could say to the curious villagers who arrived to look at me was no, I was not a priest, which was the first question they all asked. I hung dully in the background while my guides presented the villagers with some sort of explanation of who I was, what I had come for, and that I would like to stay. This story was told first to the men and women who had begun to cluster in and around the men's house, and it was carefully repeated to the relative of my guides when he emerged. This relative of theirs, my guides had decided, would look after me during my stay in Gapun.

THE VILLAGE THAT Don Laycock had never visited and didn't know anything about turned out to be a tiny windless slit in the rainforest. It was surrounded on all sides by massive trees rooted in a vast, seemingly boundless swamp. Having just sloshed my way through a gloppy, sucking, fetid stretch of that swamp to get to the village, I learned the hard way that the romantic image that many people have of rainforests is—to put it diplomatically—misguided.

Rainforests used to be called jungles. I don't know when exactly it suddenly became politically correct to say "rainforest" instead of "jungle." But I do know that the rawness and threat evoked by the word "jungle" does a much better job of covering the experience of encountering such an environment.

Rainforests sound idyllic. They are the lungs of the planet, we are frequently informed. That purifying metaphor evokes fresh air, pretty flowers, flitting butterflies, and gentle, beaming indigenous peoples who live in happy harmony with their lush, fertile surroundings.

Jungles, on the other hand, are not friendly places. Jungles conjure up images of impenetrable vegetation and venomous snakes; of shrunken heads and cannibals; of frenzied schools of piranhas stripping the flesh off a buffalo in minutes; and of waves of army ants that envelop any living thing in their path like tar and snip it to agonizing death with tens of thousands of minuscule scissorlike mandibles.

Jungles are places where people get swallowed up by quicksand and eaten by crocodiles. Rainforests are places where people commune with nature and become one with the biosphere.

The area in which Gapun lies is much more jungle than rainforest. There are plagues of mosquitos, there are crocodiles, there are black leeches that inchworm their way up into your eyes, and there are extremely venomous snakes (called, appropriately, death adders). Everywhere you turn, there are trees with needlelike spines, and hanging and creeping vines with serrated spikes that can trip you or gash your face or skin as you walk by. And there is mud, an endless expanse of mud. Mud that obscures the sharp, thorny, barbed, jagged, and sometimes poisonous critters and debris that lurk just below its surface, and that you can slip on—to fall on top of a crocodile or a death adder, or smack into a tree with needlelike spines or across a tangle of vines armored with serrated spikes.

And there is also the heat, and the oppressive, relentless, throbbing, exhausting humidity that seems to yank sweat from every pore of your body, including parts where you didn't even know you had pores.

THIS WAS THE milieu I found myself in, seated on the bark floor of the village's men's house like a lady riding sidesaddle, with my feet tucked up to the right side of my bottom, leaning slightly forward on my left hand. (Despite habitually sitting on floors during subsequent years in the village, I never managed to master the art of comfortably sitting cross-legged.) I took in the sounds around me: the shrill buzz of cicadas, the occasional squawking of parrots, and the monkey-like screeching of a colony of flying fox bats that nested upside down during the day in a gargantuan fig tree that stood just beyond the village. Occasionally, a faint gust of the bats' acrid, urine-soaked scent—burnt rubber with an undertone of dirty socks—wafted towards the men's house. It momentarily cut through the thick, overripe smell of tropical fecundity that weighed the air down like a soggy overcoat.

The villagers who streamed towards the house to get a look at the white newcomer all had neat, round helmets of fuzzy black hair and teeth that were red or black. The betel nut they all chewed gave off a faintly minty tang, and the villagers themselves smelled of fresh, clean, pleasantly pungent sweat. Children up to about age seven were naked; older boys and men wore cloth shorts in varying degrees of tatter. Women, who weren't allowed to climb up into the men's house but who were free to stand on the ground below and rest their elbows on the open-air house's elevated floor, were mostly bare breasted, a length of cloth wrapped loosely around their waists. No one wore shoes, and one of the first things I noticed about the villagers was the enormous size of their feet. They were broad and flat and commanding. They tapered off into thick flexible toes that seemed able to spread out and grip things. They were utterly unlike my own narrow extremities with their dainty compressed digits. Glancing down, I felt like a Chinese courtesan whose feet had been bound.

Most villagers (like most mainland Papua New Guineans) are short, less than five feet tall, and many of them are closer to four feet. Astonishingly, I noticed this diminutiveness only after I left the village and developed my photographs (remember, my first visit was in the mid-1980s, a primitive time of sending film to photo labs and waiting for the pictures to be sent back to you printed on paper). When I saw the photos I had taught a few young men how to take of me, I couldn't believe that most of the villagers reached only about up to my chest. My impression had been that the villagers towered over me. Granted, most of time I spent with villagers was spent sitting with them on the floor, me leaning forward in my awkward sidesaddle pose, thereby mitigating, I suppose, the difference in height that would have been more apparent if I had stood up. But I did stand up occasionally, to walk around in the rainforest with villagers and to move from house to house during visits. The pictures proved that I had stood next to them. Without noticing any discrepancy in height. I concluded that regardless of their actual physical size, the villagers did tower over me, in my psyche at least, in terms of their superior knowledge of the rainforest and in terms of my utter dependency on them to survive there.

GAPUN VILLAGE ITSELF was a hodgepodge of about twenty small houses arranged seemingly at random in the middle of a narrow clearing. The houses stood together in clusters that were separated from one another by coconut palms, slender betel palms, and crusty-barked trees that bore bunches of a waxy pink fruit called *laulau*s in Tok Pisin (Malay apples). The village area itself was free from grass and consisted mostly of mud. Unlovely, stiff-bristled black pigs wandered around snouting their way noisily through the mud, eagerly devouring any debris the villagers tossed their way. Compact, jackal-sized dogs (all of whom seemed to be covered in advanced stages of mange) hopped up into the men's house where I sat upon arriving and lay near the hearth. Whenever anyone noticed them, they were whacked with a stick. This caused them to yelp, jump up, and move a few feet away, only to move back to their original position when whomever they settled next to whacked them again a few minutes later.

Houses in the village were assembled out of bush material such as bamboo poles, vines, bark, and sago-palm leaves. They were all raised three and a half to five feet off the ground because the frequent rainstorms, which give the rainforest its name, habitually flooded the ground on which the village was built, turning it into a vast mucky pond. Some houses were walled with bamboo poles or with mats woven from split, flattened bamboo. But most were open-air structures with one or two short walls that acted as windbreakers around the hearth, which was set in the floor at one end of the house and was where most of the household's activities occurred.

The floors of the houses fascinated me. They were hard and flat, but perforated with long, thick cracks. I later discovered that the floors were made from a kind of palm tree that men prepared by first felling the palm, chopping it along the grain of the bark until it is thoroughly perforated, then making a deep cut down the length of the tree. The bark falls open and the inner pith is scraped away with a shovel. The remaining outer bark is rolled up like a carpet and carried back to the village, where it is unrolled onto runners that have been fastened with vines to supporting posts. An average house requires about nine rolls (five by eleven feet each) to make a floor.

The chops that the men make in the palm tree widen and harden as the bark dries, and these are what form the wide cracks that run the length of the floor. These cracks are handy when it comes to sweeping away scraps, and villagers always make sure to sit next to a good crack so that they can spit out the bitter red juice that accumulates in their mouth as they sit chewing betel nut. The cracks in the floor also make it easy to deal with the body waste of small children, and whenever a baby urinates or defecates on the floor, the resulting mess is splashed through a crack with a cup of water.

The insides of the houses all looked pretty much the same. None contained any furniture, although a few aluminum pots and cauldrons that women used to boil water and cook food were always strewn near the hearth. These pots were purchased with the money that villagers earned by spearing a crocodile and selling its skin or by growing cash crops like coffee or cocoa. These activities occasionally generate small amounts of money, but buyers from other places rarely find it profitable to make their way all the way to Gapun, and the villagers have no means of transporting what they grow to the buyers. Most of what the villagers grow to earn money ends up rotting on the vine or shriveling on the tree.

ALTHOUGH THE INTERNAL layout of village houses has changed somewhat since my first visit (since then, a few men who have learned that white people have rooms in their houses started dividing their houses into rooms too), the average house still consists of a single large room where all sorts of activities happen, often simultaneously. People sit eating sago, spitting betel juice, pouring water over a struggling baby, removing the midrib from tobacco leaves, shredding coconut, peeling taro, swatting a dog, rolling a cigarette, cleaning grit from their fingernails or from between their toes with the knife that they then nonchalantly use to cut up the taro they have just peeled—all that, in the same space where at the end of the day they rig up their mosquito nets, crowd onto sleeping mats with their children and go to sleep.

In addition to the houses where families live, there are men's houses. A men's house is what is left of villagers' traditional religious beliefs and political organization. Until World War II disrupted life irrevocably (in 1942 Japanese soldiers invaded northern Papua New Guinea and established bases there, one of them not far from Gapun), religious and political life in Gapun revolved around male cults. Those cults tended fearsome, bloodthirsty deities who were called forth whenever men played pairs of enormous bamboo flutes on the occasion of funerary feasts, the initiation of boys, and victory in battle. The worship of these deities—which was widespread throughout the region and is known in the anthropological literature by the Tok Pisin name as the cult of the *tambaran*—was linked to the never-ending warfare that wracked the area. It fueled the killing of enemies and the taking of heads, to feed the ravenous gods.

The *tambaran* cult also mandated a strict separation of the sexes, with women living in small houses together with their children, and men and initiated boys residing together in the men's houses. Women cooked food and sent it to the men and boys, and the men went off into the rainforest with their wives during the day to process sago flour and tend their gardens. But women were forbidden to enter a men's house, and when a men's house was sealed off with sago palm branches for the sacred flutes to be played there, women were ordered to avoid the area surrounding the house altogether, on pain of death.

A few years after World War II ended, Roman Catholic missionaries began making the trek to Gapun, and they quickly converted the villagers to Christianity. Worship of the *tambaran* ceased, for all intents and purposes, and the power of the men's houses withered. To this day, though, the *tambaran* deities have not been revealed to women, and the sacred flutes are still kept in the recesses of the rainforest and looked after by a few village men. The men's houses (at any one time, there will be two or three in the village) continue to retain an aura of taboo, and women are not allowed inside them.

Villagers built their first church in the 1950s. They erect a new one about every ten years when the old one collapses, devoured by termites and battered by tropical storms. I had passed the latest incarnation of the church on my way into Gapun when I arrived. It was on the outskirts of the village, the first building I saw when I emerged from the swamp. The church was the largest structure in the village, constructed to accommodate the over one hundred people who lived in Gapun at that time. It was the only building not elevated, which meant that on Sundays after particularly heavy rains, villagers weren't able to sit on the low benches they had fashioned. They had to spend the service standing—men on the right side of the church, women and children on the left—in stagnant pools of water.

A local man who was able to read said Mass each Sunday, and the villagers sang and prayed under the benevolent eye of a molding, bluish-tinged portrait of a once ivory-skinned Jesus that had been donated by a missionary who had visited the village at some point in the distant past.

Once I started living in Gapun, I dutifully attended church with the villagers. Each Sunday morning, a large slit-gong drum that stood in the middle of the village was thumped by the village prayer leader, summoning everybody to Mass. I followed the trickle of villagers as they slowly drifted from their houses to the muddy church, mothers carrying infants in their arms and toddlers on their shoulders; men, adolescents, and children picking their way around the inevitable puddles in groups of twos or threes. I sat or stood in the men's section in the back in respectful silence. Not a religious person myself, I at first regarded those

Sunday duties with irritation—as irksome interruptions to the work I had come to do. And truth be told, I never enjoyed the services, which consisted of leaden readings of Catholic liturgy punctuated with brief hymns sung in desultory tinny falsettos. Only gradually did I manage to peer through the fog of boredom and realize that the villagers' religious life was anything but irrelevant. On the contrary, it was absolutely central to understanding precisely what I was most interested in figuring out.

I was in Gapun to try to answer a specific question, namely: Why does a language die? It took me a long time to realize that that is the wrong question to ask. Or it is to ask a question that has an obvious answer: a language dies because people stop speaking it.

Of course, one could ask why people stop speaking a language, and that would be a bit more interesting. But when that question is asked by linguists, who are among the few people seriously concerned about language death (along with a few language activists who have discovered, usually too late, that their ancestral tongue is moribund, and brittle), the tenor of the question is always a disappointment, or a scold.

When a linguist or a language activist asks: "Why do speakers of a language stop speaking it?" what they usually really mean is: "Why have speakers of that language failed us? Why have they allowed an irreplaceable artifact, an invaluable jewel in the treasure chest of humanity, an exquisite creation that ought to have been preserved forever—or at least until we get around to documenting all its characteristic phonemes, its possibly unique morphology, and its undoubtedly idiosyncratic syntax—why have those poor shortsighted ingrates who should have known better, in spite of whatever prejudices they may have faced, maybe in spite, even, of the threat of genocide, why oh why didn't they understand how valuable their language is and teach it to their damn children?"

These days, many linguists who write about language death do so without even considering much the people who speak the languages. They are fond of likening endangered languages to endangered species: an obsolescent Uzbek language is compared to a threatened orchid; a dwindling Papuan language is like a California condor. At a time when we are all encouraged to concern ourselves with the environment and sustainability, many linguists seem to believe that the way to elicit sympathy and support for dying languages (whatever that might mean in practice) is to talk about them in terms of biodiversity and species loss.

There are certainly worse ways of thinking about languages than as fleshy flowers or rare birds. But a difficulty with comparing endangered languages to endangered species is that metaphors like those direct our attention to the natural world. The natural world, however, is precisely where we should *not* look in order to understand why languages die. After all, tender young orchids are not sent to schools where they are taught in a cosmopolitan language they've never heard, and where the only thing they end up learning is how misguided their traditional orchid ways are. California condors are not converted to Christianity and informed that their traditional condor way of life is Satanic.

To be fair, none of those things happen to languages either. But they do happen to people who speak the languages that linguists and language activists are concerned about.

By encouraging us to think in terms of ecosystems rather than political systems, comparisons of endangered languages to endangered species obscure the simple realization that *language death is anything but a natural phenomenon.* It is, on the contrary, a profoundly social phenomenon. Languages do not die because they exhaust themselves in the fullness of time or are killed off by predatory languages of greater phonological scope or syntactic richness. Languages die because people stop speaking them.

Rather than exploring why a language dies, I came to realize that the question I needed to ask, instead, was: *How* does a language die? I needed to discover what had to happen in a community, among speakers of a language, that resulted in parents ceasing to teach their language to their children. Where does language death start? How is it sustained? Does it have to involve a conscious decision on anyone's behalf? Can a language die without anybody really wanting it to?

BY MY ESTIMATE, Tayap will be stone-cold dead in fifty years' time. When I first arrived in Gapun, the language was spoken by about ninety people, out of a population of 130. Now, thirty years later, it has about forty-five speakers, out of a population of about two hundred. The village grows, the language shrinks.

As far back as anyone in Gapun has been able to remember, though, Tayap has never had more than, at most, about 150 speakers: the entire population of Tayap speakers, when the language was at its peak, would have fit into a single New York City subway car.

Tiny as that count is, such a small language was not unusual for Papua New Guinea. Most languages spoken in the country have fewer than three thousand speakers. And linguists estimate that about 35 percent of the languages (which means about 350 of them) have never had more than about five hundred speakers.

Contrary to received wisdom, and common sense, this constellation of tiny languages was not the result of isolation; it didn't arise because villages were separated from one another by mountain barriers or impenetrable jungle walls. Quite the opposite: throughout Papua New Guinea, the areas that have the highest degree of linguistic diversity (that is, the most languages) are the ones where people can get around relatively easily, by paddling a canoe along rivers and creeks, for example. The areas where travel is more difficult, for example in the mountains that run like a jagged spine across the center of the country, is where the largest languages are found (the biggest being a language called Enga, with over two hundred thousand speakers).

The conclusion that linguists have drawn from this counterintuitive distribution of languages is that people in Papua New Guinea have used language as a way of differentiating themselves from one another. Whereas other people throughout the world have come to use religion or food habits or clothing styles to distinguish themselves as a specific group of people in relation to outsiders, Papua New Guineans came to achieve similar results through language. People wanted to be different from their neighbors, and the way they made themselves different was to diverge linguistically.

Large swathes of neighboring groups throughout the mainland share similar traditional beliefs about what happens after one dies; they think related things about sorcery, initiation rituals, and ancestor worship; they have roughly similar myths about how they all originated; and before white colonists started coming to the country in the mid-1800s, they all dressed fairly similarly (and they all do still dress similarly, given the severely limited variety of manufactured clothing available to them today—mostly T-shirts and cloth shorts for men, and for women, baggy, Mother Hubbard–style "meri blouses" introduced by missionaries to promote modesty and cover up brazenly exposed breasts). Neighboring peoples hunt the same pigs and cassowaries that inhabit the rainforest; and they all eat sago, or taro or sweet potato—whichever of those staples their land is capable of growing.

In terms of the languages they speak, though, Papua New Guineans are very different from one another.

WHILE THE DIFFERENT groups of people who live in the area where the Tayap language is spoken are not isolated from one another, Tayap itself is a linguistic isolate, which means that it isn't clearly related to any other language. Its lexicon is unlike any other language's, and it has a number of other grammatical peculiarities that make it unique among Papuan languages in the region.[1]

No one can explain why Tayap is an isolate. But until the end of World War II, when the villagers began to grow cash crops and relocated their village closer to the mangrove lagoon to try (unsuccessfully) to entice buyers to come buy the rice and, later, the peanuts that they grew so hopefully, Gapun used to lie on top of the highest mountain in the entire lower Sepik basin. At only about five hundred meters above sea level, this mountain isn't particularly high today, but several thousand years ago, it was its own island.

---

1. For example, Tayap marks the subject of transitive verbs (verbs that take an object) with a grammatical construction that has the algebraic-sounding name of ergativity. So you say "the woman goes" ("*noŋor wok*"). But when "the woman" is the subject of a verb that takes an object, you mark *noŋor*, the word for "woman" with a *-yi*. So "the woman cooks sago" is " ("*noŋoryi mum nirkwankuk*"). Tayap also marks gender on intransitive verbs (verbs that don't take an object), so to call a man or a boy, you say "*Wetet!*" ("You come!"); to call a woman or a girl, you say "*Wetak!*"

That an isolate language is spoken on the site of what used to be an isolated island suggests that perhaps Tayap is a particularly ancient, autochthonous language that already was in place in some form before the sea receded and the Sepik River was formed, facilitating the various waves of migration from Papua New Guinea's inland to the coast that began occurring several millennia ago.

Whatever its origin, and despite its minuscule size, the fact that Tayap is as fully formed a language as English, Russian, Navajo, or Zulu means that it must have developed and remained stable for a very long time, for hundreds, maybe thousands, of years. All those years of efflorescence came to an end, though, suddenly and decisively, in the 1980s. By the middle of that decade, children who grew up in the village, for the first time in history, were no longer learning Tayap as their first language. What they were learning, instead, was a language called Tok Pisin.

Tok Pisin has an estimated four million speakers in Papua New Guinea, and it is the most widely spoken language in the country. Unlike Tayap or any of the other native languages that are spoken across the country, though, Tok Pisin—whose name literally means "Talk Pidgin" or "Bird Talk"—has a very short history. Like most of the other pidgin languages that still exist today, such as Jamaican Creole in the Caribbean, or Cameroon Pidgin English in Africa, Tok Pisin arose in the late 1800s as a plantation language. In the Pacific, European colonialists brought together large numbers of men from very different language groups to labor on their plantations; the laborers processed copra (the smoked and dried meat of coconuts, pressed for oil) or collected sea cucumber, a culinary delicacy in Asian cooking, which fueled a massive industry throughout the south Pacific during the mid- to late 1800s.

What did the thousands of men—who had no common language but had to work together, following orders given by their European overseers—do? They invented a new language. That language took much of its vocabulary from the language of the European order givers (so *tok* means "talk"; *sanap* means "stand up"; *pik* means "pig"; *misis* means, tellingly, "white woman"; and *masta*, even more tellingly, means "white man") But its grammar was firmly rooted in the local languages that the men themselves spoke back home.[2]

From its genesis in the late 1800s, Tok Pisin was an object of ridicule for many Europeans and Australians. The prevalence and, to their mind, the distortion of English-based words fooled English speakers into thinking (and many still think) that the language was simply a baby-talk version of English. And most of them spoke it as such, barking orders like "Bring him he come"—their tin ears and racial prejudices preventing them from perceiving the correct form, *Kisim i kam*. From the perspective of the Papua New Guinean men who spoke the language among themselves, what white people spoke to them *was* baby talk. They had a derogatory name for it: *tok masta* ("white man talk"), they called it dismissively, sniggering behind white backs at how badly white people spoke the language they used to boss black people around.

---

2. An example of how local languages influenced Tok Pisin is the way transitivity on verbs is marked. In Tok Pisin, as in many other languages spoken throughout Papua New Guinea, a verb's form varies depending on whether it takes an object. So a verb like *sindaun* means "to sit down." But in its transitive form, which takes an object (as in "to sit something or someone down"), *sindaun* becomes *sindaunim*—the *-im* at the end signals that the verb is transitive. English doesn't mark this distinction on verbs: in both "I sat down" (intransitive) and "I sat the baby down" (transitive) the verb "to sit" has the same form.

As the decades passed, this invented language set. Verbs gelled, word order settled, a grammar coagulated. Men who were released from their labor contracts brought the language back home with them, spreading it like rhizomes from the plantation to the villages. And just like the bolts of factory-made cloth, machetes, axes, and ceramic seashells that they received as payment when they were sent home, the men brought back Tok Pisin as a prestige object. It was a prized possession, the key to another world. Men who had been away on the plantation together spoke the language to one another in the village, to convey their worldliness and to intimidate their country-bumpkin relatives and neighbors who'd never ventured more than perhaps a few days' walk beyond the village into which they had been born.

Tok Pisin entered Gapun in around 1916. A year or so before the outbreak of the First World War, word spread from the coast that white men were in the area searching for young men to work for them. These white men were German labor recruiters, and the men they recruited were to be shipped off to the copra plantations that the Germans had established along the Rai Coast of eastern New Guinea (at that time, it was German New Guinea) and on various distant islands. Two Gapun men, Ayarpa and Waiki, went to the coast to find those white men. They resisted the protests of their relatives, who believed that the white men wanted to lure them away from the village to kill them. The two men were itching for an adventure. They ignored their relatives, found the recruiters, and left with them.

Ayarpa and Waiki joined the scores of men from various parts of the mainland who were taken to a copra plantation on

Kokopo near the German settlement of Rabaul, on the faraway island of Neu-Pommern ("New Pomerania"). They remained on this plantation for at least three years, and they apparently witnessed the Australian occupation of Germany's New Guinea territories at the outbreak of World War I (at which time "New Pomerania" was imperiously changed to "New Britain"). My language teacher in Gapun, old Raya, recalled Ayarpa—who was Raya's father—describing how the *inglis* (that is, the Australians) rounded up the Germans and "put them into big crates. They put them all inside the crates, nailed them shut, and sent them back to their country."

Sometime after the Australian takeover of German New Guinea in 1914, Ayarpa and Waiki came home. The stories that survive them recount how they arrived triumphantly in the village, carrying with them the fruits of their labor. Each man had a small wooden patrol box filled with "cargo": steel knives, machetes, axes, bolts of factory-made cloth, European tobacco, saucer-sized ceramic plates that looked like seashells. (Villagers throughout New Guinea regarded such flat seashells as valuable items, and knowing that, the Germans mass-produced counterfeit ones in white ceramic to pay their laborers.)

But just as impressive and even longer lasting than the goods they brought with them were the stories they told about working on the plantation. And most impressive of all was the new language the men had acquired while working for the white men.

As most people in New Guinea did at the time, Ayarpa and Waiki assumed that Tok Pisin was the language of white men. And like the steel axes and fake seashells that entered the village's redistributive networks, so did the white men's language: Ayarpa and Waiki immediately set about sharing the language with their peers.

A few years after Ayarpa and Waiki returned to Gapun, a group of Australian labor recruiters suddenly appeared in the village. This was the first time any white person had actually come to the village, and panic ensued. Most of the terrified villagers fled into the rainforest. Only Ayarpa, Waiki, and a few old people who were too frail to run fast enough to escape were left. Seeing the village thus deserted, the Australians resorted to what was presumably a time-tested technique of persuasion: they gathered together the old people who remained and prevented them from leaving, and then they waited until their anxious cries brought back a few young men. At that point, Ayarpa and Waiki did the recruiters' work for them: they told the men that if they went off with the white men, they would go to where the two of them had gone, and they would learn Tok Pisin. "We've taught you some of the white man's language," they are said to have told the men, "but you don't know it well. If you go away to the plantation, you'll learn it well."

Five men left with the recruiters.

AND SO A pattern of learning Tok Pisin became established. Young men acquired a basic knowledge of the language in the village. They then went off to work as contracted laborers to learn Tok Pisin "well." Later, when they returned to the village, they taught the language to the young men. By 1942, when the Japanese bombed the town of Rabaul, thus drawing New Guinea into the Second World War, thirteen Gapun men (out of a total adult male population of perhaps twenty-five) had spent three or more years away from the village as plantation workers, and seven of those men had returned. (Of the remaining six, five either married local women and never returned, or died on the plantation. One man returned after the war, with a wife from New Britain and two small children; one of the children was a boy named Monei, who many years later become one of my most valued language teachers.)

The war put a sudden stop to all this. Japanese soldiers appeared in the northern Sepik River area, where Gapun lies, and the Australian colonial officials all disappeared. At first, the curious villagers welcomed the Japanese and were helpful—they built them houses at their base camp, and they provided them with sago in exchange for salt. But soon, the soldiers started getting sick with malaria and other tropical diseases, and when Allied bombs cut off their supply lines, they started to starve. They grew increasingly threatening and violent, and villagers became frightened.

The villagers abandoned their mountaintop village and fled into the rainforest, where they lived in makeshift shelters and without access to their gardens for more than a year. That time was a spell of misery and death: almost 40 percent of the adult population (five men and twelve women) died, probably from a dysentery epidemic that ravaged the area. The loss of so many people, many of them elderly, meant that the number of villagers who had no knowledge of Tok Pisin was decimated. The majority of villagers who survived the war had some knowledge of Tok Pisin, and many of the men who survived were relatively fluent speakers of the language.

After the war, Tok Pisin consolidated itself in the village. Besides the deaths of many Tayap speakers, a main reason for the language's decisive entrenchment at that time was the arrival of Christianity. Villagers had known about Christianity since at least the 1930s, but it was not until after the war that any priest began coming to Gapun, which at the time was even more difficult to reach then than it is today. The villagers never returned to their mountaintop village after the war, partly because it no longer existed: the Japanese soldiers flew into a rage when they discovered that the villagers had fled, and they burned all the abandoned houses to the ground. The villagers resettled on the flat plain below the mountain, near where the Japanese soldiers had built their base camp. But even this location was remote: because Gapun was far away from the nearest navigable creek, getting there entailed an arduous three- to five-hour trek through swamps filled with chest-deep water and mud and home to large freshwater crocodiles.

The first missionary to journey to Gapun was a Canadian Catholic priest named Hilarion Morin, who came to the village in 1948. He returned a few times, and by the mid-1950s, he had baptized twenty-five villagers. All talk about Christianity was in Tok Pisin, and the villagers learned to recite prayers, sing hymns, and listen to Mass in that language.

In addition to being promoted by the church, Tok Pisin continued being learned by the young men who left the village to work as contracted laborers. During the early 1950s, virtually every unmarried male in Gapun in his late teens or early twenties (a total of fourteen out of perhaps seventeen or eighteen young men) spent at least a year working as a contracted laborer on distant plantations, as deckhands, or as road workers in the far-off town of Lae. These men all perfected their knowledge of Tok Pisin, and when they returned home to Gapun, they continued the tradition established by their fathers of using that language to speak to one another and to their children.

Each of these changes resulted in more Tok Pisin being used by more people in more contexts in the village. Tok Pisin "came up big" after the war, villagers say, and this "bigness" made it available to women and girls, who by the late 1950s had begun to incorporate it into their own communicative repertoires. A woman who I spoke to about Tok Pisin in the 1980s told me, "After the war, Tok Pisin wasn't scarce anymore. It was outside—it became like our own vernacular. And all us women who were born after the war, we grew up with it."

THE FIRST CASUALTY of the villagers' increased acquisition of Tok Pisin was their competence in other local languages. Before the arrival of Tok Pisin, Gapuners were a highly multilingual people. No one in the surrounding villages bothered to learn their little language—a situation that suited Gapuners just fine since it meant that they could employ Tayap as a secret code that nobody else understood.

To communicate with people from other villages, men and women in Gapun learned the local vernacular languages that those people spoke. During my first long stay in the village in the 1980s, I listened to old people who had grown up before the Second World War confidently speaking two other local languages that were unrelated to Tayap or to each other, and I also heard those old people responding to one or two other languages, which they clearly understood even if they couldn't speak them.

In the generation born after the war, when Tok Pisin "came up big," competence in other village vernaculars plummeted. People no longer needed to learn local languages because, at that point, it was easier to communicate in Tok Pisin. Women lagged behind men, and they continued to learn other vernacular languages for another generation, largely because women in the area generally still did not speak Tok Pisin as easily as men did. By the 1970s, though, even Gapun women's active competence in other vernaculars was eclipsed by Tok Pisin.

Once women started speaking Tok Pisin, they started directing it at their young children. This in itself didn't necessarily mean very much. Unlike middle-class parents in places like northern Europe and the United States, adults in Gapun don't spend a lot of time talking to small children. They don't use language to try to teach their kids anything since they don't believe that toddlers learn by being taught. And to try to converse with a baby is nonsensical since a baby can't hold up its end of the conversation and talk back.

But when children, especially girls, start to get pressed into service to help mothers care for a new baby, mothers begin to give the kids orders. And those orders—to fetch firewood, to hand the baby whatever it is crying for, to climb up a tree to get betel nut— increasingly got formulated in Tok Pisin. Women started doing to their small children what men had been doing to boys and young men (and their wives) for decades—ordering them about in Tok Pisin. And indeed, the men who ordered their sons, nephews, and wives around in Tok Pisin learned the language themselves in situations where they had been ordered around in Tok Pisin by white overseers.

In language death, ontogeny recapitulates phylogeny.

. . .

THIS, THEN, IS how a language dies: in Gapun, Tok Pisin was incorporated into the villagers' linguistic repertoire first at the expense of other village vernaculars, and, ultimately, at the expense of their own vernacular. There has been a steady reduction in the number of languages that villagers command, to the point where their impressive multilingualism has in the course of four generations been reduced to monolingualism. A people who used to command many languages now increasingly command only one. And that one is not their ancestral language, Tayap. It is, instead, Tok Pisin.

The longer I stayed in the village and the more this realization sunk in, it struck me that the task I thought I had come to Gapun to do—understand how a language died—was, in fact, only a small part of the enormous responsibility I naively had taken on. Tayap was not only dying—it was also completely undocumented. When it disappeared, its unique genius as a language would vanish without a trace. Unless I stepped up to the plate, that is, and started writing it down, recording it, and trying to figure it out.

Fast.

3: FIRST CATCH YOUR TEACHER

How do you learn an unwritten language?

For most people throughout most of human history, that question was one that pretty much always solved itself. You found yourself in the company of people who spoke a language you didn't know—because you were married off and had to go live with your new husband's kinfolk, or because you were captured by a marauding band of pillagers, or your country was colonized and you were sent off to a plantation to work as an indentured laborer, or because you simply moved to a new place—and you learned the new language by being forced to learn it. Sound by sound, word by word, phrase by phrase, you gradually acquired it, like a magpie collecting twigs and fluff and shiny objects in the hope of building a serviceable nest. Small children collect those snippets of language effortlessly—take a three-year-old to a new country, and she will confidently be speaking the new language within a few months.

Learning an unwritten language through immersion as an adult, on the other hand, takes a much longer time, often many years. That is fine if you have many years to learn it. I, though, didn't. I arrived back in Gapun in 1986 knowing that I had exactly fifteen months of funding to complete the research I had come there to do. I needed to learn both the local language and every-thing else about the village in that amount of time. As soon as I got there, the clock began ticking.

Before I came to Gapun, all that anyone outside the immediate area knew about Tayap was that it was a solitary little language. A few years before the outbreak of the Second World War, a German missionary named Georg Höltker passed through Gapun for a few hours and collected a brief list of words from villagers. He pub-lished the list a year later, noting that the language seemed unre-lated to any other.

The majority of languages spoken throughout Papua New Guinea are called Papuan languages by linguists. They were the last group of languages in the world to be investigated (most lin-guistic research having really started only in the 1950s), and they remain some of the most poorly known. Most of what we do know about them is from the work of missionaries who study the lan-guages in the hope of evangelizing the people who speak them and converting them to Christianity. None of the handful of mission-ary priests who came to Gapun ever attempted to learn Tayap. The language was too tiny for them to bother.

Unlike the priests, I stuck around and decided to bother.

THE EIGHTEENTH-CENTURY ENGLISH cookery book writer Hannah Glasse is famously reported to have begun a rec-ipe for jugged hare with an admonition: "First catch your hare." Apparently, this is apocryphal; Glasse never wrote it. But it prob-ably has lived on because for centuries it was, in fact, excellent advice. It still is for anyone who can't just pop down to the corner butcher's shop for a package of hare.

I thought of Hannah Glasse's apocryphal recipe when I set about learning Tayap. The thing I needed to do first was catch my teacher. This turned out to be much easier said than done, partly because it wasn't as if Gapun was peopled by idle souls who had nothing better to do with their days than sit around and chew the linguistic cud with a visiting white man. Villagers work hard. They spend several days each week wading off through mosquito- and leech-infested mud to go into the rainforest to fell, pound, and wash sago palms to produce sago flour, the primary staple of their diet. Men hunt. Women collect firewood, fetch water, and prepare meals one or two times a day for their families and a constantly varying number of relatives and visitors. During the dry season from May to November, women fish in the shallow creeks that trickle through the rainforest. Both women and men regularly tend their gardens of tobacco, bananas, and taro, which are often located more than an hour's walk from the village. They also tend whatever cash crops (coffee, vanilla beans, cocoa) they have planted in the usually delusory hope that a buyer will find his way to Gapun. On the rare occasion that does happen, villagers give the money they earn to somebody who travels to a town, enlisting that person to buy them a new mosquito net, a flashlight, or an aluminum pot.

To describe Tayap, I couldn't flit from speaker to speaker like a hummingbird and attempt to extract bits of information on the language from whoever might happen to have a moment to spare. I had to find someone who was willing to sit with me for longer than the time it took to drop a few fun facts about Tayap or provide me with some juicy obscenities. I also needed a fluent speaker. When I started learning Tayap in the mid-1980s, anyone over twenty-five would have done. The problem was that everyone over twenty-five had work to do.

That left old people.

In the village in the mid-1980s, there was only a handful of old people. Women and men in Gapun, and in Papua New Guinea generally, rarely live to see old age: a person who reaches sixty is considered old. The few tough birds who manage to survive into their seventies are regarded with a kind of awe as being almost unbelievably ancient. They are actually called "ancestor" (*tumbuna* in Tok Pisin, *apa* in Tayap) by people who address them. The reasons why most people die so relatively young are the depressingly usual ones for developing countries: chronic malaria, cerebral malaria, influenza, tuberculosis, being bitten by a venomous snake, and for women—especially young first-time mothers—death during childbirth. All these vulnerabilities are exacerbated by the total lack of even the rudiments of medical care and by the villagers' conviction that every death in the village (including the deaths of the decrepit ancestral seventy-year-olds) is murder, brought about by sorcerers; hence the way to cure anyone who is sick is to spit on them while intoning magical chants and to send money and pigs to men in the neighboring village of Sanae (where all the sorcerers live) to try to coax them into lifting their fatal spells.

WHEN I BEGAN my work in earnest in Gapun in 1986, the village population was just over one hundred people. Of those, only seven people were around sixty years old. These were:

1) Ngayam, a choleric, cross-eyed old man whom the villagers feared as an evil psychopath in cahoots with sorcerers who lived in Sanae. Ngayam's body jerked and

flailed in conflicting directions at once, and his speech was slurred. I think he was displaying symptoms of the later stages of Huntington's disease, but the villagers were convinced that his affliction was a curse that Ngayam brought upon himself and his family when, in the mid-1960s, he cold-bloodedly murdered the village headman of the time in a dispute over land.

2) Sombang, Ngayam's skin-and-bones older sister, who was afflicted with the same debilitating illness as her brother.

3) Ajiragi, Ngayam and Sombang's younger brother, who everybody thought was stupid.

4) Wanjo, an infirm man who never left his smoky, dark house—and who never spoke audibly.

5) Agrana, an old man who had a much-mocked voyeuristic *faiblesse* for young girls whose breasts "still stood" (that is, were pert), and who everybody also thought was stupid.

6) Kruni, a former headman of Gapun. In his early sixties, Kruni was powerfully built, but he was bent over at the waist. What was once a muscular back had curved into a scoliotic carapace, giving him the appearance of walking beneath the weight of a great shell.

7) And then there was Kruni's younger brother, Raya, a sinewy, wraithlike old man who suffered from tuberculosis. Raya was continually wracked by a phlegmy wet cough that left him in a perpetually foul mood. He was convinced that his illness had been inflicted on him by his ex-wife before she ran off with another man. Too

dyspeptic to spend much time around other people, Raya
had ordered his teenage son to construct a little wall-less
shelter for him just outside the village. During the day,
he would sit there—often together with Agrana, who had
been granted a special dispensation to be with him—
and whittle intricate traditional carvings of hourglass
drums and mythological ancestors. The two men sat at
opposite ends of the little shelter, their backs turned to
each other; each bent over a carving, their faces pursed
in silent rivalry, and they spoke to each other, only occasionally and tersely, in Kopar, the language of Agrana's
birth village. This largely peaceful scene was interrupted
whenever Raya shouted sharp obscenities at any child
who happened to walk by and disturb his peace—something that happened frequently since Raya's shelter was
strategically placed near the main path used by everyone
who entered or departed from the village (Raya didn't
like anyone, but he wanted to stay informed).

FACED WITH THIS restricted cast of characters, I felt
left with few choices. Ngayam and Sombang slurred their speech,
which wouldn't do if I were to ever figure out the sounds that make
up Tayap. Wanjo's frail voice seemed to seep up like steam from
some unplumbed fissured depth, and I could never quite hear him.
And Ajiragi and Agrana, while they both seemed like jovial chaps,
did indeed strike me as a bit thick.

That left Kruni and his ill-tempered brother, Raya.

The two brothers were so different from each other, both
in physical appearance and in temperament, that to this day I

doubt that they had the same father. Kruni was shorter than his younger brother, but that impression might have been due to his pronounced stoop. He had a gentle, kind face topped with short-cropped gray hair that matched the color of the milky cataract that spread like mildew over his left eye. He had a hooked nose that had a large hole through the septum—the result of an initiation ceremony long ago, intended for a thick, knitting-needle-like decoration whittled out of a cassowary's thigh bone. Kruni's ears were also holed, and he sometimes pressed the sagging perforations into service as temporary receptacles for storing half-smoked cigarettes or bits of green betel pepper. Like other villagers, Kruni had huge hands and feet that were swollen and padded with a lifetime of calluses. His default expression was one of dazed surprise, an impression he created by letting his face go completely slack and allowing his mouth to hang slightly open when he listened to anyone.

Raya looked much older than Kruni. Probably only in his late fifties in the mid-1980s, he already looked like a very old man. His body was skeletal. His hair was almost completely white. The skin on Raya's face was so thin that the exact shape of the skull underneath was visible: his cheekbones and the ridges above his eyeballs poked out from his face as bony protrusions. Raya had no eyelashes and no eyebrows, and he had a faded raccoon-like tattoo around his eyes that made them look like tiny black beads that never blinked. His nose was long and broad and curved like the noses of the traditional carvings he spent his days working on.

Whereas Kruni was humble, even obsequious, around me and in his tellings of past meetings with white people, Raya was arch. Raya enjoyed telling stories of how he had shouted at Australian patrol officers who visited Gapun after World War II, and how he had protested when white overseers did anything that displeased him during the years in the 1950s he spent working as an indentured laborer in the far-off town of Lae. He did not hesitate to inform me that I didn't seem to know very much. Seeing me return to the village soaking wet and covered in mud, he regularly observed witheringly that I certainly seemed to fall off the slippery bridges leading in and out the village an awful lot. Couldn't I even walk properly?

Raya articulated these criticisms in a coarse, wheezy voice that was muffled by the fact that his toothless mouth constantly contained a large wad of betel nut that he always, before inserting it, carefully smashed with a pestle in a little portable wooden mortar that he had carved and kept in his net bag.

Unlike Kruni, who was ingenuous and trusting, Raya was suspicious and skeptical. He regarded people with hooded eyes and a lipless scowl. He reminded me of a reptile. A raptor. He intimidated and frightened me.

Given the choice between the ingenuous brother and the scary one, I at first tried to get Kruni to work on Tayap with me. He assented, but it took me only a few elicitation sessions to realize that Kruni found it difficult to concentrate on the minutiae I was attempting to get him to focus on. He interpreted my wanting to learn Tayap as my wanting to hear the village's traditional myths. Each time I tried to get him to give me a verb paradigm—to tell me how to say "I ate," "You ate," "I will eat," "She is eating," "They will have eaten," and so on—Kruni would be reminded of an epic tale that he enthusiastically launched into, leaving me to sit in the dust of incomprehension and frustration until he finished with a broad smile in happy satisfaction that he had imparted so much Tayap to me.

After sitting patiently through a few times of that, I bit the bullet and timidly approached Raya. He grumpily agreed to work with me, but not until after he wondered caustically why it had taken me so long to come to him. He was after all, he pointed out to me, the single villager who recorded important village events. He had glasses, he said meaningfully, waving at me a pair of black round reading spectacles given to him at some point in the past by a visiting priest. He had a pen too. And a book. The "book" Raya referred to was in reality a collection of torn paper and moldy discarded exercise books that children had received from the school that existed for a few years in a neighboring village between the late 1970s and mid-1990s. But he did record important events on those pages, such as how many pigs people gave to others during funerary feasts and the dates of old villagers' deaths.

Raya turned out to be an exceptionally sharp and focused language teacher. And working with him almost daily led to both of us getting to know each other well. Raya never stopped being critical of me. He never ceased to remark how little I knew about the world, but he eventually softened, consoling himself that I was simply too young to have been told all the secrets of life by the big men in my country. On the few special occasions when I spent an entire morning preparing a dish of what I thought would be an exotic treat for the two of us to have for lunch, he inevitably disparaged whatever I put down on the floor in front of him, saying sourly that it wasn't food fit for humans (this about a vegetable stew to which I had added the one precious onion I had transported all the way from town, a two-day journey away). Once when I made him spaghetti, he blanched, saying that it looked like worms, and he handed the plate to a passing child, who also regarded it with disgust and gave it, in turn, to large pig that happened to snuffle by at that moment. ("But you people eat live, throbbing sago grubs," I remember thinking in exasperation. "And beetle larvae! What's wrong with worms? Besides which, it isn't worms!")

Over the course of the fifteen months I was in Gapun in the mid-1980s, I spent untold hours sitting with Raya in his rickety little shelter, sometimes working on Tayap but often just hanging out and talking to him and Agrana, watching them carve and listening to the stories of their lives and their usually critical views about their fellow villagers. I came to savor Raya's scabrous wit and his keen jaundiced eye. The stories he told me about growing up in prewar Gapun, his time as an indentured laborer in Lae, and about everything that had happened in the village from the time of his great-grandfathers to the time before my first visit in 1985 were vivid and rich with detail. Raya was also a well-informed, eager, and catty gossiper, which for an anthropologist is like hitting the mother lode. Furthermore, once Raya decided that I needed to be told about the world, he took on that task himself, and he would coolly explain to me things like how it is that white people have airplanes, outboard motors, cars, and all the other "cargo" that they have, but dark-skinned Papua New Guineans do not, and how it is that Papua New Guineans all eventually travel to Rome and what happens to them when they arrive there.

Soon after I left Gapun to return to Sweden in 1987, Raya died and I never saw him again. He is one of the people no longer in my life whom I think about often and find I miss most. I miss his rasping, hacking laugh, his acrid comments about my fumbling around in the village, and his mordant observations about what his fellow villagers thought about their place in the world. Raya was the only person in Gapun who ever expressed doubt to me that the villagers' understanding of how they one day will change might be misguided. At one point late in our relationship, he mentioned a memorable encounter with a young white man that had taken place in the 1950s when he was visiting the tiny rough-and-tumble Sepik River town of Angoram. This man told Raya that missionaries lied to the people in Papua New Guinea. Villagers didn't have to devalue their traditional customs, he said. Non-Christian ways of thought and black skin were not inferior to Christian ways and white skin.

This unknown white man's words could have been my own, except I would never have come right out and said that missionaries lied. Partly I had no way of knowing what past priests who visited Gapun actually had preached to the villagers (even though I did know how the villagers had interpreted what the priests said, which was disheartening). But mostly, I was in Gapun to figure out what the villagers believed; I wasn't there to try to undermine their views of the world and convert them, like an evangelist or a politician, to my point of view. When they asked me directly, I suggested to them that their understandings of the countries were not really shared by the people who actually lived in the countries. But my protestations seemed always to fall on deaf ears. Shrewd old Raya's ears, though, clearly weren't so deaf. I was moved by the realization that he had spent years quietly pondering the white stranger's admonition.

"What do you think of what that man said?" I asked him gently. "Do you think it's true?"

Raya's answer broke my heart.

He lowered his eyes and looked down. "I hope it's not true," he answered softly.

I DON'T KNOW what Raya came to think of me by the end of my stay; I never asked him, nor did he ever volunteer such information. But I do know this: on the day I left the village to return home, on a hot June morning, every single person in the village came and bade me good-bye, except Raya. He who never left the immediate vicinity of the village was suddenly nowhere to be found. I worried that Raya had fallen ill, or worse, that I inadvertently had done something to anger or offend him. I later spent many wakeful hours thinking about him and wondering what had happened to him, but there was no way I could find out since the Papua New Guinea postal service doesn't deliver to the middle of the rainforest. Even if it did I couldn't ask in a letter. In Gapun, you write a letter to ask *for* something, not about something.

When I finally returned to the village four years later, one of the first things I did was find Raya's son, who was then a young man in his twenties, and ask him if he remembered what had happened to his father on the day of my departure.

"I remember," he said. "Papa was inside his mosquito net. He was hiding. I told him you were leaving and wanted to say good-bye, but he told me no. He told me: 'I can't go see Saraki. I'm crying too much.'"

RAYA AND I would sit on the floor of his little open-air hut on stilts, and I would drill him about Tayap. I began by trying to determine which sounds make up the language's contrastive repertory. Every language makes limited and particular use of all the possible sounds that humans are capable of making. Some of the world's languages are lavish in this regard (an African language called !Xóõ has 112 contrastive sounds, or phonemes); others are much more modest (Rotokas, a Papuan language spoken on the Papua New Guinean island of Bougainville, has twelve).

English has about forty phonemes. English contrasts *s* and *z*, for example (so "sip" and "zip" mean two different things). What sort of contrastive sounds did Tayap have? Did the language distinguish between things like long vowels and short vowels? Did it have unusual sounds, like a glottal stop? Did it, God forbid, have tones? I had to find all that out, and the only way to do that was to ask someone a litany of tedious questions.

First, I'd elicit a monosyllabic word, for example *nam*, which I discovered means "talk." Then I'd open my lined notebook and begin to make a list. "Does *num* mean anything?" I'd ask, pen poised. "Yes? It means 'village'? Duly noted." "OK. What about *nom*? Wild taro? Great, let's keep going. *Nim*? Doesn't mean anything? What about *nem*?" And so on.

It turned out that Tayap isn't a particularly complicated language in terms of the sounds that compose it. It doesn't have tones, or glottal stops, or any other sounds or phonemic contrasts that aren't readily perceptible and pronounceable by a speaker of English. It doesn't have some of the distinctions that exist in English—for example, Tayap (like most Papuan languages) doesn't distinguish between *r* and *l*; either sound will do.

But Tayap does have two sounds that aren't represented in the English alphabet. Consequently, in writing the language, I had to use phonetic symbols to denote them. The two sounds are the

vowel *ɨ*, which is pronounced like the *u* in "urn," and the conso-
nant, *ŋ*, which is the phonetic symbol for the sound *ng*, as in "sing."
Tayap has many words that start with *ŋ*, including the first-person
pronoun, "I," and the first-person possessive pronoun, "mine." In
Tayap, those words are *ŋa* ("I") and *ŋaŋan* ("mine").

ONCE I FIGURED out the basic sound system of the
language, I went on to elicit different areas of vocabulary: How
do you say "mother"? What about "father"? "Sister"? "Brother"?
"Daughter"? "Son"? What about food: What do you call "sago"?
"Banana"? "Coconut"? "Those boiled bugs I was given to eat for
breakfast this morning?"

Thankfully, I didn't have to learn Tayap monolingually; in
other words, I didn't have to learn it *through* Tayap. That would
have taken forever. I communicated with the villagers in Tok
Pisin, so I could ask them in that language: "How do you say 'X' in
Tayap?" That sped up the process of acquiring the language significantly, but a problem with Tok Pisin is that as a pidgin language
of recent historical vintage, its vocabulary is not exactly vast. So a
word like *gutpela* (literally, "good") covers everything from "OK"
to "fantastic," including "beautiful," "happy," "delicious," "well
done," "healthy," and "calm." *Mekim* (literally, "make something")
means "make," "do," "cause to happen," "accomplish," "act," and
"force," among other things. *Brukim* means "break something,"
but it also means "fold," "tear," "bend," "split,"—and "reveal," "go
across," and "take a shortcut."

This kind of polysemy isn't too much of a problem when one
speaks because the meaning of most words is apparent from the
context. If I went to bed before the moon rose and asked a villager

the next day whether the moon the previous night was *gutpela*, it would be obvious that my query didn't concern the moon's tastiness or its happiness: I wanted to know whether the moon was full. In language elicitation sessions, however, the fact that many words in Tok Pisin have a wide range of meanings often made it difficult to be precise. It was hard to elicit a difference between the moon being full, for example, and it being pretty, enchanting, romantic, arresting, picturesque, grand, dramatic, poetic, and so on since all those words are conveyed by Tok Pisin's *gutpela*.

Over the months, I gradually progressed from monosyllabic words and vocabulary items such as food names and kin terms, and I began to discover the features of Tayap that make it so distinctive.

The most obvious way that Tayap differs from those spoken around it is in terms of its lexicon. A comparison with a few languages spoken in the lower Sepik area where Gapun is located shows how dramatically Tayap differs from the languages of Gapun's neighbors.[1]

	Yimas	Angoram	Murik	Tayap
"one"	*mba-*	*mbia*	*abe*	***nambar***
"two"	*-rpal*	*-(li)par*	*kompari*	***sene***
"three"	*-ramnaw*	*-elim*	*kerongo*	***manaw***
"male"	*panmal*	*pondo*	*puin*	***munje***
"star"	*awak*	*arenjo*	*moai*	***ŋgudum***
"louse"	*nam*	*nam*	*iran*	***pakind***

---

1. This table is adapted from: William A. Foley, *The Papuan Languages of New Guinea* (Cambridge: Cambridge University Press, 1986), page 215.

	Yimas	**Angoram**	**Murik**	**Tayap**
"eye"	*tuŋguriŋ*	*tambli*	*nabrin*	**ŋgino**
"ear"	*kwandumiŋ*	*kwandum*	*karekep*	**neke**
"tree"	*yan*	*lor*	*yarar*	**nim**
"tomorrow"	*nariŋ*	*nakimin*	*ŋariŋ*	**epi**
"snake"	*wakin*	*paruŋ*	*wakin*	**aram**
"mosquito"	*naŋgun*	*wawarin*	*nauk*	**at**

In addition to its distinctive lexicon, Tayap also differs from all the languages spoken in the surrounding area by the way it marks gender. Whenever villagers talk about their language, a fun fact they merrily tell anyone willing to listen is that Tayap "is broken in two, into a woman's language and a man's language." If you want to talk to a woman, the villagers explain patiently, you have to use the "women's language." If you want to talk to a man, you have to use the "men's language."

When they say this, the villagers are referring to the different endings that the imperative forms of an intransitive verb take depending on whether the speaker is talking to a male or a female. In other words: the command forms of verbs that don't take objects (such as "Go!" "Come!" "Talk!" "Look!") are different according to the gender of the addressee.

Male Addressee	*o-tet*	*muŋgo-tet*	*pruk-tet*
	"You go!"	"You stand up!"	"You work!"

Female Addressee	*o-tak*	*muŋgo-tak*	*pruk-tak*
	"You go!"	"You stand up!"	"You work!"

The difference between these two forms is not complicated: you simply add *-tet* to the verb stem when you give a command to a boy or a man, and *-tak* when you order a girl or a woman to do something. The dramatic way villagers describe this feature of their grammar, though—that you have to speak to men and women using their specific "languages"—makes it seem as if the entire Tayap language is "broken in two." The villagers' story about their language carries the unspoken implication that even parts of speech like nouns have different forms for females and males, and that both those forms have to be mastered to say anything at all.

Non-Gapuners who listen to Gapun villagers describe Tayap in this way always react with understandable dismay, and they inevitably shake their heads in wonder that a human language could possibly be so complex.

WHILE THE WAY Tayap marks gender is much easier than villagers acknowledge, I rapidly discovered that another feature of the language that nobody reflected on was formidably knotty. That feature is the way Tayap makes words.

When linguists describe a language, one of the basic things they look at is how words are constructed. The way words are formed is called morphology, and the building blocks that construct words are morphemes. An example of a morpheme is the *-s* on "dogs" or "houses." That *-s* is a morpheme of plurality. Speakers can playfully or poetically segment words in ways that make morphemes that they then can use creatively to form new words. In recent years, English speakers have identified word segments like *-gasm* and *-zilla* as morphemes, and they have used them to build new words, like "shoegasm" and "bridezilla."

The world's languages vary vastly in relation to how complex their morphology is. Languages like Chinese and Vietnamese have very simple morphology. In those languages, there are no endings, and most words are a separate morpheme: so to say "dogs," you say "many" "dog"; to say "ate," you say "eat" "already." These languages are called isolating because a word's form never changes.

At the other end of the spectrum of complexity are languages called synthetic. These kinds of languages exist all over the world, but some of the most complicated ones are Native American languages like Lakota. Anyone who has ever seen a Hollywood Western has perceived a whisper of synthetic languages, in the translation of Native American names. For example, "Crazy Horse" and "Sitting Bull," two renowned warriors, are Anglicized versions of single Lakota words that mean, respectively, "his-horse-is-crazy" (*t͟hašúŋkewitkó*) and "buffalo-bull-who-sits-down" (*t͟hat͟háŋkaíyotaŋka*).

Names like "His-horse-is-crazy" and "Buffalo-bull-who-sits-down" illustrate how single words in highly synthetic languages can correspond to entire sentences in English. Highly synthetic languages construct words out of morphemes that mark things like person, number, gender, and direction, and that get inflected to signify things like tense, duration, and mood (which is the technical term for how a language grammatically encodes a speaker's attitude towards an utterance, expressed in English by verbs like "can," "will," and "must").

Tayap is synthetic language like those, and even compared with other Papuan languages (which generally speaking are characterized by intricate morphologies), it is elaborate. Tayap can combine different morphemes, none of which, in themselves, can stand on their own as words (just as *-s*, *-gasm*, or *-zilla*, on their own, aren't words in English) to create words of extravagant complexity. An example is "She intends to carry him down on her shoulders." English needs a whole sentence to express that action. Tayap can do it in a single word.

That word is *tapratkɨŋgiatikɨtakana*. This word consists of the following elements:

tapr-	-at-	-ki-	-ŋgi-	-ati-ki-tak-ana
verb stem *tap-* "carry on shoulders," with /r/ inserted at morpheme boundary	object morpheme that occurs only with nonfinal verbs, inflected for "him"	dependent verb root *ki-* "bring," which can occur only together with a verb of motion	object morpheme used with independent verbs, inflected for "him"	independent verb of motion *atiki-* "go down" inflected in the future intentional mood for "she"

Translated literally, this word means "Carry-him-on-shoulders-bring-him-go-down-she-intends-to-do."

Perhaps unsurprisingly, it took a long time before I progressed to the point by which I figured any of this out. For months, I struggled to dissect the verbs I was getting from Raya and others, wondering what parts were what and why the forms changed in the way they did. Why was "she came" *wokara*, but "she will come" *aikitak*? What part of those words was the verb? What was the difference between verbs like *pokun* and *poiatan* since people insisted they both meant that someone speared a pig? Why did some speakers say *akrɨknukun* to mean "I would have eaten it," whereas others said *akkun* to mean exactly the same thing?

I spent uncounted hours poring over my notes from my sessions with Raya, and from my talks with Kruni and other older speakers. I also combed through my transcriptions of the tapes I spent several days a week recording of mothers and caregivers talking to children. I made lists, I drew charts, I designed tables. I wrote out flash cards. My notebooks are filled with underlining, arrows, circles, crossed-out transcriptions. They are garlanded with comments like "Strange." "Tense marker?" "Counterfactual?" "Why do some verbs have 3 'they' forms?" "What is this?" "Check this again." "Why this weird exception?" "Did I hear this right?"

I eventually came to understand most of what makes Tayap a unique language. Despite thirty years of work on the language and many months spent in the village, though, I never learned to speak it. Like the children I studied in the 1980s, I have good passive competence; I can understand most of what people say. But also like those children, who are now all adults, I never needed to say much—except, that is, when people from other villages came to Gapun to visit. Then, inevitably and to my great exasperation, the villagers resolutely brushed aside my protestations and insisted on exhibiting me like a trained parrot. They took enormous pleasure in showing off their resident white man, and they delighted in the fact that I was able to awe their easily impressed guests with my ability to respond to commands in Tayap and mouth a few stock phrases.

THROUGHOUT OUR MONTHS of language tutorials, Raya and I had many misunderstandings. He got cross when I asked him how to say nonsensical phrases like "my three eyes" (to test whether possessive pronouns and nouns changed when they co-occurred with different kinds of adjectives). A recurring misunderstanding centered on the fact that I was able to produce sentences that he hadn't taught me to say. Reading from my notes, I became increasingly able to predict a particular verb form, and sometimes—thinking that I would speed up the elicitation process and also show off to Raya that I actually was learning something—I would tell him the form of a verb I wanted, rather than ask about it. This always disquieted him.

"How do you know that?" he would say disapprovingly. "I haven't told you that yet."

A particularly memorable misunderstanding occurred one afternoon when I was trying to figure out the correct forms for the verb "send." This verb didn't seem to fit any of the patterns I had spent months working out. Like other Tayap verbs, it clearly changed its stem form to signify different tenses (so a verb like "cut" was *pu* in the past and *wu* in the future; "eat" was *ka* or *o* in the past and *a* in the future, and so on).

But I couldn't understand what Raya was saying when I asked him to translate sentences like "He sent the pig to Sanae yesterday" and "He will send the pig to Sanae tomorrow" into Tayap. The future, I thought, I got: it was *mbudji*. But the past I couldn't hear clearly no matter how many times Raya repeated it. It sounded like the same form, *mbudji*, which didn't make any sense.

I asked Raya to take a short break. He crushed a betel nut in his little wooden mortar and slid the pulverized mass into his mouth. I paged through my notes. Suddenly, I thought I saw what the form must be.

"Is 'sent the pig' *mbuspikun*?" I asked him. "Is 'sent' *mbus*?"

"Yeah," Raya replied. Then, after a pause, he added tartly: "That's easy for you to say. You have teeth."

ANSWERING MY QUERIES about verb declensions—and being made to recite them mechanically, one after the other (I go, you go, he goes, she goes, we go, we two go . . . (in Tayap: *ŋa mbot, yu mbot, ŋi mbot, ŋgu wok, yim wok, yim sene woke . . .*)—was mind-numbing work; sooner or later, it was bound to anesthetize even the most enthusiastic language teacher into a state of glassy-eyed somnambulism. Which probably was why Raya would sometimes take charge of our sessions and ignore the questions I asked him, instead telling me things he thought I should know. Unfortunately, most of those initiatives were fruitless because I couldn't comprehend what he was saying. Once, he instructed me how to say (I later understood): "He went and has gone altogether—he isn't coming back."

I had no idea what Raya was going on about with his sudden stream of impenetrable loquacity; I'd only asked him how to say "Don't go" in Tayap.

Seeing my confusion, Raya snorted impatiently. He planted his right hand on the floor. "You look," he said.

"This is all the big talk you write down." He grasped his extended arm with his free hand. Raya ran that hand along his arm, down to his crumpled arthritic fingers that were spread out like a spider's legs on the floor. "But all this little talk," he said, stroking his fingers, "you haven't gotten it yet. You don't know it."

"But that's not how I learn language," I objected. "I learn language the other way around. I start with the little talk and I work my way up to the big talk."

Raya and I spoke past one another here. By "little talk," I meant that I began with the smallest building blocks of language, the elements of its sound system, and worked my way forward to the "big talk" (words, sentences) from there.

That way of seeing a language as a disembodied system, as a grammar, was foreign to Raya. For him "little talk" was the core of language. You might know some "big talk"—like how to say "I go, you go, he goes, she goes," and so on. But if you couldn't use the right words in the right situations, you were a blockheaded boob. It didn't matter that you could conjugate a verb like "to go" flawlessly. If you didn't know how to order a child to go get you a burning ember to light your cigarette—or if you didn't know that when referring to someone who has died you should say, "He went and has gone altogether. He isn't coming back."—all you could do was sputter gibberish.

Raya, of course, was right. Many years after my language elicitation sessions with him were but fading memories, I finally published a grammar of Tayap. It's big: at over five hundred pages, the book is the linguistic equivalent of a meticulously mounted fossil skeleton. Like a museum display of brontosaurus bones, my grammar exhibits the structure of Tayap. It showcases the language's impressive architecture and suggests its once-formidable power to breathe and move. But my grammar, like all grammars, lacks the crucial feature that Raya was pointing at with his remark about the importance of "little talk": a grammar lacks life. It lacks a language's guts, it lacks its nerves, it lacks its spit and its spark. All of that goes when a language dies.

When Raya died, for example, a vital piece of Tayap's heart stopped beating forever.

4: MOSES'S PLAN

THE DESTRUCTION OF the village happened, as most destruction has in recent years, during a drinking binge.

Moses, the one with the plan, had prepared. He spent a day brewing several buckets of "white soup," a liquid that is actually not white, nor is it soup. It is a kind of cheap jungle wine, yellowish in color and smelling of bread. Moses and the other villagers had acquired the knowledge to make white soup only a few years previously. They learned the recipe from Moses's cousin Kak, who brought it back from one of his travels to a village along the Sepik River, where he met a man who had served in the Papua New Guinean army during the country's decade-long civil war (1988–1998) with the secessionist island province of Bougainville. When the war ended, the man returned to his village penniless and broken. He spent his days cajoling cigarettes and betel nut off other men, and he paid for them with braggart stories about how he and his mates raped countless women and made alcohol out of coconuts.

The recipe for white soup was two pounds of sugar per gallon of liquid spilled from split coconuts, and nine to twelve spoonfuls of yeast. Moses made his batch of white soup with almost double that amount of yeast, not caring that the result would taste sour and rancid. He wanted quick fermentation and a powerful brew.

Moses was the village *komiti*—a title that comes from the English word "committee," but in Tok Pisin, the word refers not to a group but to a single person, a village's elected headman. Once every five years, government officials, accompanied by armed policemen, make an appearance in the village for one brief morning; they distribute and then hurriedly collect ballots on which villagers mark their preference for members of their provincial parliament and their national parliament, which sits in the faraway capital city, Port Moresby. At this time, villagers also vote for a *kaunsil* ("council"), a man who is supposed to lead the local area (in this case, three villages, of which Gapun is one), and a village *komiti*.

The *komiti*, like the *kaunsil*, has no real power. Both positions are a holdover from the Australian colonial administration (1914–1975), when patrol officers designated particular men in every village as leaders, largely to have someone to blame whenever villagers did anything the officers didn't like. Today, with the colonial administration only a distant, faded memory, *kaunsil*s and *komiti*s have no patrol officers to answer to, and what they do is up to them.

Nobody really knows what a *kaunsil* is supposed to do, or sees any evidence that anyone elected to the position ever actually does do anything. But there is a general feeling that a *komiti* should take the lead in organizing village work parties to do things like cut grass on overgrown footpaths or repair bridges that have floated away after heavy rains. Whether a *komiti* actually does that varies. Over the years in Gapun, the office has alternated between men (always men) who are belligerent and pushy, and who regularly beat a slit-gong drum to harangue villagers into doing community work, and "closemouthed" (*mauspas*) men (whom the villagers usually vote for after getting sick of having had a pushy *komiti*), who spend their five-year term doing nothing.

Moses was a *komiti* of the belligerent and pushy variety. He was in his early forties, thin and wiry like everyone else in Gapun, but at about five foot four, he was several inches taller than most villagers. He also considered himself to be several degrees smarter than everyone else because he was the single villager of his generation who had passed his sixth-grade exams and left the area to go on to high school in the provincial capital of Wewak. He attended school for one and a half years, until his parents stopped sending him money to pay the fees. After he dropped out of eighth grade, Moses floated around for several years, living off the largesse of people he met in town, and then working as a laborer on a copra plantation outside Wewak.

Towards the end of the 1980s, Moses spent four years at the Catholic mission station at Marienberg, where a Hungarian priest who was stationed there identified him as attractive and clever, and took him on as a kind of personal servant. The priest had Moses accompany him to the various Sepik River villages that made up his parish. He also taught Moses to strip naked and flagellate him with a rubber hose during full moons—a time, the priest said, when his desire for women (yeah, right) was most intense but unattainable since he was a man of God.

When the Hungarian priest was posted somewhere else, Moses married a woman from a coastal village and returned with her to Gapun.

Soon after he came back to the village at the beginning of the 1990s, Moses overheard a remark that incensed him. Men from the neighboring village of Sanae—the home of "Big Belly" Onjani and all the sorcerers in the area—were sniggering at Gapun men behind their backs, calling them *bus kanakas*—a derogatory term in Tok Pisin, an old colonialist slur that means "uncivilized savages."

Moses overheard a group of Sanae men mocking Gapuners as bony stupid *bus kanakas* who lacked knowledge of the outside world. This insult wounded him. As the only villager with an eighth-grade education, and with the intimate experience of having lived in close contact with a white priest, Moses decided that it was his responsibility to prove the Sanae men wrong.

Sitting alone with damp, ant-nibbled paper salvaged from old notebooks, and with red and black markers pilfered by one of village children from the elementary school that still existed in the 1990s, in another village a two-hour journey away, Moses drew a map. The map radically reimagined Gapun.

The Gapun village where Moses sat drawing his map was composed of a jumble of houses of various sizes and facing various directions, grouped close together in small clutches. The clutches of houses were separated by narrow footpaths bordered by coconut palms and betel palms, giving the villagers easy access to the two staples they most depended on in their day-to-day lives, and by a variety of fruit trees: mangoes, soursops, and *laulaus*, that in addition to providing refreshment, also supplied much-appreciated shade from the relentless tropical sun.

In Moses's plan, all that had to go. The random and organic layout of the village would need to be replaced by one regimented by "order." In his schoolbooks, Moses had seen pictures of neat

Australian suburbs, with identical houses lined up in tidy rows. He had learned that this kind of community had a name: "modern living."

Moses's plan was to bring modern living to Gapun. Doing so would require razing the existing village and building a new one from scratch. First, all the trees would be felled. Then each village family would be allotted a "block," which he calculated would measure exactly twenty-nine by sixteen meters. These blocks would be lined facing one another in two single rows separated by a broad road that would be cut through the center of the village. Each house would be the same size, and all would be built facing the road. The former easy open access between houses would be replaced by boundaries made of croton plants, which grow rapidly and would enclose each block like an impenetrable fence.

This complete redesigning of the village was not just Moses's personal aesthetic preference. It was an expression of the village conviction, which I heard expressed many times throughout my stays in Gapun, that function follows form. Moses was convinced that once all the houses were lined up in an orderly fashion, once all the blocks were separated from one another by croton-plant fences, once all the coconut palms and fruit trees were chopped down and a road was carved like an airstrip down the center of the village—once, in other words, the village was turned into a simulacrum of a what he imagined a white suburb looked like—then the rest, the sought-after change, would inevitably follow. Cars would materialize; water and electricity would flow into the houses; a shopping center would appear in the village; the dead would arise from the graveyard, bringing with them endless reams of money; and the villagers would metamorphose and turn white.

That would show those bellicose Sanae men who the stupid *bus kanaka*s really were.

MOSES DREW HIS map in the 1990s, but he hid it, biding his time. Once he was elected as the village *komiti*, he used his platform to regularly harangue the villagers about the need to change, never missing an opportunity to remind them that he had an eighth-grade education and therefore knew more than they did. He hinted mysteriously that the Hungarian priest he had spent so much time with had given him a "booklet" that contained powerful secrets that he could use to hurry along the change that all the villagers desired. He also began to mention his plan, telling the villagers that the time had come for them to make modern living in their village.

The villagers responded to Moses's harangues by doing what they usually do when men harangue them, which is: nothing. They would listen, lament laconically that the village was still waiting for change, and then mosey off back up to their houses to chew betel nut or prepare to process sago flour. Most Mondays, at least some of them allowed themselves to be conscripted when Moses beat the slit-gong drum right after sunrise to summon them for communal labor. But his talk of razing the village and building a new one fell on deaf ears.

Then something unexpected happened.

A man from a coastal village called Watam arrived in Gapun one day bearing a letter, which was an invitation, typed up on official stationery, encouraging village headmen in the area to send six villagers to Watam to attend a course. The course was to be given by an NGO with the name Elti Ailan ("Healthy Islands").

I later looked up this name on the Internet and discovered that Healthy Islands was a World Health Organization initiative to promote public health throughout the Pacific Island countries. Its goals were to support existing health systems and reduce the spread of communicable diseases like tuberculosis, and of non-communicable diseases, in particular diabetes.

By the time those worthy ideals dribbled down to the under-paid Papua New Guinean Catholic mission workers who had been employed by the National Department of Health to spread them, they consisted mostly of windy exhortations to cut down trees. Trees, the villagers who took the course in Watam were informed, are the source of illnesses that kill people, especially children: rainwater collects in the leaves and at the base of trees. This encourages mosquitos to breed. To make each village into a "healthy island," therefore, the villagers needed to cut down their trees. The cover picture of the book that the NGO workers passed around to the villagers who had come to Watam showed them what an ideal healthy village should look like.

The picture showed a neat village, made up of identical boxlike houses, perched on what looked like a golf course devoid of trees.

As the village headman, Moses was one of the six Gapun villagers who went to Watam to attend the course. And he learned there that a healthy village was exactly what he had envisioned: a place denuded of trees, isolated in the middle of a vast savanna of neatly manicured lawns. This message delivered by an NGO that had appeared out of nowhere was not just a coincidence. It was a sign.

The Elti Ailan course ended on a Saturday and Moses was back in Gapun by nightfall, with four plastic jars of dry yeast and forty pounds of sugar that he purchased on credit from one of his wife's relatives in Watam. He spent Sunday quietly mixing buckets of white soup.

On Monday, he was ready.

DARKNESS WAS JUST draining away into the gray light of dawn when Moses beat the slit-gong drum that called the villagers to a meeting. As they drifted down to the end of the village where the Monday morning meetings took place, they heard Moses already shouting. The time has come, he was screaming in loud, plangent tones. Now was the time to bring on change. Not tomorrow, not next week, not next year. Now. The course in Watam he had just come back from was proof. The villagers had to step out of darkness. "Modern living" must come to Gapun.

Moses spoke fast, unrelentingly, accusatorily. He had been telling the villagers for years what the workers from the NGO course had just come and told them. So he, Moses, was right and the villagers were wrong! They were lazy! They were primitive! They were Satan men! Moses sat in his men's house and bellowed himself into a froth of self-righteous indignation and condemnation.

It didn't take long for Moses's pistonlike exhortations to begin to achieve their intended effect. His younger brother, Rafael, the village prayer leader, grabbed his ax and ran over to the betel palms beside his house. One by one, the elegant slender trees crashed to the ground. Rafael shouted at some of the young men standing around watching him in dismay to help him cut down the rest of his trees. His brothers and a few of his cousins went to their houses and came back with their axes. They set upon the coconut palms in front of Rafael's house. All the while, Moses was screaming at them, yelling at them to follow his plan, hollering that the time for modern living had finally come inside the rainforest to Gapun and that they were going to make it happen *now*.

By the time all the trees had been chopped down in front of Rafael's house, the young men had worked themselves into a kind of frenzy. They whooped and hollered, hacking and chopping at everything in their path. Betel palms continued to fall, mango trees crashed to the ground, huge coconut palms trembled and collapsed.

The men continued, hacking their way through about a third of the way into the village. But then they were stopped.

Sixty-five-year-old Samek stood with feet apart in front of the betel palms that grew beside his house, brandishing a long grass knife. "Whose trees are these?!" he shouted. "Are they yours?! Did you plant them?! These are my betel palms! My coconuts! My father planted them for me and for my children and for their children! You will not cut them down!"

A fight broke out. Rafael cursed Samek, shouting at him that old men like him were the reason why the village hadn't yet changed. Samek's son, Abram, a muscular man who had a reputation as a tough and tireless fighter, made a rush for Rafael. Rafael's brothers jumped in front of him and held up their axes. Abram's cousins started raising their machetes. Some of them ran off to get their "wire catapults," which are slingshots that fire steel darts filed into cruel barbs fletched with cassowary feathers. Men say they use these slingshots for hunting, but their true purpose is as a weapon intended to grievously injure other men during drunken fights that spin completely out of control.

A few punches were thrown, but before the fight could develop into a full-scale melee, Rafael and the young men who had wrought destruction on a third of the village backed off. They turned around and walked down to the far end of the village where they had started.

Moses was waiting there, beside his plastic buckets full of white soup.

MOSES HAD KNOWN that carrying out his plan would not be easy. He knew that not everyone would be willing to chop down the trees that provided them with coconuts they used to prepare practically every meal, with betel nut they chewed and exchanged with one another constantly, with fruit their children loved to snack on, with shade, with air. He had been expecting conflict and trouble.

That is why he brewed the hooch.

Soon after Rafael and the others returned to where Moses sat, he told the young men to cut off a large branch of betel nut from one of the palms that now lay strewn across the ground in front of Rafael's house. He tied some leaves of tobacco onto it and a few sheets of newspaper. This is a *kup*, the villagers say, a peace offering. He sent it up to Samek, saying that he was sorry for the disturbance that his brother had caused, and asking Samek and the other men who supported him to come down to his house and speak to him.

They came. They carried a similar peace offering of their own and gave it to Moses. They said they were sorry too. They said they were willing to listen.

And so Moses began talking. He quietly shamed Samek and the other old men in the village. "You all haven't succeeded in changing Gapun," he told them. "We're the same now as we were in the time of our ancestors. We pound sago flour, we hunt in the rainforest with dogs. Where's the money? Where's the houses made of corrugated iron? Where's the change?

"I'm a child of this village," Moses said. "I'm talking because I want to help this village. I want to help it change. If I leave you to do what you want to do, you'll never change. But you can't stay primitive. Now is the time to use your head. Modern living has to come inside Gapun. The time of you old men is over."

Moses spoke calmly but firmly. His conviction was compelling. He spoke of the change that would happen if only the villagers would follow his plan. He talked about the water supply that he said the NGO would build as soon as the villagers lined up their houses and planted fences. He talked about the shopping center that was waiting in the wings to appear. The cars that would soon be driving through the village on the road that they would build once all the trees were gone. The dead people who would return from the countries, white skinned and laden with money. It was all there, waiting to happen, Moses explained. And when the village was remade, it would.

By appealing to the change that everyone in the village agreed they wanted, Moses won Samek and the others over. They capitulated. They gave their consent to chop down all their trees.

And before they could think twice and change their minds, Moses unveiled his buckets of white soup and made sure that all the men got roundly drunk.

THE DRINKING CONTINUED for four days. As soon as the plastic buckets of white soup that Moses had prepared were empty, he split more coconuts, spooned in sugar and yeast, and brewed more. As a result of being continually smashed, the young men worked with energy and strength that they would have had trouble maintaining otherwise. The drinking stimulated and enlivened them, and the work seemed like play. By the time they were finished, every tree in the village had been chopped down.

On the fifth day, the villagers woke up with a collective hangover from which they have yet to recover. They looked around them and saw a cataclysm. Their once verdant village had been transformed into a barren desert. The ground was littered with tree trunks that still needed to be carried away, heavy work that ended up taking another month to complete. Coconuts lay everywhere, as did betel nut and mangoes and other toppled fruit. Several houses had been crushed when drunken men carelessly cut down trees that fell on top of them. It was a wonder that nobody had been killed. The houses would have to be rebuilt. The entire devastated village, in fact, would have to be rebuilt.

Which, of course, was precisely Moses's plan.

OVER A DECADE has passed since the felling of the trees, and what happened during those four drunken days in 2007 is not a popular topic of conversation in Gapun. I wasn't in the village during the destruction; I returned two years later and heard the stories then. When I asked the villagers what had happened, they were either shamefaced or critical. Hardly a day went by when somebody did not loudly lament the loss of his or her betel palms. Now villagers have to send their children deep into the forest to get the one thing that they really cannot ever be without, and there are constant conflicts about betel nut theft because a resource that once was plentiful has been made scarce. The vast road that bisects the entire length of the village—cynical villagers have dubbed it their "highway"—is a hot barren grassland. People avoid walking on it because there is no shade. They instead walk up and down the length of the now-elongated village at the edge of the rainforest behind the houses. Women complain constantly about having to cut the grass, which they have to do practically every day—standing bent over at the waist and swinging long, daggerlike grass knives—since the fast-growing tropical grass takes only a few days to swell up into an impassable field.

The highway never attracted any cars, but it does attract death adder vipers, which like to lie in the middle of the road sunning their fat bodies on stiff patches of warm grass. Fear of treading on these snakes with their bare feet gives the villagers another reason to avoid walking on the road. Houses that had been constructed in accordance with Moses's plan to face the road are turned in the wrong direction to protect them from the rain that blows down from the mountain, or in from the mangrove lagoon. The peaks in the thatch face the direction of rain, instead of being turned against it. So every time it rains, the insides of houses get soaked. The croton-plant fences between the villagers' "blocks" are a source of continual bickering. Village pigs squeeze through the plants and defecate inside what now are known as people's *premisis* (their "premises"); children run around playing break the plants, which creates gaps that cause loud acerbic arguments between neighbors.

Moses is no longer the village *komiti*. He was replaced by a closemouthed man who never does anything. After the destruction, Moses left the village and moved with his wife into a house he built inside the rainforest. His new house is surrounded by coconut and betel palms, and by the kinds of fruit trees that he made sure were extinguished from the village landscape. Moses is bitter, but for different reasons than those of people like Samek, who looks out from his house across a parched wasteland and weeps over the loss of his father's beloved trees.

Moses is bitter because the villagers didn't follow through with his plan. They didn't understand that the cutting down trees and the rebuilding the village according to the principle of "order" was simply the first step towards transformation. There were other steps that needed to be completed before modern living could be achieved, before the money would start appearing, and before the villagers' skin would change. The villagers needed to buy a chain saw to cut down even more trees in the rainforest to sell as timber; they needed to erect a *pementeri* (a cement furnace) to dry their cocoa beans; they needed to obtain a windmill to entice the NGO to produce a water supply. Maybe Moses neglected to mention those other steps during the heady four days of drinking and felling trees—as he reluctantly conceded when I asked him to tell me what happened—but he later told the villagers about them.

They, however, don't care. They've stopped listening.

So Moses sits in his house in the forest, fingering his map and paging through the soiled booklet that the Hungarian priest gave him. It is a pink mail-order catalogue from a company in Britain that sells bogus novelty items like X-ray glasses, as well as magic mantras and spells that will fullfill all wishes and conjure instant wealth, power, and beauty.

Moses writes hopeful letters to this company in his best school English, and whenever I traveled into town to get supplies, he asked me to buy envelopes and stamps for the letters, and to post them to England for him.

Meanwhile, Sanae men still snigger at Gapun villagers and call them *bus kanaka*s behind their backs.

5: THE BURDEN OF GIVING

I HAVE OFTEN wondered why Gapuners were so tolerant of having a busybody anthropologist living in their village. From the moment I first arrived, unannounced and seemingly out of nowhere, the villagers were welcoming. And even as the realization must have gradually dawned on them that the mysterious activity that I called my work consisted mostly of butting into their business, eliciting gossip, and gently pumping them to tell me their secrets, they remained good-natured and gracious.

To accommodate me, the villagers built me a house three different times during the years I visited them (one in 1986, one in 1991, and one in 2009). Every time I arrived, many of them collected at the point where a canoe could penetrate no farther, and they unloaded my cargo and carried it on their backs and on their heads for an hour through the swampy rainforest, across tenuous slippery pole-and-bark bridges. In the village, they fed me—women and girls taking it upon themselves to send me plates of food throughout the day, or else they called me to come and eat with them in their houses when they had cooked a fresh cauldron of sago jelly or boiled some banana stew.

If I had let them, they would have fetched water for me from their shallow wells, and they would have washed my clothes. (Since fetching water and washing my clothes were about the only two activities that I could successfully carry out by myself in the rainforest, I didn't let them.) The villagers made sure I was clean and tidy, continually exhorting me, whenever they saw the faintest splash of clay on my legs, to hurry up and wash it off, even while their own bare feet and legs were caked with mud. A woman with whom I was sitting and chatting once reproached me when she noticed that my fingernails were dirty.

"Why don't you wash them so they are white?" she asked me in a concerned voice.

I told her that because I was living in the rainforest, my fingernails would inevitably get dirty just like hers did.

She didn't like this answer. "We want everything about you to be white," she explained patiently, making it clear that by not cleaning my fingernails I was being either dim-witted, or inconsiderate.

ONE REASON WHY the villagers were so solicitous about my well-being was, of course, because they thought that I was a harbinger of the change they want so badly. But that can't be all there was to it because though the villagers have many virtues, patience is decidedly not one of them. If the only reason they tolerated my presence was because they were waiting for me to get on with it and call down the cargo from Heaven, they would have given up on me a long time ago.

Over the years, I concluded that the villagers put up with my helpless, prying presence in their village for other reasons as well.

The first was because I provided reliable entertainment value. People in Gapun aren't exactly bored (they may have no books, radio, television, or films, but they keep themselves entertained with stories of sorcery, of adventures in the rainforest, of gossip about one another). They do, however, tend to lack a lot of novelty in their lives. Whenever I was in the village, I provided them with that novelty. With my white skin, my unfamiliar habits, my excessive belongings, and my inscrutable gadgets, I was so foreign to them that I might as well have been an extraterrestrial alien.

A favorite pastime of young men and children was to watch me work. This sounds exactly as boring as it undoubtedly was. The work they liked to watch consisted of me sitting in a blue plastic chair at a lopsided, poorly nailed-together plank table (one of my hand-iworks) in the middle of my house, writing: either typing into my computer or, more often (since there was frequently some problem with the solar connection that powered the computer), writing by hand with a pen in my notebooks and journals. This activity was excruciatingly uneventful; personally, I'd rather watch paint dry. But something about me sitting silent and hunched over a computer or a notebook, writing, seemed to hold an irresistible allure for the villagers. They clearly found me as exotic as I found them.

Especially during the first few weeks following my arrival, after which even they got benumbed, groups of adolescent boys would crowd into my house, and the toughest two would shove the others away and plant themselves next to each other, occupying one half each of the other blue plastic chair on the opposite side of my table, facing me. (The chair's purpose was to provide a seat for the various women and men I worked with when I transcribed audiotapes I made of the villagers' talk.) The two triumphant boys sat in this chair and stared across the table at me. The other boys, who were prevented from sitting in the blue chair, fanned out on the floor and sat cross-legged or lay down on their backs, positioning themselves so that they also had a good view of me. And they stared too.

I grew used to being glared at like a monkey in a zoo, and learned to accept it. Sometimes, I became so immersed in my writing that I managed to forget the boys were there. I'd suddenly look up to meet the eyes of an entire household of young men watching me as intently as if I were a movie. I often felt like I should sell popcorn.

Children, likewise, slipped into my house whenever they could, hoisted themselves up into the blue plastic chair and stared. They were small enough to walk around under my house, which like the other houses in the village was on stilts. From under the house, the kids peered up through the cracks in my bark floor and watched my every move. They provided one another with a kind of running sports commentary about my activities. "Saraki is boiling water," I'd hear tiny voices whispering under my floor as I pumped up my little kerosene stove. "He's looking for something in his boxes." "He's shaving." "He's eating a banana." "He's combing his hair."

THE SECOND REASON why the villagers tolerated me, I think, was that I asked them to talk about themselves and was interested in what they had to say. Since the 1980s—when anthropologists were informed by postcolonial scholars that what they had always assumed was a benevolent and progressive project of studying human diversity was in reality an Orientalist mode of subjugating people by producing colonialist knowledge about them—anthropologists have become anxious about getting people to talk about themselves. They worry that they are imposing, that their very presence in a place outside their own familiar milieu is somehow an exploitative exercise of power, an objectionable tool of oppression.

Maybe because I started working in Papua New Guinea before the wave of recriminations that paralyzed a whole generation of my younger colleagues and drove them to stay at home and study only people like themselves, I never felt particularly guilty about going to exotic places and asking the people I've worked with nosy questions. And contrary to what students learn in many anthropology classes these days, I have found that this is not an especially difficult thing to do; people, generally speaking, like to talk about themselves. They like talking about themselves, in fact, more than they like talking about almost anything else.

When I first arrived in Gapun in the mid-1980s, some of the people I ended up hanging out with the most were the old men, largely because they were the ones who sat around not doing very much. Old men like Raya and Kruni had a lot of time to kill, and they enjoyed spending it with me, talking. In addition to teaching me the rudiments of the Tayap language, they shared memories of their lives. Nobody else in the village was asking them about the old initiation practices that the villagers had abandoned before World War II, practices that both brothers had either undergone themselves or—if the practices had been abandoned before they could undergo them—they knew all about from their father's and uncles' stories. Nobody else wanted to hear them talk about village origin myths or *tambaran* song cycles. Nobody else cared about the syntactic intricacies of the Tayap language. But I did. I recorded the stories, the myths, the song cycles, and the language, not so much because I always was captivated (I wasn't, myths and song cycles of any variety bore me to death) but because the two old men clearly wanted to tell someone about these things.

Today, those recordings are all that remains of their stories, songs, and explanations.

WE NOW COME to the third—and, I don't for a moment doubt, the most important—reason why the villagers tolerated me living in their village, being a burden and nosing around. That third reason is because I gave them things.

Constantly.

Whenever I was in the village, it was like Santa Claus had set up his workshop in the rainforest, and treated nobody as naughty and everyone as nice. From the second I opened the door to my house at about six thirty in the morning until I snuffed out my kerosene lantern and crawled into my mosquito net to sleep at about eleven at night, a steady stream of men, women, and children came to inform me quietly that they had (or, more often, their mother, their husband, their brother, their uncle, their grandmother, and so on had) a "little worry" (*liklik wari*).

The little worry was always for some item they knew, strongly suspected, or hoped that I had tucked away somewhere in one of the boxes or containers they had carried from the creek to the village. The things they asked for when they came to my house were generally small—cigarette lighters, salt, some kerosene (they would bring a small plastic bottle for me to fill)—and as long as my supply lasted, I gave. Sometimes, I brought dozens of items that I knew the villagers valued. Those items included butcher knives (which really are used to butcher, in this case, the pigs, possums, and cassowaries they hunt in the rainforest) or files that they used to sharpen the knives, or stacks of *The Sydney Morning Herald*, which villagers carefully rip into strips and use to roll the tobacco they grow in their gardens into the skinny cigarettes they all smoke constantly. I distributed items like those among all the households in the village as soon as I arrived. But no matter how much I bought, there was never enough, and, inevitably, individuals who felt they should have received a knife, a file, or a few sheets of newspaper, but hadn't, showed up at my door with a "little worry."

Villagers asked me for big things too: a *reda* (i.e., a "radar," by which they meant a metal detector that they wanted to use to locate the cache of canons and bombs that they were convinced the Japanese had buried somewhere before they left Papua New Guinea at the end of the Second World War), a tractor, a windmill. At one point a group of men asked me, seriously, to bring them a submarine. The rebel leader of Papua New Guinea's breakaway province, Bougainville, had been given a submarine by the countries, the men had heard. They wanted one too.

During one of my stays in Gapun after the villagers had cut down all the trees and made their highway, they pestered me to buy them a lawn mower, which a couple of men who had traveled to a town had seen in action and been duly impressed by. I got so sick of hearing villagers complain about all the grass they had to cut and lament that if only they had a lawn mower, their lives would be so infinitely easier that I actually broke down in the end and bought them a lawn mower (well, a weed whacker). They filled it with the petrol I also bought and used it about five times before it exploded trying to slice through the fibrous tropical stalks that no machine will ever succeed in subduing.

When the villagers asked me to give them things like tractors and submarines, I didn't mind so much. I could usually point out the logistical problems of transporting objects like a windmill through the swampy rainforest across hastily constructed bridges that could barely hold a child without cracking or floating away. When they asked me for things like a *reda*, it gave me the opportunity to ask them questions about topics like World War II and what happened afterwards.

The continual giving from my house every day, on the other hand, drove me crazy. It drove me crazy partly because the never-ending requests reminded me, never-endingly, of my white, first-world privilege.

But it also drove me crazy because of the way the villagers request things.

A group of four young women would arrive at my door. Then it went something like this: They step inside the house and stand in the door opening, staring at me sitting at my table writing. They don't say anything.

I learned that, to break the silence, I was expected to ask: "What's your worry?"

One of them, the one who had been designated by the group to be the spokesperson, clears her throat and says timidly, "Musuma has a little worry about a rubber band."

"All right," I say.

I get up from my table and start trying to remember where I have put the bag of colored rubber bands I bought in town, knowing that villagers like to collect them on their wrists.

I root around in the big plastic containers in which I kept everything shut to prevent things from being stolen by sticky-fingered adolescent boys, or, if it was food, to prevent it from being devoured by ants or by the mouse-sized roaches that started roaming through my house like a herd of grazing buffalo the moment my lantern was blown out at night.

After a few minutes of opening and closing various containers, I find the bag of rubber bands. I extract one, close the bag, put the lid back on the box, and walk over to Mususma with the object that will "finish her worry."

I hand the rubber band to Mususma, who takes it without saying anything and looking down, which is the polite way in which villagers receive something from someone. She twists the rubber band onto her wrist and the group of women turns to leave. Before they reach the door, though, they pause.

"Jipanda too has a little worry about a rubber band."

I HATED THE unrelenting stream of little worries that every day flowed up into my house like a lapping tide, but the situation was partly of my own making. During my first long stay in Gapun, I decided that it wasn't morally justifiable to just freeload off the villagers and give them nothing but the promise of a PhD thesis that they would never be able to read in return for everything they did for me. I didn't want to pay them, though, because money wasn't (and still isn't) an appreciable part of life in the village. Also, to pay some villagers (for rent, for example, or to make me food) would have generated enormous jealousy among the rest of them, and that would have resulted in conflicts, which in turn result in sorcery, which results in sickness and deaths . . . And so largely to ease my own guilty conscience, I started buying small things I observed that villagers wanted or needed, and I made those things available to anyone who asked for them.

The things I gave villagers in exchange for everything they did for me weren't exactly payments. They were gifts; they were a way to acknowledge my relationship to them, and to encourage it to continue. That is the essence of what gifts do. One of the most famous books ever written in anthropology makes this point: titled *The Gift*, the book was written by a French sociologist and anthropologist, Marcel Mauss, and was first published in 1925. *The Gift* is the English translation; the title in French is *Essai sur le don*. The word *don* means "gift," but it has always leapt out at me, and I have always read the book in a rather more self-referential and self-interested way. I amuse myself by fantasizing that the book is actually a treatise about me, at least during my time in Gapun. Its argument is certainly pertinent: Mauss says that a gift is never just an expression of generosity, concern, or love. Instead, whatever else it might be, a gift, first and foremost, is a sign that the giver and the receiver are engaged in a social relationship. A gift is received, in Mauss's felicitous phrase, "with a burden attached".[1] A gift (in distinction to a payment) implies reciprocation; it compels a countergift.

In Gapun, like it is everywhere else, the burden of the gift is double-edged: the things villagers did for me compelled me to reciprocate, and the goods I gave them, likewise, obliged them to continue looking after me. That ceaseless cycle of gift giving was the glue that bound us together.

Anthropologists are generally quite vague about the exact nature of that social glue: of who gave what to whom in order for them to continue being able to live among the people who provide them with the information they use to write their books. I'm not entirely sure why this is so, but it probably has something to do with the fact that anthropologists are still fond of cultivating the impression that people talk to them because they (the anthropologists) are so friendly and receptive and really, genuinely caring. Or even more cloyingly,

---

1. Marcel Mauss, *The Gift: The Form and Reason for Exchange in Archaic Societies*, translated by W. D. Halls (London: Routledge, 1990), quote from page 41.

they claim that the people they work with enthusiastically embrace them into their familial bosom and magnanimously adopt them into their Amazonian, or Nepalese, or whatever families; hence the adopted anthropologist waxes on as though the confidences that their "sister" or "mother" or "brother" divulge to them are bestowed out of familial affection, not pecuniary or some other interest.

For an anthropologist to reveal that he or she actually exchanged goods for the hospitality and the information they received happens almost never. It is considered vulgar.

At the risk of seeming vulgar, then—and to lift a tiny corner of the enigmatic veil of what this anthropologist, anyway, actually had to do to maintain social relationships with people who couldn't have cared less about the books and articles I wrote when I got back home—here is an itemized list of what I gave and what I received in the course of five days of a typical week in Gapun (in this case, the week of June 22–26, 2009):

MONDAY

Don gives:	*Don receives:*
• 1 sheet of newspaper for rolling cigarettes to Yaman	• 1 sago ball with 5 boiled clams from Mbup
• 1 cigarette lighter to Kema	• 1 sago pancake with 3 boiled clams from Ndamor
• 1 cigarette lighter to Egraya (Kema's sister)	• 1 plate of sago jelly topped with 4 boiled sago grubs from Kiki
• 1 butcher knife to Kiki	
• 1 butcher knife to Ebranja	• 1 plate of sago jelly topped with 6 boiled sago grubs from Kambema
• 1 balloon to Kuriŋ (Yaman's four-year-old nephew)	
• 1 balloon to Dgamok (a ten-year-old girl)	• 1 bowl of sweet potato soup with 4 boiled clams from Ndamor
• 1 file to Maŋai	• 1 plate of sago jelly topped with a bit of boiled brush-turkey egg from Egraya

TUESDAY

Don gives:	*Don receives:*
• 1 sheet of newspaper for rolling cigarettes to Mbit • 1 sheet of newspaper for rolling cigarettes to Mbanu (Ndamor's husband) • 1 cigarette lighter to Karepa (Mbit's daughter) • 1 cigarette lighter to Kema (who insists that she didn't ask me for a lighter yesterday and that I must have mixed her up with Nano) • 1 sheet of newspaper + 1 cigarette lighter to Mbawr • 1 balloon each to Poniker, Mbulu, Apop, Kamek, Kape, Ɗawr, Atani, Samai, Ŋgure, Kem, Manup • 1 butcher knife to Mbobot & Mopok (Ndamor's daughters, to share)	• 1 bowl of soup made with taro and a boiled bandicoot from Ndamor • 10 laulaus (Malay apples) from Mopok (Ndamor's daughter) • 1 plate of sago jelly topped with 3 boiled mangrove slugs from Ndamor

WEDNESDAY

Don gives:	*Don receives:*
• 4 AAA batteries to Mbowdi • 1 sheet of newspaper + 1 cigarette lighter to Mesam • kerosene poured into a small plastic bottle to Ŋgandu • salt poured into a bottle that formerly held cough syrup to Ngandu for Atani • 1 sheet of newspaper to Ebiyana • 1 cigarette lighter to Pasi • 1 cigarette lighter to Mbit • 1 sheet of newspaper to Moses • 1 piece of tape to Ebiyana	• 1 plate of yam soup from Erapo • 1 slice of papaya from Kama • 1 sago pancake and some pig-meat broth from Kambema • 1 small papaya from Mbonika • 1 plate of sago jelly topped with 5 boiled sago grubs from Yapa • 1 sago pancake and some pig meat broth from Ndamor

THURSDAY

Don gives:

- 1 sheet of newspaper to Kamik
- 1 sheet of newspaper to Paso (Kamik's mother)
- 1 sheet of newspaper to Ariba (Kamik's father)
- (1 cigarette lighter) to Kema who came again and tried to convince me that I hadn't given her one. This time she wasn't successful. "It's in the book," I told her portentously.
- 1 balloon each to Mopok, Mbulu & Mbajina
- 1 sheet of newspaper + 1 cigarette lighter to Egraya for her husband Mesam
- 1 sheet of newspaper + 1 cigarette lighter to Entomoya
- 3 used D batteries to Simbwira
- 1 piece of tape to Ebranja (Simbwira's wife)
- kerosene poured into a small plastic bottle to Kiriŋ

Don receives:

- 1 plate of sago jelly topped with 3 boiled clams from Nano
- 1 bowl of banana stew with some boiled pig meat in it from Erapo
- 1 plate of sago jelly topped with a small chunk of boiled pig meat from Yapa & Mbonika
- 1 sago pancake with pig meat soup from Kama

FRIDAY

Don gives:

- 1 sheet of newspaper to Saraki
- 1 razor blade + 2 teabags to Saŋgi
- 1 rubber band to Kak
- 1 sheet of newspaper + 1 razor blade to Morabaŋ
- kerosene poured into a small plastic bottle to Sopak

Don receives:

- 1 plate of sago jelly topped with a piece of boiled possum from Ndamor
- 1 plate of sago jelly topped with a small piece of boiled fish from Kama
- 1 plate of sago jelly topped with a small piece of boiled fish from Kiki
- 1 bowl of sweet potato soup from Ndamor

6: DINING IN GAPUN

THE CONSTANT GIVING wasn't the only part of life I found difficult to adjust to in Gapun. In addition to that, I also had to get used
to the lack of sex, the mosquitos, and the mud. And then there
was the single hardest part of spending long periods of time doing
fieldwork, namely eating the local food.

I couldn't really do anything about any of those discomforts.

As far as sex is concerned, I was never propositioned by a villager. And while I found many of them attractive, I figured that
what with me being dead and all, I had enough on my plate to
worry about, let alone throwing in a romantic entanglement
(which, for all I know, the villagers might have regarded with disgust, as a form of necrophilia).

All I could do about the mosquitos and the mud was curse
myself for choosing to spend years studying a dying language
spoken in a swamp, instead of one dying under more convivial
circumstances on a beautiful tropical island.

The food situation was also beyond my control. I couldn't bring
my own food to the village because to do so would have been
expensive and bulky. But much more important, doing so would

have isolated me from the villagers and insulted them. Sharing food with people is one of the most basic forms of establishing social relationships. To refuse to eat food that someone offers you is a serious affront. The French gastronome Jean Anthelme Brillat-Savarin's famous culinary dictum "Tell me what you eat, and I will tell you who you are" isn't just about individual taste. It has a social meaning too. It means that if I reject your food, I'm really rejecting you.

The staple food in the village, and along the entire Sepik River, is sago. Sago is eaten every single day of the year, ideally at least twice a day; once in the morning and once in the late afternoon. Its raw form is a flour that resembles wet compacted cornstarch. This flour can be made into a kind of rubbery pancake by flattening it out and heating it on a broken pot shard or a frying pan; it can be tossed onto the fire raw in a tennis-ball-sized chunk (the resulting meal, a charred membrane on the outside and a dry powder on the inside, is called *muna kokɨr* in Tayap, which literally means "sago head"); it can be wrapped in a leaf and cooked in a fire, or it can be crumbled into a bamboo tube and thrown onto a fire to congeal.

Its most common and most appreciated form, though, is what, in English, is usually called sago pudding or sago jelly. Those designations are grossly misleading, however, because they imply (a) that said food item has the consistency of pudding or jelly and (b) that said food item is appealing in the way that pudding or jelly can be.

Both those implications are screamingly false. The texture of the foodstuff referred to as sago "pudding" or "jelly" is actually much closer to slime or phlegm. Its consistency is such that some of a mouthful will be in your mouth at the same time the rest of it will be dangling down into your throat, like a long, thick strand of sputum. This is not a consistency that many people in the West even identify as food. When we have something runny slipping down our throat that feels like mucus, our reflex is to spit, not to swallow.

And appealing, sago jelly is not—unless, of course, one happens to be a Sepik villager raised on it from birth (villagers in Gapun start feeding their babies sago jelly already a few days after they are born). It is tasteless, which is the only thing about it that is not objectionable—unless it was made by being washed in unclean water, in which case it can taste like furniture polish. The color of sago jelly varies from light pink to dark red or even black, depending on the quality and character of the water in which it was leached.

Sago jelly, perversely called *mum* in Tayap (I say "perversely" because in Swedish the word for "yum" is *mums*), is served in large shallow plates or washbasins (members of one household in the village regularly served it to me in a square plastic foot basin they had obtained from somewhere) in big viscous globs. On top of such a glob, women will place a few leaves of some vegetable and/ or a few boiled larvae and/or a small piece of boiled fish and/or a tiny chunk of boiled meat—like a cherry on top of an ice-cream sundae (although, again, that image is deceptive because it suggests something tasty). On top of that, a few spoonfuls of "soup" will be poured. Soup consists of the coconut milk (i.e., the liquid produced when a coconut is grated and squeezed in cold water) in which the vegetables or meat served on top of the *mum* has been boiled. If the villagers have salt, they will use copious amounts of it to flavor the soup. Aside from too much salt, or none at all, no flavorings, spices, or herbs of any kind are used in Gapun's cuisine. This isn't because none are available—many of the spices used in kitchens around the world, after all, originate in rainforests. Villagers, though, are not interested. They like their food either unseasoned or oversalted.

Villagers produce sago in a process so complicated that it makes one wonder how human beings could ever have discovered it. To begin with, most sago palms are far from inviting: they have long, sharp cactus-like needles covering their trunks and their leaves. Nevertheless, at some point in the distant past, people somehow realized that an edible starch could be wrested from the inner bark of those spine-covered palms. But that starch doesn't come easily. First, a man must fell the sago palm and use his machete to strip it of its needles. Then, with an ax, he chops a slit lengthwise down the outer bark. He uses his ax and his machete to pry open this tough bark, gradually creating a gash that he widens until it opens like a shell, thereby exposing the palm's pale interior.

At that point, the man takes a tool that looks like a cross between a pickax and a large chisel, and he begins to chip away at the palm's innards. He starts at the base of the tree and hacks his way upwards, towards the crown of the palm. The scraped-away inner bark that he produces with this tool looks like coarse pink sawdust.

The man's wife takes it from there. She carries the pink-sawdust-like substance to a rough well dug somewhere near the sago palm (because sago palms grow in swamps, there is usually plenty of water on hand). She puts handfuls of it into a long funnel constructed from the base of one of the sago palm's leaves. She attaches a coconut-fiber strainer to the end, and she pours water into the funnel. She then squeezes and kneads the sago pith in the funnel, releasing the starch the pith contains. The starch runs through the strainer along with the water, and it is collected in buckets made of palm fronds.

The sago pith, once it has been leached of its starch in this manner, is tossed away. Each handful of sago pith is washed four or five times to ensure that it has been completely leached.

The sago starch that has run through the strainer with the water settles on the bottom of the palm frond buckets, and the water rises to the top. The water is poured off, and what remains are dense cakes of wet flour. The woman covers the cakes with leaves and hot ashes; the heat from the ashes extracts the remaining water. Once they are dry, the cakes of sago flour are carried back to the village and are used to prepare the villagers' meals.

The entire process, from felling the sago palm to producing the cakes of sago flour, takes an entire day, from about eight in the morning to three or four o'clock in the afternoon, for two people to complete. And this day's work will usually result in only half the sago palm being processed—the other half remains for the following day. One day's work by two people produces five to eight large cakes of sago flour. Depending on how much of that sago one distributes to relatives, this amount of sago will last a family of eight two to four days.

Sago jelly is made by breaking off a mound of sago flour, putting it in a pot, and diluting it in a small amount of cold water. This produces a watery paste that is strained so that most of the remaining impurities (insects, needles, ashes) are removed. Next, the cook pours a large amount of boiling water onto the paste, stirring vigorously all the while. The steaming water and the stirring cause the sago paste to coagulate and become the viscous mass so beloved by villagers. This pot of gummy mucous is twisted like taffy onto the basins it will be served in; it is topped with the requisite few leaves, larvae, or small chunks of meat and fish, and— *voilà, bon appétit*!

THE FIRST TIME I ate *mum*, which was only a few hours after I first arrived in Gapun in 1985, I nearly vomited. I struggled to control my gag reflex when I saw how the pink goo stretched from the basin in snot-like ribbons when I managed to lift some up with my spoon. As it filled my mouth and started sliding down my throat, I started to retch. I was already covered in sweat from the heat and from the trek through the swamp to get to the village. But now, my sweat glands started gushing like fountains with the realization that I was about to throw up the first meal I was served in the village where I wanted to spend at least a year doing research. I somehow managed to swallow a few dainty spoonfuls and say I was full.

In the weeks that followed, I had a lot of practice suppressing my gag reflex because I was served *mum* for practically every meal. At the time, I didn't know that there were other ways to prepare sago; nor did I know that *mum* was the prestige variety—it is the village version of an omelette compared with a fried egg, of a filet mignon compared with a hamburger. Naturally, the villagers wanted their mysterious white guest to eat the food that they were most proud of. And naturally, their mysterious white guest came to eat it, because he was starving and he had come to discover that there was nothing else on the menu at Chez Gapun.

. . .

WHY IS IT that food regarded by local people as delicacies is often stomach-churningly repellent? In Sweden a food trumpeted by diehards as a quintessentially Swedish delicacy is a fish dish called *surströmming*. This is a word that translated literally means "sour herring"—but "sour" as in *rotten* herring, not "sour" as in tart-tasting, lemon-flavored herring. It is made by putting freshly caught herring into a strong brine solution that draws out the blood, then beheading the fish and gutting them, putting them into a weaker briny solution, leaving them to ferment for several weeks, and then canning them so that they can continue fermenting in the tin.

This process putrefies the fish and makes the tins they're packed in buckle at the seams. The tins are not allowed on airplanes because of the risk that they will burst. But of course such prohibitions don't stop the cognoscenti, and every year in August—the time of the annual *surströmming* premiere—there are bemused accounts in Swedish newspapers about how *surströmming*-loving Swedes who live abroad get reported to the local police and health authorities when they open the tins containing their beloved rotten herring.

The reason the police are called is because the putrefied fish smells magnificently of shit—of baby feces, to be exact.

I tasted *surströmming* once, a few years after I moved to Sweden. Sooner or later, all foreigners do; they do it as a kind of dare that Swedes (most of whom never go near the stuff themselves) enjoy challenging non-Swedes to take. I smelled the fecal odor of the fish, but I did as I was told and lifted one out of the tin and obediently laid it on a piece of crisp bread that had been garnished with slices of boiled potato and raw onion. I put the *surströmming* to my lips, thinking that surely the smell of shit couldn't also translate into the taste of shit.

I was wrong.

THE VILLAGERS OF Gapun also have delicacies. The primary one is boiled collared brush-turkey eggs. Collard brush turkeys are pheasant-sized birds that are a species of megapode, which means "large foot." The birds use their unusually big feet to scrape together huge nest-mounds of decaying vegetation, in which the females lay their eggs. Buried in the mounds, the eggs incubate, and when they hatch, the chicks claw their way to the surface. Unlike the chicks of other birds, which are born unfeathered and unable to fend for themselves, brush-turkey chicks hatch fully feathered and are already able to live independently from their parents from the start.

When women and girls in Gapun spy one of these nest-mounds in the rainforest, they carefully scratch away at the surface to find the eggs inside without cracking their delicate shells. The eggs are large—about twice the size of a duck egg—and they have an attractive ochre shell. The villagers cook the eggs the way they prepare nearly all their other food—they boil them, and they usually serve them on top of sago jelly with a section of the shell peeled off so that the egg can be eaten easily with a spoon.

All that perhaps sounds innocuous enough. The problem, however, is that because the eggs are found randomly, they also are at random stages of development into chicks.

When I arrived in Gapun in 1986 for my first long-term stay, women told me that brush-turkey eggs were a delicacy, and they would do their best to find one for me to eat. Thinking that anything resembling an egg would be more palatable than the boiled sago grubs or mangrove slugs that I was often presented with atop my daily *mum*, I enthusiastically responded that I looked forward to eating one.

One afternoon, a child arrived at my house carrying on her head an aluminum basin on which a broad *kapiak* ("breadfruit tree") leaf had been placed to shield the food inside from flies. As she handed me the basin, she murmured that her mother had found a brush-turkey egg for me and that she had put it on some *mum*. "Oh good," I said. Then I lifted the leaf.

The room closed in on me. In the middle of a basin full of pink phlegm lay the egg, and staring up at me from inside the shell that the girl's mother had helpfully broken open was a large, fully formed eye. I swear I heard the screeching violin strings of the shower scene in *Psycho* when I looked down into that eye—or rather, when the eye looked up at me.

I was horrified. I had to think fast because I knew that I had to at least appear to eat the long-promised egg. Throwing it away was impossible—I would need to smuggle it into the rainforest, which I couldn't do since I was virtually never left alone unobserved. And even if I did manage to somehow get it out of my house and into the forest, I was afraid that somebody would eventually find the shell and somehow trace it back to me. Also, I had made a big deal about how much I looked forward to eating a brush-turkey egg—and now I had one to eat. I couldn't suddenly remember that I was allergic to eggs, or fake an attack of malaria or a sudden brain hemorrhage.

The little girl who had brought me the egg in a basin on her head had gone and was halfway down the notched pole that led up to my house, but I called her back. I told her to wait so that I could send back her mother's basin with her. Holding the basin above her head so that she couldn't see what I was doing, I cracked open the egg with my spoon and watched, sickened, as a fully formed boiled baby brush turkey spilled out. I quickly forced down a few spoonfuls of *mum*, which by that time I had been in the village long enough to be able to swallow, usually without gagging. With a space made in the basin by the slurped down *mum*, I cunningly lifted the sago goo and maneuvered what I could of the boiled chick under it, like a maid slipping a stolen package under her employer's Oriental rug.

I then looked down at the little girl and told her how much I had enjoyed the egg, but I had, unfortunately, just eaten another basin of *mum* sent to me by another mother, and so I was full. Did she want to help me eat the egg?

The little girl's eyes lit up. The boiled chick was consumed faster than I could say "Norman Bates."

It could have all ended there, but idiotic me then made the classic mistake. Instead of telling the girl's mother, when she later asked me whether I liked the egg she had prepared, that I discovered that brush-turkey eggs made me break out in hives, or that they upset my stomach, or made me temporarily go blind, I thought it prudent and polite to express appreciation of the local delicacy. So I gritted my teeth and lied, thanking her profusely and telling her that I thought it was very tasty.

After that, every time I arrived in Gapun, the first thing women always gleefully told me was, "I'm gonna find you a brush-turkey egg." They said it as a gesture of hospitality; I heard it as a threat. And throughout my stays in the village, I was confronted by a procession of boiled brush-turkey eggs on *mum*, each one unique in its own state of development, from a big orange yolk to a fully feathered boiled chick.

The BRUSH-TURKEY EGGS, though, were one of the few things I ate in Gapun that hadn't passed through a larval stage.

Villagers use spears to hunt mammals like wild boars, arboreal possums, and big ratlike bandicoots, and they have recently learned how to set traps for large birds like crowned guria pigeons and cassowaries. They also fish in rainforest streams, and they collect a slimy kind of slug from the mangrove lagoon that, when boiled, tastes like a rubber pellet encased in mud. They kill and eat monitor lizards. But insects, both boiled and raw, make up a substantial part of their diet.

Most common are sago grubs. These are fat, ringed white grubs, about the size of a large strawberry. They have small, hard brown heads. They pulsate. Villagers snack on live sago grubs when they find them in the rainforest, but they also collect them and boil them to put on sago jelly. They taste vaguely nutty and buttery in both their raw and cooked forms. They also leave a lingering aftertaste, so that hours after eating them, you walk around with hearty sago grub breath.

Like everything else consumed in the village, sago grubs are an acquired taste, but I was able to eat them relatively unperturbed as long as I managed to repress the thought of what exactly it was I was eating. What, after all, is inside a larva? It isn't meat, and it isn't anything like a shrimp's tail. It isn't an oyster. All I can think of is pus. Which is why I had to carefully think other thoughts whenever I put a palpitating sago grub into my mouth, bit down, and chewed.

BUT THERE ARE things far worse than sago grubs.

Once, a woman named Ebranja came to my house with a stew that she had prepared, she told me with a flourish, especially for me. She had been in the rainforest and come across some beetle larvae, and she didn't know whether I had tried them yet. She extended the bowl she held in her hands under my face, and I looked down into a soup made of what looked to me like jumbo-sized maggots. In fact, I had seen them on other people's plates in the past, but I had successfully managed to avoid eating any myself. Now, though, with smiling Ebranja standing in front of me holding out a plate of maggot stew and staring at me expectantly, I realized with a sinking feeling that my time had come.

I chose the smallest specimen—one that was still the size of my thumb—closed my eyes, and put it in my mouth.

At first it tasted like a normal sago grub. But as I continued chewing, a rancid taste of something putrid filled my mouth. I quickly swallowed the larva and said it was good (I never learn), but added that I wasn't particularly hungry right then, so if Ebranja could just leave the plate of food with me, I would eat it later and return the plate to her the following day. She cheerfully agreed and went off back to her house.

As soon as Ebranja was out of sight, I discreetly carried the plate up into my neighbor Ndamor's house and asked her children if they were hungry. They said, "Ooh, beetle larvae," and fought over the biggest one. I confided to Ndamor that I hadn't found the larvae particularly tasty.

She picked one up out of the stew and examined it.

She said, "Ebranja didn't make these well. She didn't cut out their shit. You have to cut open their stomachs and pull out their shit. She left it in."

The charming conclusion I drew from Ndamor's culinary critique was that I had not only just eaten a massive maggot. I had also eaten massive maggot feces.

In a stew.

Mums.

But the single most appalling culinary experience I ever had in the village occurred one morning when a woman brought me—for breakfast, no less—a *mum* topped with three large larvae, one of which was sprouting antennae, mandibles, and legs. It looked like the early life cycle of the creatures in Ridley Scott's *Alien* film—the icky one that scuttles around on arachnid-like appendages and tries to shove its ovipositor down people's throats to squeeze out a carnivorous spawn into their abdomens.

I accepted the plate of food, but the boiled alien surpassed even my well-honed ability to eat unbelievably disgusting things. As soon as the woman was gone, I ran down with the plate to give it to my other neighbor, a woman named Paso.

Paso immediately gobbled down the larva with the legs. I asked her what those particular insects were called in Tayap, and she told me.

"*Uruk uruk,*" she said.

That name struck me as fittingly onomatopoetic: it is the sound of a person vomiting violently.

7: "I'M GETTING OUT OF HERE"

ONE FEATURE OF life in Gapun that made the food and all the other discomforts I experienced bearable was the village children. They are the opposite of the coddled, overprotected middle-class kids in the United States and Europe that I encounter in my friends' homes and in public spaces such as shopping malls and parks. Children in Gapun are exuberantly independent. By the time they are four years old, children can light a fire, shimmy up a betel palm, and whack open a coconut with a machete. Young girls can fish from a stream, cook simple food, use a grass knife, chop firewood with a small ax, and be trusted to look after their younger siblings. Young boys can aim at small birds with slingshots and throw short spears fashioned from stiff stalks of grass or bamboo. Kids joke, scold, threaten, and swear like tiny adults. They know secrets about others that they have to be cajoled to reveal. They are irrepressible, tough, and undaunted. They delighted me.

The children liked me too. I was popular because unlike most other adults, who shouted at them and chased them away whenever they gathered in groups and started making too much noise, I welcomed them to play on my veranda and underneath my house. I also always made sure to include them in my gift-giving activities.

I gave kids things like marbles, rubber bands, playing cards, and child-sized balls to kick. I inflated balloons for the youngest toddlers, and I blew soap bubbles to entertain them.

I always took care to learn each child's name. This was not a particularly easy task, partly because at any given time there were close to one hundred children under age fifteen in the village; but the effort was all the more difficult because villagers usually marry one another, and their kids all tend to look remarkably similar. Keeping track of who was who among groups of siblings and cousins who all looked more or less like twins was taxing. Everybody in my neighbor Ndamor's family, for example, looked virtually identical. Ndamor's youngest boy, Amani, at age four, looked exactly like his older brother Mbulu had looked when he was four. Mbulu, in turn, looked exactly like both boys' still older brother, Ngawr, had looked when he was Mbulu's age. The boys' mother, Ndamor, looked exactly like her own mother, Sopak, had looked when she was Ndamor's age, and when Ndamor gets to be an old woman, she will look exactly like Sopak. I often thought about how villagers didn't need photographs to remember what they had looked like when they were younger—or what they would look like in the future. All they had to do was look around them, and they would see themselves cloned.

Another reason why children liked me was because I was the only person in the village who never threatened them or hit them. My lack of aggression perplexed them, and I would sometimes overhear them discussing this bewildering behavior among themselves. They never understood it, but they seemed to appreciate it. I think they saw me as a kind of harmless, ditzy, permissive, spinster aunt who turned a blind eye to behavior—swearing vigorously, smoking little hand-rolled cigarettes—that would get them scolded and probably smacked by any other adult.

Throughout my stays in Gapun, there was always one little boy who for some reason took a particular shine to me and decided that he was my special friend. In the mid-1980s, a ruminative three-year-old boy named Mbini took to reaching up and holding my hand whenever he saw me, and to contentedly falling asleep on my lap whenever I held him. During my long stay in 2009, a two-and-a-half-year-old boy named Njimei started eluding his mother every morning to clamber up the notched wooden pole that led to my house, where he snuck in the door and hoisted himself up onto the blue plastic chair at my makeshift table. Njimei would sit in the chair singing softly to himself until he decided it was time to climb down onto the floor to curl up and take a nap.

During my last trip to the village in 2014, my neighbor Ndamor's boisterous four-year-old, Amani, announced one day that he would be my *sukuriti* (my "security guard"). After that, whenever he saw that I was about to ascend the pole that led to my house, Amani would run ahead of me and scramble up the pole first, insisting on opening my door for me (I had to lift him up so that he could reach the block of wood that secured the door). Amani also insisted on holding my flashlight whenever I walked anywhere at night, something which was, in fact, of only minimal help since most of the time he just shined it into his own eyes, greatly enjoying, as only a four-year-old can, the sensation of bright light followed by temporary blindness.

My fondness for the village children and my solicitous engagement with them wasn't entirely disinterested. I realized that to understand why Tayap was disappearing, I needed to pinpoint how the break in transmission had occurred: How had it come to pass that, for the first time ever, village children were no longer learning the village's ancestral language? To try to resolve this, I needed to overhear what children said when they spoke to one another. I also needed to understand how they came to speak at all.

It was in observing mothers and other caregivers interact with preverbal infants that I discovered the central role that lies and lying play in village social life. For the first several months of their lives, mothers respond to fussing babies by unceremoniously stuffing a breast into their mouth to quiet them down. When babies are about six months of age, and this strategy no longer reliably works, mothers in Gapun start telling their babies lies.

A favorite way to distract a baby is to turn him or her outwards to face the village or rainforest, and to point dramatically.

"Em ia!" ("Look!") a mother will say, with an outstretched arm and adding in a soft, singsong, rising intonation, "Look, a pig. Look at the pig. Oh, it's eating a baby chicken. Look, the pig. Pig. You see the pig?"

The child will stop fussing and strain to focus in the direction of the mother's gesture. Nine times out of ten, though, the child doesn't see a pig because there is no pig to see.

The mother is lying.

IT IS LATE one evening, and Masito's nerves are fraying. Her three-year-old daughter, Pero, has been whining for almost an hour. Pero has been doing this a lot lately. She plays happily during the day, but at night when she gets tired, she starts to fuss and cry.

"During the day, you're a big woman but at night you turn into a little baby," Masito snaps irritably at her daughter. Then she shouts at her to "Shut up!" several times. When Pero keeps on whining, Masito growls through gritted teeth, "Tomorrow when you're playing, I'm gonna beat you."

Then, suddenly, she changes tack.

Masito cranes her neck towards the rainforest and says in a quiet, urgent voice, "Yooo, a woman has gone into the forest to have a baby. Her baby is crying. Look," she says, pointing into the darkness, "you see the light inside the forest?"

Without waiting for her daughter to answer, Masito then calls the name of a woman who recently gave birth. "Ampamna's baby died. Its ghost is coming," she says urgently.

Then she says: "Oh, men from Sanae have come and have grabbed hold of Sakap (Pero's four-year-old cousin and playmate).

"Poor thing, they've tied him up and they're carrying him away like a pig. They're looking for children who cry. They're gonna take them away."

"Sleep now," Masito orders her daughter. "Sorcerers from Sanae are coming!"

A few minutes pass, and Pero remains seated on the bark floor next to her mother by the hearth, continuing her quiet whining. Masito's fourteen-year-old nephew, Telega, climbs up into her house and sits down.

"Telega," Masito says in an anxious whisper just loud enough for her daughter to hear, "did the Sanae men tie up Sakap and take him away to their village?"

Catching on quickly, Telega answers: "Yeah, they came asking for children who cried."

Masito calls softly, using the vocative "O" to convey to Pero that she is addressing people standing right outside her house. "O, my baby is in her mosquito net-o. I put her there and she's asleep-o."

Telega joins in, "You can go-o. Pero is asleep-o."

"My baby is asleep-o!" Masito calls out. She wraps her arms protectively around Pero and widens her eyes to signal that the girl better shut up fast if she doesn't want to get trussed up like a pig and carried off by a band of roving sorcerers.

EVERY SINGLE THING Masito says to her daughter to get her to stop whining is a lie (*giaman* in Tok Pisin, *takwat* in Tayap). No woman is going off into the forest to have a baby; there is no light to be seen inside the forest; Ampanna's baby has not died, and no one from Sanae has come to Gapun to carry away children who cry.

It's all lies.

Villagers merrily admit that they lie freely—vigorously even—to their children. They do so because they want to distract them and get them to stop whining. Everyone in the village who lies like Masito does (which is to say, every single person in Gapun) doesn't mind that the things they point to for a child to see aren't really there. That would bother them only if they imagined that the point of talking to children were to teach them something. But villagers don't see themselves as teaching children anything—for example, instructing a child what a pig looks like, what color it is, or what sounds it makes. Questions like "What color is the pig?" or "What does a pig say?"—so common in Western middle-class talk to children—are absent in Gapun. Talk that asks children questions like those is both engaging and instructional. But that kind of talk isn't necessary in Gapun because villagers don't believe that small children learn by being taught.

Children learn on their own, villagers say, when what they call their *save* (pronounced sáv-ei), their "knowledge," breaks open.

Save is a Tok Pisin word, derived, in the winding and circumlocutory way that many words in pidgin languages have their origin, from the Portuguese verb *saber*, "to know." The word in Tayap is *numbwan*, which means "thought." Small children up to about age four don't have any *save*, villagers say. They have no thought, no knowledge.

A BABY'S FIRST word in Gapun isn't the equivalent of "Mommy" or "Daddy" or some version of either, such as "Mama" or "Papa." Instead, villagers agree that the very first word all children utter is *oki*. (That letter *i* is pronounced like the *u* in "urn.") *Oki* is the stem of the Tayap verb "to go." When a baby says "*Oki*," it means "I'm leaving." Or, more to the point: "I'm getting out of here."

Oki is followed by a second word, *minda*. When a baby says "*Minda*," it means "I'm sick of this." A baby's third word, villagers say, is "*Ayata*." This means "Stop it."

Babies everywhere babble, and parents everywhere interpret their baby's babbling to suit their ideas of what a child is. When middle-class parents in Los Angeles or London fasten on sounds that they can interpret as meaning "Mommy" or "Daddy," they reveal less about the minds of their children than they disclose about their own minds. The first words that people attribute to children say a great deal about what they think about children's nature, and how they think children perceive the world they are discovering around them. In Gapun, words that sound like "Mama" or "Papa" are filtered out by people who hear them: babies make those sounds because babbling babies sputter whole con-stellations of different sound combinations. But the villagers don't notice sounds like "Mama" or "Papa". They pay them no attention. Instead, from a baby's incoherent babbling, villagers extract those three words—*oki*, *minda*, and *ayata*—that they reckon express a baby's way of engaging with the world.

From those three first words, it is easy to see that a baby in Gapun is considered to come into the world in a very foul mood. A baby is ill-tempered, cranky, and already thoroughly fed up with everything that goes on around it. Babies are born with exceptionally determined small wills. They are born, villagers say, with a lot of "head" (*hed* in Tok Pisin, *kokɨr* in Tayap).

Because babies are all thought to be born splenetic and bigheaded, the point of talking to them is not to have conversations with them (what's the point of that, when babies can't talk back?) or to teach them anything. The point of talking to them at all is to get them to stop being petulant. Mothers talk to infants for three reasons: to distract them, to confirm that they have interpreted the child's cries correctly ("You want a betel nut, ah?"), and, when all else fails, to threaten them ("Sorcerers from Sanae are coming!").

For the same reason, because babies are grouchy and willful, everyone who cares for a baby during its first years of life constantly placates him or her. Babies get whatever they want. Whenever a baby fusses, its mother is always there to quickly push a breast into its mouth. If the child reaches out for anything, she or he is handed it. If the person who happens to be holding whatever the baby wants hesitates to give it, that person will be coerced to do so by whoever is caring for the baby. If the person is one of the baby's brothers or sisters, then the baby's mother or one of its older sisters will roughly snatch whatever the baby wants out of the hands of the other child—and will usually smack that other child as well, for being slow to respond to the baby's wishes.

This generosity extends to everything, even to objects that may seem inappropriate, to put it mildly, for babies to handle—a cigarette lighter, for example, or a rusty battery. The pair of scissors owned by the man who functioned as the village barber was a favorite plaything of babies, and it was frequently seen in their mouths. Whenever I brought plastic bags into Gapun, people always asked me for one, to cover up a foot with a sore to protect it from the mud, as a waterproof container in which to store their clothes—or as a plaything they would give their babies to amuse themselves with.

Similarly, whenever I bought butcher knives for the villagers and went around to the houses to hand them out, the first thing that inevitably happened was that a baby sitting on a mother's lap or being held in her arms was attracted by the shiny new object and grabbed for it. Invariably, the mother to whom I had just given the knife impassively passed it on to her baby.

Before handing the knife over, the mother would usually say sharply, "You better not bugger up my knife." But then, without any hesitation, she would hand the knife to her delighted, gurgling infant.

Watching a preverbal baby being handed a butcher knife as a plaything was a jolting experience for me at first. It took me a while to appreciate that a reason why villagers were seemingly so incautious is because no baby is ever out of arm's reach of their mother or older sisters—more often than not, the child is usually in someone's arms or on someone's lap. (Very young children in Gapun don't go through a stage when they crawl on their hands and knees, and they begin to walk later than most Western babies—because they don't need to: they are carried everywhere they might want to go in the arms or on the back of their mother or older sisters.) The baby's mother or sister is ready to intervene in the blink of an eye if a child does anything that looks like it might be harmful. I also gradually came to see that the style of caregiving practiced in Gapun resulted in extraordinarily capable and competent young children. Children who handle knives from a young age become proficient at handling knives at a young age. They do occasionally hurt themselves—my "security guard," four-year-old Amani, severed a quarter of his thumb when he was three, bashing away at a coconut with a machete that was as long as he was. But the wound healed quickly and life went on.

THE PRELAPSARIAN BLISS that infants experience during their first years of life ends dramatically when a new baby comes along. This is changing today because the Catholic Church encourages people to disregard traditional taboos, but in the past, a new baby usually didn't come along until the older child was about three, because couples didn't start resuming sexual relations until at least a year (and more often closer to two years) after a baby was born. New mothers were considered "hot"—not as in "sexy" but as in "scalding"—and any man who even glimpsed a woman during the first several months after she gave birth ran the risk of being stricken with a potentially fatal case of asthma.

Women have always given birth in the rainforest assisted by their mothers and other female relatives, and they still do so today. When a woman has had her baby, she takes the infant and climbs up into a usually cramped little hut that her husband has constructed for her and the newborn on the outskirts of the village, near the areas that villagers go off into to urinate and defecate. In the past, women used to remain in these maternity huts for up to six months, until their baby could sit up and laugh. By the mid-1990s, though, the old men and women who policed such things had all but died off, and women started leaving their poky little huts much earlier to go return to their houses. These days, most women remain isolated with their newborns for only two or three weeks before they reemerge with their infants.

Once a new baby appears on the scene, an older child's days of being pampered are over. All attention is turned to the new arrival, and the older child is suddenly in the position of being an older sibling who gets things snatched from his or her hands and smacked whenever the new baby reaches for whatever those alluring items might be.

This is the point when children's "knowledge," their *save*, is expected to begin to break open. They are expected to begin to listen to others instead of just being mollified by them. Instead of being distracted and placated, kids are now ordered around—and threatened with violence. They start hearing their mothers shout at them with menacing warnings like: "Shit will shoot out of your asshole [when I hit you!]" (*"Pekpek bai sut long wul bilong yu!"*). This is also the age at which the nonexistent pig pointed at in the forest becomes the marauding Sanae sorcerers come to tie a crying child up and carry her off, like a pig.

One pitch-black evening a few months after her baby brother was born, three-year-old Kape was sitting next to her mother, Ndamor. Ndamor told me and another woman who was sitting on the floor with her that Kape had been startled that same afternoon by a gecko that ran across her hand. Kape was terrified and cried, Ndamor said, laughing.

As soon as Ndamor finished telling us this story, she turned to Kape and said to her softly: "The gecko is up in the thatch and he's watching you. If Kape tries to sleep on my lap, he'll come down and bite her. That gecko that bit your hand and made you afraid, he's up in the thatch watching you. When Kape wants to go sleep, she has to go inside the mosquito net to sleep. You try to sleep on my lap, the gecko will come down and bite you. You'll die."

Later that evening, Kape started to whine because she wanted to crawl up onto her mother's lap to sleep. Ndamor cried out in an alarmed voice, "The gecko! The gecko is there! Come down and bite Kape!"

Kape was being given a lesson on how to grow up. She lay on the bark floor the rest of the evening, shivering in quiet fear.

CHILDREN LIKE KAPE display their *save*, their "knowledge," mostly by doing what they are told. They are not expected to say much, and, in fact, until they are about four years old, most children in Gapun say very little. Before they were displaced from their infant thrones by a new baby, they needed only to whine to be given whatever their mother or older sister(s) thought they wanted. By the time they're age four, though, they find that the same cries and whines that once resulted in rewards are roundly ignored, and if those whines continue for too long, they will elicit shouts from their mothers, and maybe also sharp smacks. In Gapun, girls have to grow up faster than boys because they are pressed into service by their mothers to help them with each new baby, and to do things like collect firewood and fetch water. In a pattern that was familiar to me from my own culture, boys will also be asked to help occasionally, but for the most part, they are left to amuse themselves with other boys who are the same age.

During my first long-term stay in Gapun in the mid-1980s, I discovered that the way parents talk to their children subtly changed when the child reached this stage and began responding to orders. At that time, parents were still using a lot of Tayap when they spoke to their children, so a mother would order a three-year-old to do something like "Go fetch a burning piece of firewood!" (to light a cigarette), in Tayap, *"Otarkut kukuwe!"* But then, especially if the child didn't respond right away, the mother would repeat the same command in Tok Pisin—*"Kisim hap paiwut i kam!"*— usually with more emphasis.

Children quickly learned that whatever was said in Tayap would soon follow in Tok Pisin. And the Tok Pisin was emphasized more because if the child didn't do what had been asked after the command had been spoken in that language, the mother would threaten the child—also in Tok Pisin, saying something like *"Bai yu kisim pen"* ("You're gonna feel pain" [when I hit you!])—or she might throw something across the room aimed at the disobedient kid. So children realized that they had to pay attention to things said in Tok Pisin.

The Tayap they could ignore.

I asked parents why they spoke Tok Pisin to their children and not just Tayap. Their response was unexpected: they explained that they spoke Tok Pisin because their children were *bikhed*— meaning they were "bigheaded," stubborn. Parents insisted that for some reason known only to the kids themselves, their children had rejected Tayap and decided to respond only to Tok Pisin.

This was a surprising and original explanation. But I knew that, scientifically speaking, it was nonsensical. How could barely verbal children not only have separated the two different languages— the Tayap and Tok Pisin they heard spoken around them—but also made up their minds to reject Tayap?

The more I learned about how babies emerge from the womb with big heads and strong wills of their own, the more I was able to make sense of the idea that young children could decide what language they wanted to speak. From the perspective of village parents, it wasn't so strange that tetchy babies who announced that they were sick of everything and were leaving also would have firm opinions about which language they preferred. And that parents would accommodate their children by speaking to them in the language the kids had decided they liked best also made sense since everyone who looks after babies strives constantly to placate them.

But I also knew that two- to three-year-old toddlers do not, in fact, make decisions about which language they prefer, especially not when two languages are spoken around them constantly, as Tayap and Tok Pisin were in Gapun. I knew that if children had received sufficient input in Tayap—and if they had needed to use the language—they would have continued to acquire it, just as children in the village always had done until then.

Preverbal babies' attitudes towards language had not mysteriously altered; instead, parents were gently—and unconsciously—teaching their children to attend to Tok Pisin and to disregard their ancestral language, Tayap.

MONUMENTAL CHANGES OCCURRED in Papua New Guinea during the course of the twentieth century. Saying that the country has traveled from "Stone Age to Space Age" in a single generation is an overly fondled platitude—and an inaccurate one besides, given that most communities in the country hardly have access to space-age anything, including services like primary-school education or basic medical care. But the tired cliché does nevertheless express the magnitude of the impact that white people have had on the lives of everyone in Papua New Guinea.

In Gapun, the impact of white colonialism and the postcolonial state is seen not so much in terms of material improvements. Villagers these days may have steel tools and wear Western-style clothes. But they still grow and hunt all their own food, they still have very little money, and their day-to-day activities in their swampy village are not appreciably different from those of their great-grandparents.

The impact of white people is instead most evident in how the villagers think about things like knowledge.

Before the coming of white men, the kinds of socially prized knowledge that children were expected to demonstrate as they matured would have been expressed through Tayap. But the arrival of white men and the changes they brought with them meant that the whole basis of what counted as knowledge also irrevocably changed. The painful old initiation rituals that both girls and boys had to endure to acquire knowledge about how to behave as adults were abandoned. So, too, were the stories and myths and magical chants that used to signify that people were knowledgeable. With them, gradually, went the spectacular practices like grand funerary feasts, which demonstrated that the people who had managed to mount them had supple organizational skills and vast social networks. The Australian-enforced "pacification" of the area after World War II meant that the crucial knowledge of how to fight, and how to survive, in the midst of the perpetual warfare that had existed throughout the area since time immemorial became superfluous . . . and was lost.

What supplanted all those traditional ways of being in and knowing the world were the new ways of life that had been introduced to Papua New Guinea by white colonialists: Christianity, growing crops like coffee or cocoa beans for sale, the desire to acquire all the goods that the villagers saw or imagined white people had—and more broadly, the desire to change into something other than what villagers were. Those new ways of life all came linked like train carriages to the locomotive of a new language: Tok Pisin.

By the 1980s, Tok Pisin was firmly entrenched in Gapun as the language of the church, of modernity—of the sought-after change the villagers all wished for so badly. Even though most village women by that point had learned Tok Pisin and spoke it fluently, the language was still steeped in the juices of the masculine history that had first brought it to Gapun from the plantations and anchored it in the village. Men had always been stereotyped as having more knowledge than women, and the fact that they had brought Tok Pisin to the village and taught it to others both confirmed their superior knowledge and extended it to new domains. Men also actually used more Tok Pisin when they spoke than women did, and they made a special point of speaking in the language whenever they made speeches in a men's house about how everyone should stop being heathens so that the village might change.

But even as the villagers' understandings of *numbwan* ("knowledge") shifted towards Tok Pisin and became reimagined in a new framework as *save*, their perception of *kokɨr*, or "head"—the willful stubbornness that children are born with—remained tied to Tayap. The first three words that babies uttered: "*Okɨ*" ("I'm leaving"), "*Mɨnda*" ("I'm sick of this"), and "*Ayata*" ("Stop it") were in Tayap—and they were all expressions of pure head. Women swore vociferously in Tayap, and they were generally blamed by men (and other women) for being repositories of the old ways—and for holding the village back from changing skin and becoming white.

Tok Pisin came to symbolize all the desirable goals in the good life while Tayap increasingly came to represent the irrational, negative qualities—qualities that villagers agreed they needed to suppress so that they might all change.

These understandings of the relationship between "knowledge" and "head" seeped down to how mothers and other people in the village interacted with their babies.

Even though no parent in Gapun thinks of how they talk to their children as having any overall direction or plan, it was clear to me that the goal, such as it was, in bringing up children there, was always to get them to suppress their "heads"—and instead display their "knowledge." The goal has always been to convince or coerce children to transcend their own infantile sense of entitlement and dissatisfaction and engage with others as they mature.

In the new world that had come to entrench itself in Gapun after World War II, how could children do this? How could they display their knowledge?

Simple: by speaking Tok Pisin.

And so parents began imperceptibly, casually, to encourage their children to speak Tok Pisin. They did this first of all by not expecting children to speak Tayap. Once parents had identified the first three words that all children supposedly say in Tayap—*oki*, *minda*, and *ayata*—they never interpreted any other sounds made by their children as Tayap. Instead (to the extent that parents paid any attention at all to what their children said), they heard everything as Tok Pisin. So a one-year-old's babble like "*tatai*" would be interpreted as Tok Pisin "*Tata i go*" ("Older sister is going")—even in the absence of a sister who is going, rather than the equally plausible Tayap phrase "*Ta taitukun*" ("Take the knife")—even in the absence of a knife.

At the same time, parents used Tok Pisin when they spoke to their children, to accommodate what parents thought was their children's language preference and to emphasize commands that the kids ignored when they were uttered in Tayap.

By the mid-1980s, a tipping point had been reached. The first generation of children who were not learning the village language had been produced: when I arrived in Gapun in 1985, no child under the age of ten actively spoke Tayap, and some of the youngest children seemed not even to understand it well.

It turned out that a few of those children did end up learning Tayap. But those now-adults never speak it to anyone for fear that a nitpicky older villager will shame them for getting a word wrong or stumbling over a verb inflection. Most of the kids I knew in the mid-1980s never acquired anything more than a passive competence in the language. When they today, as parents, speak to their own children, they do so entirely in Tok Pisin.

ONE RESULT OF being raised on a diet of lies is that children in Gapun learn very quickly that everyone around them lies. Their mother lies, their favorite older sister lies, their father lies, their aunt lies—everybody lies. As early as the first distracting routines, when a mother turns her preverbal infant outwards and enthusiastically points out into the rainforest at a nonexistent pig, children become attuned to the fact that there is an often irreconcilable gap between what people say about the world and the actual state of the world.

Children eventually perceive that the pig pointed out to them so insistently isn't actually there. They see the baby whom their mother has declared to have died being serenely carried around the village. They realize that the threat that they will be trussed up like a pig and kidnapped by Sanae sorcerers is a bluff. By the time they are two years old, children have learned that much of what everybody says to them is a lie. They learn that they have to watch carefully, listen closely, and pay keen attention to what people do—not to what they say—in order to be able to judge for themselves the state of the world.

At the end of every day, before my little security guard, Amani, fell asleep at night, his mother, my neighbor Ndamor, always tried to coax him to let her pour a bucket of water over him to wash him off. Ndamor insisted on washing her son partly so that the sweat and most of the mud that had stuck to his little body during the day wouldn't get tracked onto her sleeping mat, but also because villagers think that taking baths makes one grow. Referring to me by my Tayap name, Ndamor repeated to Amani almost daily: "If you want to be tall like Saraki, you have to wash yourself. If you wash, you'll grow quickly and get big."

Amani, though, like most other four-year-olds, usually had other ideas, and when his mother appeared with a bucket and summoned him, he often ran away and hid, frequently in the darkness underneath my house.

One evening, Ndamor went through her entire repertoire of lies to get Amani to appear. She told him that Sanae sorcerers were coming to shoot him with ensorcelled hooks; that his dead grandfather's ghost had appeared out of the rainforest and was coming for him; and that his sick uncle had died, and the whole village had gone down to his house to cry over his body.

Amani responded to each of his mother's threats and entreaties by shouting "*Giaman!*" ("That's a lie!")

Giving up on trying to coax Amani out from under my house herself, Ndamor whispered to a nephew who was sitting nearby on her veranda to tell Amani that his mother had left without him to go cry over his uncle's body. The nephew repeated this lie, and it struck a nerve. Worried that Ndamor might have abandoned him in the darkness, Amani poked his head out from under my house, looking for his mother. When he appeared, Ndamor was waiting. She made a rush for him and tried to grab him. But he eluded her grasp and ran away, scampering back under my house again.

At that point, I joined in the campaign to "butter up" (*grisim*) Amani. In my best buttery voice, I cooed to him that I, too, was going to follow his mother down to his uncle's house to cry over the supposedly dead man's body. Knowing how much the boy liked to hold my bright flashlight at night, I told Amani that if he came out from underneath my house, he could carry the flashlight and guide us both through the darkness to get to his uncle's house.

Amani's response, delivered in crystal-clear Tok Pisin from somewhere underneath my house, was the obscenity: "*Opim wul bilong yu!*" ("Open your hole!").

Standing next to me hearing this, Amani's mother was momentarily shocked. "Amani told Saraki to open his hole," Ndamor called out in openmouthed astonishment to everyone sitting next door in her house.

Then she and everyone else collapsed into a screaming fit of hysterical laughter.

Hearing the hoopla, Amani emerged, beaming, from under my house. Ndamor ran to him and hugged him tight. She lifted him up into her arms and kept repeating in delighted guffaws that he had told me to open my hole. She was proud of her little son. Not only did Amani correctly identify the fact that I was lying to him. He also knew to tell me exactly where I should stuff the lies.

Amani had shown *save*.

8: OVER THE RAINBOW

ONE MORNING AFTER a night of heavy rain, a broad, vibrant rainbow appeared in the sky. On my way to wash my clothes at one of the village water holes, I looked up and saw it, and I realized that I didn't know what a rainbow was called in Tayap. So I asked the first person I saw—Rafael, the village prayer leader, who I knew was fluent in Tayap—what the word for "rainbow" was.

"*Renbo*," he responded, without missing a beat.

"Um, no," I said, that must be the Tok Pisin word—the Tayap word had to be something else.

"Oh," he said. In that case, he added, he didn't know—and suggested I should go ask his father, sixty-five-year-old Monei.

MONEI WAS AN exotic villager. His father had been a Gapun man, but his mother was a woman from a faraway island. Monei's father met his wife while working on a plantation before the Second World War, and uniquely among the village men who left the village as indentured laborers and married local women while they were away, Monei's father brought his wife and their two children back to Gapun.

Both parents died soon after returning (sorcery, everyone agreed). I like to think, though, that Monei's mother must have been a gentle woman who had a formative influence on her children. Because what made Monei exotic wasn't anything about his physical features (he looked pretty much the same as other village men); it was that both he and his younger sister had placid temperaments and calm demeanors. I never heard either of them threaten to hit another adult and they seldom raised their voices, even to children. In situations of conflict, Monei tried to reason with his antagonist. If that didn't work, he withdrew. Over the years, this strategy led people to see Monei as a reasonable man, a person one could turn to for sensible advice and prudent views. He was also articulate and thoughtful, and after Raya and Kruni died, I often sought out Monei when I had questions about Tayap.

ON THE MORNING I saw the rainbow, in early 2009, Monei was sitting in his usual morning spot on his veranda, chewing betel nut. I bade him good morning and told him I had a question. "What is the Tayap word for 'rainbow'?"

Instead of simply saying the word, as I expected he would, Monei paused and put a finger to his chin. He pondered. After a minute, he told me he couldn't remember the word offhand; he needed to think about it. I thought that was odd. On the other hand, it isn't as though rainbows are exactly common occurrences in the rainforest. I saw only that one the entire nine months I was in the village that year. I thought that maybe Monei was just having a senior moment or had been caught off guard by my unexpected question about a word that villagers didn't have occasion to use very often.

It turned out that Monei's thinking about rainbows took several days. Late one afternoon on my way to my daily wash at the water hole, Monei called me over to his house and told me that "rainbow" had no single word in Tayap. Instead, "rainbow" was expressed through a verb phrase—*akin tamtiek*—that meant "cloud is marked with color."

This sounded reasonable to me, and I duly recorded it.

But when I repeated the phrase to other people to check their reactions, I was universally met with disdain. "*Em giaman,*" everyone I asked responded with a sneer, using their favorite expression—meaning "He's lying"—to dismiss another speaker's expertise in Tayap. Even though no one could think of the correct term, they all told me they knew that the phrase Monei had volunteered was wrong.

I had encountered this kind of collective disagreement several times before. People disagreed testily on the Tayap word for "caterpillar," for example. And then there was the wind problem. There are four named winds in Tayap: *awar, ŋgamai, mbunim,* and *mbankap.* On this, all the older villagers agreed. They also agreed that the winds are differentiated primarily by the direction of the origin of each. What they absolutely could not agree upon, however, was what those directions of origin are. One old man was adamant that the *ŋgamai* wind came from the mountain to the south of Gapun. An old woman was equally adamant that the wind came from the sea, which lies to the north of the village. Likewise, the *awar* wind was held by some people to come from the mountain (i.e., the south) and by others to come from the mangrove lagoon (i.e., the north). Old people argued vigorously with one another whenever this topic came up, but they never resolved it.

By sheer luck, the four winds are listed and defined in the short list of Tayap words that German missionary Georg Höltker had published. In 1937, Höltker traveled to Gapun in the company of a fellow missionary, thereby becoming one of the few white people to ever actually visit the village. He and his companion spent only three hours in Gapun. Höltker took two photographs and collected a word list. A year later, he published the list, together with the weary remark that "it will be a while before any other researcher 'stumbles across' Gapun, if only because of the small chances of worthwhile academic yields in this tiny village community, and also because of the inconvenient and arduous route leading to this linguistic island."[1]

Aside from Don Laycock's unpublished word list that he gathered from two Gapun villagers whom he met in Wongan village in about 1971, and my own work, Höltker's word list is the only documentation of Tayap that exists. Having been gathered by someone who had never before heard Tayap (and who would never hear it again), Höltker's list is impressively accurate. To resolve the controversy regarding the four winds, I decided, therefore, to go with his definitions. He had, after all, spoken to language informants who still lived in a more or less completely Tayap-speaking village. Also, one of the oldest speakers in Gapun whom I asked defined the winds as Höltker did. So the problem of the winds was solved, to my satisfaction, at least.

Unfortunately, though, "rainbow" wasn't on Höltker's list.

---

1. Georg Höltker, "Eine fragmentarische Wörterliste der Gapún-Sprache Neuguineas," translated by Agnes Brandt. *Anthropos* 33 (January–April 1938): 279–282, quote from page 280.

DAYS WENT BY, and no one could come up with the Tayap word for "rainbow." Old villagers explained to me that their parents and relatives had warned them about rainbows, saying they should never walk underneath one because if they did, their minds would become clouded and confused. But even though they remembered these cautions, nobody could recall the word their parents and relatives had used for rainbow. The word, villagers told me, *i hait*: it was "hiding."

Eventually, Monei's old wife (and my neighbor Ndamor's mother), Sopak, had a dream in which she said the true word for rainbow was whispered in her ear by a dead ancestor. The word, the ancestor had revealed, was *minuomb*—a word that otherwise means "large round lake." Sopak said that the way to say "rainbow" in Tayap was to say "*akinni minuomb utok*" ("a large round lake appeared in the clouds").

I told other old people in the village about Sopak's revelation. They were unmoved. "*Em giaman*," they declaimed impassively.

A few days after Sopak recounted her dream, one of the oldest men in the village told me that he had remembered the word—it was *wagurmos*.

The other speakers' judgment fell predictably: "*Em giaman*," they all intoned. They explained that *wagurmos* meant the white film of stars that appears in the sky at night—it is the Tayap word for the Milky Way. It doesn't mean rainbow at all. Many also took the opportunity to disparage the linguistic knowledge of the old man who had offered *wagurmos*. That man may be old, they said belittlingly, but he's *lapun nating*—which means he's grown old without having learned anything. All he has, people said, is *bebi sens*—the sense of a baby.

Weeks passed and frustration grew. Finally, a man in his thirties came to my house one day and told me that he remembered once having heard his grandfather, old Kruni, say the word for rainbow.

The young man reported that as a child, he had been paddling in a canoe with Kruni through the mangrove lagoon. In the middle of the lagoon, they were approached by a canoe full of women from the neighboring village of Wongan who were talking about rainbows. In the Kopar language spoken in Wongan, rainbows are called *mamor*. The young man remembered that the women had called out to Kruni and asked him what the word in Tayap was. Kruni told them that it was *mamar*.

Rather than being the happy breakthrough that I thought this was, *mamar*, too, was rejected.

Without telling them why and hoping to jar their memories, I asked the old people to define *mamar*. "It means 'banana,'" they all responded dryly.

And indeed, the word does mean a kind of banana. But lots of words in any language are homonyms. The word "mole" in English, for example, has a number of different meanings: a small burrowing mammal, a raised blemish on the skin, and a unit of measurement in chemistry, among others. Couldn't *mamar*, in a similar way, mean more than one thing? Might it not maybe also mean rainbow?

Nope. Kruni *giaman*. Or the young man who reported what Kruni said *giaman*. Somebody, in any case, was lying, the old speakers agreed.

In the end, after a month of quarreling—unable to come up with a word or expression that satisfied them all, and growing annoyed at my persistence in questioning them—the older villagers begrudgingly allowed that *mamar* must be the word for rainbow since Kruni apparently (and here several of them rolled their eyes furtively) had claimed it was.

My own conclusion is that *mamar* probably is the correct Tayap word for rainbow. Tayap and the Kopar language spoken in Wongan are completely unrelated, even though the villages where they are spoken are only two hours apart on foot and then by canoe. But because speakers of the two languages have been in contact for a very long time, they share quite a few nouns that are similar.[2]

I told the villagers that I would enter *mamar* in my dictionary as the word for rainbow. This announcement was met with muttering.

I WAS SURPRISED that a word for something as striking and lovely as a rainbow could somehow slip away from village memory. I think I secretly wanted Tayap to have a beautiful word for the beautiful phenomenon, and it was difficult for me to believe that a whole population of speakers could simply forget a word—especially that word. That no one could remember the word for "rainbow" was comical, given the parental cautions villagers told

---

2. The kind of slight phonetic variation between *mamor* and *mamar* are common in the words shared by Tayap and Kopar. For example:

	Tayap	**Kopar**
crocodile	*orem*	*oreo*
cockatoo	*kaimwa*	*keimwa*
turtle	*pawp*	*pup*
lorikeet	*njijerik*	*njijeriŋ*
hook	*pipiŋgabu*	*bibigabu*

me about, that walking under a rainbow clouded your mind and made you forget things. It was as if everyone in the whole village of Gapun had passed under a rainbow together and suffered collective amnesia—about the word for rainbow—as a result.

Old villagers' squabbles over the rainbow helped me to see how their inability to agree on proper Tayap was a feature of village life that was contributing to the language's demise. I was continually struck by how vigorously (and, to my mind, how gratuitously) the old speakers of Tayap discounted and ridiculed one another's linguistic competence. Early on during my stay in the village in the 1980s, I stopped trying to discuss Tayap in groups of old people because discussion of any aspect of the language would inevitably result in bickering. Speakers might eventually, and grouchily, agree on whatever it was I was asking them about, but later on, they would always arrange a private moment with me to heartily dismiss the knowledge and opinions of their fellow speakers.

It escapes no one's attention in Gapun that Tayap is a tiny language spoken nowhere else but there. But unlike people in many other communities around the world, Gapuners do not regard language as a communal, shared possession. Like everything else in the village, knowledge of language is considered to be private property. Gapun villagers would shake their heads in absolute bewilderment at the persistent Western stereotypes about how a rainforest-dwelling people like themselves supposedly eschew ownership and magnanimously share their natural resources in a kind of socialist ecological bliss.

On the contrary. In Gapun, *nothing* is communal, nothing is equally owned and shared by everyone. Everything—every area of land, every sago palm, every coconut palm, every mango tree, every pot, plate, ax, machete, discarded spear shaft, broken kerosene lamp, and every anything else one can think of—is owned by someone. This includes people's names and the right to bestow them, as well as knowledge of myths, songs, and curing chants. Villagers always know who owns what. They have to know who owns what in order to take things freely, or steal them with relative impunity. They guard their rights of ownership energetically, and they defend them fiercely. I have heard bitter arguments and shouts that "It's not yours, it's mine!" over objects as trivial as a discarded piece of string that a woman who had thrown it away saw her sister salvage from the rainforest.

Understandings like those of possession and proprietary ownership have consequences for language: they mean that the Western truism of a common "shared" language has little purchase in Gapun. In their own view, villagers don't "share" a language. Instead, each speaker *owns* his or her own version of the language. The older those speakers become, the more they regard their version as the proper one and everyone else's as a "lie."

And so speakers are predisposed to not regard the loss of Tayap as particularly traumatic. Fluent older speakers still have "their" Tayap; if younger speakers don't possess a version of it as, well, *wari bilong ol*—that's their problem.

9: THE POETICS OF SWEARING

THE DAY I arrived in Gapun the very first time for my month-long reconnaissance visit to the village in 1985, the distant relative with whom my two guides left me turned out to be a man named Alan from a Sepik River village called Mangan. Alan was married to a Gapun woman named Sake, and Sake had "pulled" Alan, as villagers say, to live in her village, where she, like all the other villagers, had access to a great deal of land.

Sake was a small, tightly wound woman who reminded me of the cartoon character Popeye the sailor. She had a bulbous nose and close-set eyes, between which she had tattooed a blue daisy. She squinted like Popeye, but instead of a pipe, she had a sloppily rolled newspaper cigarette perpetually clenched between her betel-stained lips. Her voice was raspy and throaty like Popeye's, but with a shrill, metallic edge. When she shouted, she sounded like an angry duck.

Sake seemed unsurprised to suddenly have a young white man from nowhere foisted on her, and she calmly took me under her wing. One reason she was so unperturbed was perhaps because she had no children of her own to look after. Sake was unable to bear children, which is a condition that villagers are convinced is always self-induced, by eating too much of a kind of tree bark that village women consume to prevent pregnancy.

But there was another reason why Sake was unfazed: the dead villager whom Gapuners decided I was the ghost of was her son. Or to be precise, I was the son of her older sister, Aioma, who had died in the early 1980s while giving birth to a boy. Sake adopted the infant and took on mothering responsibilities for him. The baby lived a few months but then, sadly, he died too. The villagers decided that I was that child. This was obvious, they told one another (I later discovered), from the way I had marched into Gapun demanding to see my mother, Sake. In fact, I had done nothing of the sort—I had not marched into Gapun at all (a more accurate description would be that I pitiably dragged myself in, splattered with mud, drenched in sweat, and almost delirious from hunger). The ones who did all the talking, furthermore, were my two guides, who summoned their relative, Sake's husband, not Sake, to look after me.

None of that mattered, however; my arrival got reedited and recomposed in numerous retellings. What actually happened was quickly and resolutely forgotten by everyone.

When I first arrived in the village, Sake was in her midthirties. I came to be grateful that fate had passed me to her because if I hadn't had been assigned a special connection with Sake, I would certainly have been afraid of her. Despite her relative youth, Sake turned out to be the most dominant woman in the village. She had this status because of the tornado-like intensity with which she could hurl invectives. Whenever Sake decided that someone else's actions or words infringed on her—and Sake decided this frequently—the entire village reverberated with her sharp, loud,

vituperative, and searingly obscene shouts at the person she identified as the culprit.

Sake's swearing was legendary. When she fought with her
husband, Alan, she would call him things in Tayap like "dog's
vomit face" and "fucking grandfather balls" whose "prick is full
of maggots." To her younger sister, who she thought was too pro-
miscuous, she screamed, "You walk around like a porcupine with
pricks sticking out of you everywhere!" She called this sister "cat-
fish cunt" whenever she argued with her. She once quacked at her
older sister, with whom she also frequently clashed, that her "cunt
sagged like loose mud on a riverbank!"

Sake's gargantuan displays of anger won her renown in several surrounding villages. Her most spectacular display occurred
a few months before I arrived, when, during a quarrel with her
older brother, she marched over to her own brand-new house—the
result of six months of heavy work by her husband and the villagers who helped him—and set it on fire, hacking at it with an ax as
it burned to the ground.

Sake died in about 2004 of a hereditary shaking sickness that
villagers attribute to a curse on her maternal line, but that I think
was Huntington's disease. (Sake's mother was Sombang, one of the
seven old people still alive when I started my work in Gapun in the
1980s, and who also suffered from the same incapacitating symptoms.) I missed Sake's decline and death because they occurred
during the nearly fifteen-year period when I stopped going to
Gapun because Papua New Guinea had become too dangerous to
work in.

When I began returning to the village in 2006, another woman
stepped forward to take primary responsibility for looking after

me. This was Ndamor, the mother of Amani, my little security guard. Ndamor started looking after me by default. When the villagers decided where they would build my third house (the other two having long-ago disintegrated in the rainforest's exuberant putrescence), they chose a spot right near the house that Ndamor shared with her husband, Mbanu, and their six children. This close proximity led Ndamor to treat me as a family member; whenever she made food, she included me, even though I also regularly was sent food by other women or summoned to their houses to eat with them and their families.

Ndamor and her three preteen daughters also landscaped the area surrounding my house. They patiently scraped at the ground with the blade of a shovel until every last piece of vegetation was gone, leaving a yard of bare black dirt in both the front and back of the house. My protestations, which I voiced every time the grass started growing and the shovels started scraping, that I actually would like grass in front of my house, instead of dirt, were always roundly disregarded. Ndamor and her girls had a reputation to maintain, and they wouldn't tolerate other villagers criticizing them for seeing my house *kamap bus*: "turn into jungle."

I had known Ndamor as a twelve-year-old girl during my first long stay in Gapun in the mid-1980s, and I had noticed nothing unusual about her. At some point during her adolescence and early adulthood, though, Ndamor blossomed into a character. Like other villagers, she was short, tough, and muscular. She moved languorously, with straight-backed dignity and raised-chin poise. She had a wicked sense of humor and a loud, infectious, whooping laugh. But she could turn on a dime and was also quick to explode into ferocious anger. And even though it was highly unusual for a village woman to hunt, Ndamor hunted. She frequently carried a spear and went off to hunt for pigs, bandicoots, and arboreal possums together with her husband, and sometimes by herself. The villagers, who are tolerant and accepting of individual eccentricities, shrugged when I asked what they thought of a woman hunting. "It's her way," they said reasonably.

Ndamor, as my Irish American mother back in the United States would say, "had a mouth on her." She could irradiate the air with her swearing. She would sometimes joke that she was Sake's child because she swore as much as Sake did. She summoned her children by distractedly calling out things like "Where is cunt lips?" referring to one of her daughters, or, to any of her sons, "Balls, you come here and take this knife over to Papa." Ndamor was creative with her obscenity. She enjoyed swearing, and she was good at it. Like Sake, she used obscenity as a kind of poetics. She sometimes refused her husband Mbanu's requests to do something by telling him, "Go rub your foreskin back and forth."

Once, Ndamor had an argument with Mbanu because he had promised a man from a coastal village that he and Ndamor would go into the forest and process sago for a day, and give the man the cakes of flour they produced. Her husband hoped that the man would do him a favor in return. But Ndamor had been burned twice before by this same man, who had promised to do something for them but never came through. She refused to do another minute of labor for him. The women in the coastal village the man came from often stood up to their waists in the mangrove lagoon, fishing, and when her husband persisted in nagging her, Ndamor shot back that her husband and his friend "were born by being pulled out the assholes of women whose clits are snipped at by crabs."

IN WESTERN COUNTRIES like the United States and in Europe, there are plenty of foulmouthed women. But the people in those places who use the foulest language and the harshest obscenities tend to be men. In Gapun, this polarity is reversed. In the village, men are expected to refrain from obscenity, and women are expected to luxuriate in it. The reason for this is that men (again, in a pointed reversal of Western views) are supposed to be the more cultured sex. Men, say villagers, have more knowledge (*save* in Tok Pisin) than women. Men are supposed to be diplomatic, calm, measured, and reasonable. They are supposed to share with others, never get angry, never swear, and, these days, generally be exemplary Christians. When men give speeches in a men's house about communal work, or carbon trade, or the reason why someone has fallen sick and looks about to die, they like to portray themselves as speaking on behalf of the common good. Men spend a lot of time denying that they have any disagreements with anybody, and reminding one another that they are all in agreement—even when it is patently evident that they have completely opposing views on the topic being discussed.

Women, on the other hand, are stereotyped as being big-mouthed bickerers. Women are not expected to understand or speak in favor of the common good of the village because they, supposedly, don't have knowledge. Like children, they have only "head" (*hed*). They are thought to fly off the handle at the slightest of provocations, and they are expected to swear.

Of course stereotypes like these disguise the fact that men are not, in general, calm, diplomatic, and reasonable. Some men, like Raya, who was a notorious curmudgeon, swear like women. Men get angry, too, and they fight with one another, often violently.

Those fights may sometimes be started by women, or be about women, but it is men who wreak havoc in the village by attacking one another, especially after drinking, with machetes, axes, and steel-dart-shooting "wire catapults."

A time-tested trick that men somehow learn, though, is to let their wives handle minor infractions. The thinking goes like this: If my cousin borrows my ax and is slow to return it, or returns it with a broken blade or shaft, I will not make a public scene—I'll inform my wife about the ax and let her take it from there. When she starts screaming obscenities at my cousin, I can retire to a men's house and chew betel nut with my fellow men and rise above it all, shaking my head and tsk-tsking at how quarrelsome women are.

Gapun men do swear, but they swear much less than Gapun women. And when they swear these days, they tend not to swear in Tayap. Instead, they swear in Tok Pisin.

Swearing in Tok Pisin is similar to swearing in Tayap as far as general themes are concerned. In both languages, the lower body and its functions feature prominently when people hurl abuse at one another. But a difference is that whereas swearing in Tayap involves verb phrases of great complexity (saying something like "Your mother gave birth to you through her asshole, together with a pile of shit, while lightning flashed!" requires both imagination and linguistic dexterity), in Tok Pisin, swearing consists of plain unimaginative nouns. These words have the same affective force as the Tayap obscenity, but from a linguistic perspective, they are boring. There is nothing resembling poetics. *Pekpek as* ("shitty ass") is a common swear, as is *wul* ("hole").

The single most popular obscenity is *kaikai kan* ("eat cunt"). This phrase has the same status in Gapun as the word "fuck" has in English-speaking countries: it is a swear that can be directed at another person (as in "fuck you"), and it can also express private frustration or disappointment, as in muttering "fuck" when you drop an egg on the floor or when the doors of the train that you have run to catch close in your face.

"Eat cunt" is used in Gapun in both these ways. The people in the village who use it the most are children, who are quick to express their frustration and anger about not being given something they want. In fact, I am convinced that even though villagers claim that a baby's first word is *Oki* ("I'm getting out of here"), the first word that babies, these days, *actually* utter is *kaikaikan*. (Their second word is *Giaman*, "That's a lie.")

A LANGUAGE DIES by contracting, by having its layers of complexity peeled off like an onion skin, getting smaller and smaller until there is finally nothing left. Some of the first things to go are the esoteric words for cosmological myths, or for obscure kinship relations. These are the dimensions of language loss that are most lamented by linguists and language activists who write about language death. They represent language at its most august, its most respectable, its most jewellike.

Nobody cares much about the obscenities, the linguistic equivalent of gravel.

But I mourn the impending loss of Tayap obscenity. I rue the disappearance of the impressive lyrical arsenal of vulgarity that the little language has at its disposal. Some obscenity will live on as mummified formulaic phrases—even ten-year-olds in the village can shout *kwem petiek* ("wanker") at someone who has done something they don't like. But they can't use the phrase productively; they can't do anything with it except holler it out in someone's direction to call that person a bad name.

The creative use of Tayap obscenity is restricted to a handful of women who, these days, are in their midforties and older. Even men who are excellent speakers of Tayap are unwilling to avail themselves of the language's arsenal of obscenity, perhaps because they don't want to sound like women. Or maybe they just aren't imaginative enough to formulate the kinds of incandescent zingers that flew so easily from the mouths of women like Sake.

Ndamor in that sense really is Sake's child. She and a few other village women continue Sake's legacy of poetic swearing. Sadly, though, she and those other women are the last generation of Tayap speakers who will have the competence to be able to tell their husbands: "Stuff your sago into the opening of your friend's prick and get a thread and sew it up so he can carry it down to his village in his balls!"

After them, all that will be left is "shitty ass" and "hole."

10: MATTERS OF THE LIVER

BEFORE PAPUA NEW Guineans encountered white people, they didn't have writing. Their history and traditions (and their languages) were all oral. They were embodied in art and ritual, remembered by old people and passed on in stories and initiation practices. Literacy arrived with colonialism, especially with missionaries who set about devising orthographies—alphabets, ways of writing—for local languages that were spoken by enough people to justify the considerable effort it took for the missionaries to learn the languages from scratch. They learned the languages to translate the Bible in order to facilitate conversion to Christianity. Later, when the colonial government established schools in various parts of the country, students were taught how to read and write in English, which was the national language of Australia, Papua New Guinea's colonial caretaker.

Living far away from the concern of missionaries or the government, most villagers in Gapun never became literate. A few old men like Raya learned to read and write when they worked as plantation laborers in the 1950s. And for about fifteen years from the late 1970s until about the mid-1990s, a small government-run school did exist in the village of Wongan, which is a two-hour journey from Gapun—an hour's walk through the swamp and then another hour of paddling across the mangrove lagoon in a dugout canoe. At its apogee in the mid-1980s, when I was living in Gapun for the first time, the school was staffed by three teachers who taught grades one through six. I spent several weeks in the school observing what went on, and I came away feeling depressed. The teachers—who were all men from villages along the Sepik River—could barely speak English, the language of instruction, and the pedagogy they used consisted entirely of repeating by rote. They wrote sentences (that were often ungrammatical and nonsensical) on fragments of blackboard in the front of classrooms that had been constructed out of poles and thatch, and they read aloud what they had written, ordering the kids who sat desultorily on bark benches to repeat back at them exactly what they had said.

Children from Gapun went to school only sporadically because they could see no real point in attending. I agreed with them—it was obvious that they acquired much more useful knowledge cavorting in the rainforest than they ever did sitting bored in a stuffy, dark classroom, where they got shouted at by ill-natured teachers and arbitrarily struck with a length of stiff cane for being "disobedient." The teachers, furthermore, frequently went on strike because of non-school-related conflicts that they had with various villagers. For most of the 1990s, they stopped teaching, then two of them left. The one who remained in Wongan because he married a local woman hasn't taught a day since 2009.

As far as I was ever able to tell, the children who attended Wongan Community School during the years it existed learned only two things. The first thing they learned was to be dissatisfied with their life in the village. The crumbling Australian-made schoolbooks they passed around in the classroom contained drawings and photos of things like highways and cities—providing the pupils with glimpses of a life of opulence that they couldn't really imagine but that, clearly, existed *somewhere else*.

The second thing that some of the more industrious children learned at school was basic literacy skills. They learned to read and write. They never learned much of the meaning of the texts they were ordered to read in school because those texts were in English, and the teachers commanded the students only to repeat after them, not to actually comprehend any of the words they mouthed.

Without ever receiving any formal instruction to do so, however, some young people put their reading and writing skills to use to read and write Tok Pisin. There wasn't ever much to read in the village aside from a little booklet of Catholic hymns titled *Niu Laip* (*New Life*) that a visiting priest at some point had brought and distributed to most households. But villagers who acquired literacy skills started writing notes to others asking them for things. A few also made sporadic lists, like Raya did, of important events that occurred, especially noting the names of men involved in large-scale village fights (keeping track of such things made it easier to remember who should later compensate whom with pigs). And at some point in the 1990s, some resourceful young people put their literacy skills to a novel, creative use: they started writing love letters. These missives opened up a whole new way for young villagers to court one another.

But because the words used in the love letters were written down, they were also harder to take back, or deny, when mix-ups occurred and things went awry.

IN THE MIDDLE of the mangrove lagoon, paddling home, Saragum suddenly realized he had given his girlfriend Bebs the wrong love letter. He stopped paddling and reached into the back pocket of his shorts to check. Sure enough, he pulled out the letter he had written to Bebs. That meant that he had given Bebs the love letter he had written for his other girlfriend, Pemela.

Kaikai kan.

Saragum put the love letter to Bebs back in his pocket and thought, "How am I going to get out of this one?" He took up his paddle again and started singing "Meri Morobe" ("Morobe Woman"), a Tok Pisin song by a popular group called Skwatas, under his breath. He replayed the events of the morning and tried to think how he could have been so careless as to give a love letter to the wrong girlfriend by mistake. "'*Yu belhat long mi / na yu bin kolim mi clown,*'" he sang, smiling to himself with bemused self-pity. ("You got angry with me / and you called me a clown.") His dugout canoe glided through the still waters of the mangrove lagoon in the crisp early-afternoon light.

How *would* Saragum get out of this one? He would need to draw on his experience juggling girlfriends. And he certainly had ample experience with that.

Saragum was the village Casanova. He was a popular lover, and at age nineteen, he had already reputedly fathered at least two children, even though he admitted nothing. Several young women in Gapun regarded Saragum as a boyfriend. He let each of them think what she liked, making each feel special every time he met with her in private, even as he imperiously ignored them all in public.

Like most true charmers, Saragum wasn't conventionally handsome. He had a broad, slightly upturned nose and small eyes that were too close-set for his big, blockish face. The eyes and the piercing intensity with which he looked at people through them gave him an air of menace. But he had a wide, sensual mouth, and when he smiled, he flashed his teeth all the way back to his molars. When he did that, his face creased upwards from the corners of his lips, and his eyes crinkled into two shiny, mischievous buttons. The combination of impishness and menace gave Saragum a strong erotic aura. He moved casually and confidently, in a swaggering way that made it clear that he would have sex at the drop of a hat. But he was self-centered and fussy, so it was also clear that he would have all kinds of idiosyncratic ideas and rules that would make the experience of having sex with him strange and demanding, but also utterly captivating.

Saragum was one of the few villagers who had completed sixth grade in Wongan Community School. He was accepted to a high school in the tiny town of Angoram on the Sepik River. The year that he attended the high school, the teachers were on strike much of the time because most of the students, including Saragum, never paid their school fees. So instead of spending his time getting an education, Saragum spent his time in Angoram getting laid.

A few months into his first semester, Saragum had to leave Angoram because he had gotten a young woman pregnant and her parents were demanding that he marry her. He fled home into the rainforest, banking on the girl's parents not being able to find him in Gapun. Once back in the village, he continued to correspond with one of his other girlfriends in Angoram (this was Bebs) by way of friends who traveled up and down the Sepik River transporting betel nut in rowboats powered by outboard motors. Those young men would take the letters that Bebs and Saragum wrote to each other, giving his to her in Angoram and delivering hers to Saragum's relatives in the coastal village of Watam; those relatives would eventually pass them on to Saragum in Gapun.

But even as Saragum kept his Angoram flame burning bright, he also quickly found a new favorite—Pemela—in the neighboring village of Wongan.

On the day of the fateful missive mix-up, Saragum went to Watam for the opening of a newly built village church, which the priest in the far-off mission settlement of Marienberg had promised to come to consecrate. Bebs had told Saragum by letter that she would be traveling from Angoram to Watam to meet him. He also knew that Pemela was going to be there, too, with the excuse of attending the church consecration but really to indulge in more profane activities with her boyfriend. Saragum decided that if he spoke to either of his girlfriends in public, he would risk being seen by the other, and the result of that would be awkward. So he wrote them each a letter proposing to rendezvous with them in private later for—in a charmingly louche phrase that practically demands to be sung by Barry White—a "love meet."

Soon after Saragum arrived in Watam the morning of the consecration, after having paddled his canoe across the mangrove lagoon for three hours to get there, he spied Bebs. He strolled past her nonchalantly and surreptitiously handed her what he thought was his letter to her. That mission accomplished, he decided that seeing Bebs made him feel nervous, and he didn't want to stick around in case she insisted on hanging around him when his other girlfriend, Pemela, turned up.

So he got back into his canoe and paddled home.

. . .

By the time Saragum arrived back home in Gapun, he had considered his situation carefully. He thought of several possible lies he could tell Bebs. His first idea was to tell her that the love letter he had given her was from someone else to that person's girlfriend, who was named Pemela, and that he, the mere messenger, gave it to Bebs by mistake. But then he remembered that he had penned his love moniker, "Sont" (for "Spirit of Night Time"), several times throughout the letter.

So that option, unfortunately, was out.

Then he came up with a better plan. He would tell Bebs that the letter really was from him to her, and that despite looking suspiciously like a woman's name, the word "Pemela" wasn't; it was a word in his mother's local language that means "true love." So every time Bebs read "Pemela," she should read the word as addressing Bebs as Sont's "true love." Saragum's mother had been born on a faraway island; she was Monei's sister, the child of the Gapun man who worked as a plantation laborer in the 1940s and a local woman whom he married and brought back to Gapun with him. Saragum knew that there was no way to check the veracity of what he said about the meaning of "Pemela" in his mother's local language.

It was a brilliant, foolproof plan, in other words.

Despite that, though, Saragum worried that the lie was a thin one since the letter he had given Bebs didn't mention anything about her. Plus, all Bebs had to do was ask anyone who Pemela was, and it would take her no time at all to discover that she was a young woman in Wongan who, everybody knew, slept with Saragum.

In the end, Saragum thought that maybe he shouldn't do anything at all. Or, better yet, maybe he should do what villagers who find themselves in a pickle often do, which is to "run away" to another village and lie low for a while until things cool down back home.

LUKE WAS ALSO a diligent writer of love letters. The same age as Saragum, nineteen, Luke had never spent much time outside the village, but he came from a family with older brothers, all of whom actively read and wrote. Luke's oldest brother was Moses, the man who had orchestrated the destruction of the village in 2007. Moses used the literacy skills that he had acquired to draw maps of the village and write to a mail-order catalogue company in England that sells magic mantras to fulfill one's fondest wishes.

Luke's second-oldest brother, Rafael, was the village prayer leader. He regularly read parts of the New Testament—his favorite verse (in fact, every villager's favorite verse—the only one they all could quote, especially to me) was Matthew 7.7: "*Yu askim bai yu kisim*" ("Ask, and it shall be given you"). Rafael was the contact person for the priest who lived in the Marienberg mission station, and he sometimes wrote letters inquiring when the priest would come to the area, or asking him for assistance with petrol so that Rafael could travel on a motor canoe to Marienberg on some errand.

Luke's third-oldest brother, Kosai, was the head of the village "police." This was a completely nominal group consisting of four men who had no authority whatsoever and who never did anything except bemoan the fact that they didn't have uniforms. "If only we had uniforms," they would lament whenever anyone noticed that the so-called police were never anywhere to be found when violent fights or disruptive drinking bouts occurred. In fact, if the disturbances involved anyone related to the policemen (which, in a place as small as Gapun, was virtually assured)—or if they involved the policemen themselves (which also happened often)—the policemen would invariably "run away" and disappear for a while until the conflict blew over.

Still, in a large bound notebook that I had given him for the purpose, Kosai occasionally wrote down reports of infractions, such as thefts of betel nut and major village fights.

As for Luke himself, pretty much the only thing he ever wrote were love letters.

Like Saragum, Luke was popular among the young ladies in Gapun and the surrounding villages. But whereas Saragum, not yet even twenty years old, was already a jaded rake, Luke gave the impression of cherubic innocence. He was thinner than most village men his age, and he looked more adolescent and several years younger than he really was. He had a round, open, boyish face, with wide eyes and the downy suggestion of a mustache on his upper lip. Luke didn't stare at people intently like Saragum did. When Luke looked at you, he tended to look up with a downturned chin and upturned eyes. He seemed both sorrowful and cheeky at the same time, like the proverbial little boy who has been discovered with his hand in the cookie jar.

If Saragum was the Marlon Brando or the Mick Jagger of Gapun, Luke was the village's James Dean.

And Luke was equally successful at seducing young women. Like Saragum, he had multiple girlfriends whom he struggled to keep track of—and keep apart. And like Saragum, Luke wrote love letters to his girlfriends to arrange meetings with them. Luke's letters were different from Saragum's. Saragum opened his love letters with Marvin Gaye–worthy lines in Tok Pisin like "*Gutpela sweetpela love de stret long yu*" ("Good sweet love day right to you"). He signed off with poetic flourishes in capital letters, in English. Saragum didn't know what the flourishes meant, but he liked the way they sounded. One ending read: "YOU ALREADY TAKE PLES IN MY SUPPER HEART ALREADY"; another one crooned: "YOUR VOICE NEVER ABANDON IN MY THOUGHT."

Luke was more pedantic and less polished. Into an old notebook that he still had left over from his school days, he had composed in English what he considered to be the proper form of a love letter. It read:

> Dear my derling,
>
>   What situation you are in there. I hope you are 100% fine. At this moment, I hope, you are enjoying your life with your friends. and this time I have nothing much to say. but just to let you know I realy want to make friendship with you. I want to check your mind. Are you want me to make friendship with you. It's okey. Are you dont want me to make friendship with you That's okey. Makso replly my letter with Person name

That last sentence ("Makso replly my letter with Person name") meant: "Send your reply with the person who gave you this love note." Luke was so proud of this paragraph that he used it verbatim in letters to five different young women. He sometimes repeated it in letters he wrote to the same woman. In one letter he wrote to a girl named Magret, he began in Tok Pisin by saying that Magret hadn't responded to Luke's previous letter, "I think because you don't know how to read English." He asked her in Tok Pisin to come to Gapun, and he finished the letter by reiterating the same paragraph in English that he already had determined that Magret couldn't read—because she didn't understand English.

As stilted as it was, Luke's letter writing style was positively Shakespearean compared with what some of the other young men produced. Pukos, a twenty-three-year-old villager, began his love letters to young women with the salutation he remembered from school: "Dear Sir." This was always followed by a direct proposition (and creative capitalization) in Tok Pisin: "Hello AND Really good morning or Afternoon to you. I Want you (*mi gat TinTing long yu*) AND I'm JUST ASKING you IF you lust (*las*) after me, alright tell me straight tell the man who brought this letter to you."

Pukos's younger cousin, Konjab, who was twenty years old, wrote similar proposals in Tok Pisin, embedded in long, summer-saulting requests: "Anduwara I think about you and I'm just ask-ing you if you lust OK answer my letter I'm just asking if you read it and you think of me alright tell me straight and I'll know that you lust I'm just asking."

How is it that I am privy to such private correspon-dence from so many young men and can legitimately reveal the contents?

Through what I like to think of as anthropological ingenuity.

Love letters are a relatively new phenomenon; they didn't exist when I lived in Gapun in the mid-1980s. At that time, about the only thing the few villagers who could write used their writing skills for was to send short notes to people (again, especially to me) asking for something that they felt embarrassed to ask for in person. Throughout my stay in the village, in addition to the daily visits requesting things, I received a steady stream of small handwritten notes informing me that the writer had a "little worry" about "a little rice" (which, translated, usually meant the writer wanted me to give him or her a fifty-pound sack of rice), "a little money" (usually several hundred kina to buy a pig for a funerary feast), and so on.

By the time I returned to the village for my second long-term stay in 2009, the notes to me requesting a little rice, a little money, sugar, coffee, salt, etc., still flowed reliably in, but some young villagers were also writing to one another to establish and maintain relationships, and to arrange "love meets." Most young men didn't write love letters for the simple reason that most young men weren't literate enough to write them. They arranged meetings with young women in the old-fashioned way, through intermediaries or by speaking to them discreetly when no one else was within earshot. But the young men who did write love letters discussed them with one another; they shared formulations (Luke's paragraph that begins with "Dear my derling, What situation you are in there. I hope you are 100% fine . . ." was especially popular and occurred in numerous love letters written by a variety of young men); and they pressed one another into service as messengers to deliver their letters and, hopefully, also collect a written or verbal response from the young women who received them.

I overhead young men talking about the letters they wrote, and I saw them sitting close and giggling together as they checked the insect-ravaged notebooks in which they had composed or copied down formulations to put in their letters. I was dying to know what the letters looked like, and in what language, or languages, they were written in. But I couldn't think of any good reason to ask the men to show them to me.

Then I hit upon an ingenious plan.

In the middle of my long stay in the village in 2009, I went to Australia for a week to attend a conference, and while I was there, I purchased a little portable printer and a box of paper. When I returned to Gapun, I hooked the printer up to my solar-battery-powered laptop and let it be known that I possessed the means of transforming any handwritten letter into a beautifully printed billet-doux. The conditions of enlisting my printing services were that I got to keep the original letter, I could use its contents in my work, and I could publish it if I wanted to.

The young men I explained this to were perplexed as to why in the world I was interested in their love letters. They were used to me working with old people on the vernacular language that none of them could speak. The letters they wrote to young women had no respectability; they were just trivial rubbish, they told me, embarrassed. But once they saw the notes that they had laboriously scrawled out with fading ballpoint ink on scraps of molding paper transformed into neatly printed epistles on crisp white sheets, they began pouring up into my house with their love letters in hand. And they discussed them with me with gusto, carefully explaining the meaning of various abbreviations (such as Sont, for "Spirit of Night Time"), and sharing the details of their relationships with the young women they wrote to. I showed them different fonts I could use to print out their letters and I let them choose the one they liked best. Most surprised me by selecting what I thought was the gayest and most curlicue font of them all, one called *French script*.

Young women write love letters, too, in response to the ones they receive or to initiate a contact with a young man they fancy. Like the young men, young women have a variety of individual letter-writing styles, ranging from the more direct to the more prosaic. They frequently talk about how the young man they write to is their liver. This is the Papua New Guinean equivalent of the heart. In Papua New Guinea, emotion flows from the liver, not the heart. Perhaps the floridity of the French Script font best approximated the flutter of their livers that young people felt when they wrote love letters. Magret, the young woman from Watam who Luke thought couldn't read English, once wrote to him in Tok Pisin to say: "I really long (*mi wari tru*) to see your face. So in term 3 I'm gonna come to Gapun. MBAW [Luke's love moniker, a shortened form of his Tayap name, Mbawi], I just hang around, I don't eat. I always really long to see you term 3 I'm gonna come to see you my liver Brother Mbaw." ("Brother" and "sister" in love letters are murmurs of endearment; they aren't kinship terms.)

Young women use their letters, more than young men do, to try to gauge the true depth of the men's feelings for them. One young woman wrote to a young man she had heard was interested in her. In her letter, she reported that someone had told her of the man's interest, and that she thought that was "all right" (*orit*). But she wanted to know: "And I want to ask you this do you have a girl friend here too or not. If you have a girl friend here alright write a letter back to me and tell me straight that I have a woman here."

The man responded that he didn't have any girlfriends, and the couple agreed to rendezvous. A few months later, they married, which in Gapun means simply that they started going off into the rainforest to process sago flour together, and they began sleeping together in the same mosquito net at night.

The letters that Saragum's girlfriends wrote to him are full of this same concern. One he received from Bebs prior to the mix-up informs him in Tok Pisin of her discovery that people in Angoram were saying that he got one of her schoolmates pregnant. "Sont why when I started having sex you (*prenim yu*) you were supposed to tell me that you already had a woman and you had a baby with her. SONT honest when I heard that my liver really broke." (Saragum replied by admitting that the woman in question had been his girlfriend, but he rejected the idea that he could have been responsible for getting her pregnant. The girl had "a secret boy friend," he wrote cryptically, and that unrevealed man was the father of her child, not him.)

Pemela's letters to Saragum also question the status of their relationship. One has a long passage in English that says, "Sont when the sun godawn from the west I was remember your movement and I diden't talk with anyone sometime I cryed. somtime in the class I was tink about you and I dident listening to my teacher. I don't know you love me or you diden't love me. My love from me to you is that when the rain full dawn from the cloud that is my love for you. You get and drink." The letter continues in Tok Pisin: "Please Brother sont if you like me or not OK you write a letter and send it to me."

LOVE LETTERS FROM both women and men contain coded messages. Villagers write only on one side of a piece of paper. The reason for this is because there are no envelopes in Gapun; when a letter is written, it is folded up into a little square and the name of the recipient is written on it. Experienced love-letter writers like Saragum or Luke, though, frequently embellish the blank back page with what Saragum told me are called "Expression." These include bon mots like "Action speak louder than voice" or "I will never miss you a lone," and "Love Words," such as "When the golden sun rise from the east to the west, the tears will fall as rain when you think of mi" (Pemela used a variation of this phrase in her letter to Saragum; it clearly circulated widely, and young people seemed to like it a lot).

The blank back page of a letter is also the place where writers will include words or the names of towns or countries that knowing readers understand are acronyms to be deciphered. Merangam, a twenty-year-old village youth, had a notebook in which he had written the meaning of some of the most popular acronymns. YAM, for example, according to Merangam's notation, means "You Are Mind." ITALY should be read as "I Truthly Always Love You." WABAG, a town in the highlands of Papua New Guinea, stands for "We Are Boys And Girls." BOGIA, a small settlement on the east coast, means, mysteriously, "Boy o Girl In Acident." Then things get even more mysterious. WEWAK, the capital of the province in which Gapun lies, is an acronym for "When Eating We Always Kiss." CAMBRIDGE is, inscrutibly, "Come Any Moment But Remember I Don't Forget Another." The offshore island MANUS is short for "Man Always Neked Under the Chair."

THE DAY AFTER his mix-up with the love letters, Saragum scurried out of Gapun to avoid a potential scene and hiked to a village near the Ramu River—a seven-hour trek through the rainforest—where he had a friend from high school he knew he could stay with. On his way out of Gapun, though, who should he pass on the trail but Bebs, who had traveled to Gapun to see him.

As he hurried past her, she handed him a letter.

Bebs's letter was a whole double page torn out of a school exercise book, plus another single page. Either she had read his letter and not understood that it was not intended for her, or else she somehow hadn't yet read it. Her return letter made no reference to his, and it was full of love. "Memories of you will be my life story," she wrote in Tok Pisin, and she ended in English with: "I LOVE YOU THATS SOL." On the back she wrote "I ❤ U so muck." Saragum read the letter when he got to his friend's village, and he was so relieved that he cut his stay short and returned to Gapun four days later.

As he was about to enter Gapun, though, fate determined that Saragum again met Bebs as she marched down the road on her way to the creek that leads to the mangrove lagoon. She was leaving. As she passed him, she shoved another letter into his hands, hissing, "Now we know all the secrets of you and your girlfriend." The letter she handed Saragum was short and written in red ink, a color that, in the arcane language of love letters, villagers told me symbolizes anger. It was clear that Bebs had now read the letter that Saragum had given to her by mistake in Watam, and she was not happy. "Dear the pathna [meaning "partner"] of someone else not me," her letter began acidly in English. Then she switched to a brisk, no-nonsense Tok Pisin, which, translated, reads:

> I got the letter you gave me it isn't a letter to me it's a letter to your beloved Girl Pemela you tell her that you like her better than me that's alright, don't worry. it's God's plan [in

his letter to Pemela, Saragum had waxed lyrical about how it was God's plan that she and Saragum should be together. He also wrote, using a line he cribbed from Luke's corpus of love letters, that "Pemela love for you it's like a mother cares for little babies."] last night God called me and told me that Pemela came according to my plan. you were really bad to give her letter to me I read it and I got really mad if you had given it to her I wouldn't be angry. So you can't worry about me, she's your true love. it's alright I don't fit your style you said its God's plan. You like her like a new born baby of yours. and you love her more than me. it's not a mistake because its God's plan. your heart [Saragum had used the English word "heart" in his letter to Pemela] breaks because of her. Thank Q truly AND I DON'T HAVE ANYTHING TO SAY TO YOU

Bebs finished her letter in English: "END OF ALL THINGS." She signed it: "BEBS FUUL CRUZER OF APMA LEND [Apma is the name of the village Bebs was from] LIVING WITH NO STYLE BUT LOVE THE WAY I' AM B COZ."

SARAGUM'S FACE FELL when he read Bebs's letter. The game, it seemed, was up. I asked him what he was going to do. He said he would have to talk to Bebs in person; he was sick of writing letters. He would explain to her that he was a young man, he wasn't married, and he could have other girlfriends if he wanted. She would have to accept that. Imagining the scene in his head, he suddenly perked up. He flashed his seductive alligator grin. She'll accept it, he said with the jaunty self-confidence that only a true heartbreaker (or in his case, a true liverbreaker) could summon under such circumstances.

But to be honest, Saragum confided, he was a bit tired of trying to please all his girfriends. Couldn't I try to find him a female pen pal when I went back to my country? He would write to her and tell her to come to Papua New Guinea on the cruise ship that arrived about once every six months and stopped for a few hours in Watam. He would wait for her.

It would be hard to spot her, though, he told me thoughtfully, scratching his head after some consideration. Because at the end of the day, Saragum said, smiling brightly, all white people kind of look exactly alike.

11: YOUNG PEOPLE'S TAYAP

AFTER MANY YEARS of doing anthropological fieldwork, I have reached the conclusion that the secret to being a successful anthropologist is to overstay your welcome. Since the whole purpose of anthropology is to try to understand not only what people say they do but what they actually do do (knowing full well that those two activities are often divergent or even contradictory), an anthropologist rarely just interviews someone or hands out a questionnaire and then leaves. Instead, we stick around. To do the job well, an anthropologist has to have as a natural talent—or develop as a skill—the ability to hang around unobtrusively.

Overstaying one's welcome is a painful process for everyone involved. Imagine befriending an anthropologist who turned up in your neighborhood one day and made it known that he wanted to write a book about people like you. You might invite him out to lunch one afternoon, out of politeness, curiosity, or pity. The anthropologist would show up early, draw out the lunch all afternoon by listening with avid intensity to the stories you tell about yourself and about anything else. Suddenly, you'd find that you had somehow invited him to dinner at your place. There, he'd engage your spouse in friendly banter, play with your kids, coo over your pet parakeet, and become best buddies with the family dog. After all the dinner dishes had been washed and put away, you'd turn around to find that the anthropologist was still in your kitchen, or your living room, bright-eyed and eagerly hanging out. Eventually, you'd announce that you were tired and needed to go to bed. The anthropologist would take courteous leave. Only to turn up again at your doorstep the next day.

And the next.

From the point of view of the anthropologist, the goal of such shaggy-dog behavior is to wear you down—to help you understand that an anthropologist doesn't want to be treated like an invited guest who gets accorded special treatment every time he turns up. He wants to be treated as an unremarked-upon regular: not necessarily like a family member; more like a comfortable piece of furniture or a potted palm.

This role—what in the jargon of the discipline is grandly called participant observation—is not a particularly pleasant one to establish, and the absolute worst parts of fieldwork are always the first few months when everyone is still working out the boundaries for what is acceptable. I can remember many, many times in the various places I have done fieldwork sitting with people I barely knew, in front of an empty coffee cup or scraped-clean plate of food, thinking, "They really want me to leave now"—and consciously resisting what I knew perfectly well would be the normal, sensible, and polite consequences of that insight. I knew that if I could overstay my welcome just a little longer, the quicker I could convey to my flustered hosts that I was undemanding and harmless, and that I didn't mind at all if they got on with their lives and paid no attention to me at all.

That, in fact, was the whole point.

During the fifteen months I lived in Gapun during my first long-term stay in the mid-1980s, I devoted hundreds of hours overstaying my welcome, much of it spent recording how mothers and other people talked to babies. I followed a strict schedule: three days a week, I would arrive before dawn in the house of one of the five bewildered families that had agreed to let me record them, and I would settle down in an unobtrusive corner with my tape recorder and my notebook. I'd sometimes follow mothers and their children on their visits to other houses or to their gardens, and a couple of times, I went with a married couple when they took their children with them into the rainforest to cut down a sago palm and process sago flour. For the most part, though, I sat in my corner of the house all day long, turning on the tape recorder whenever anything interesting was going on, and noting things like the names of the children and adults who came and went, and where people were positioned in relation to one another when they spoke.

I didn't sit in the houses I visited pretending to be a fly on the wall—I ate with the family and chatted with the mother, her children, and anyone who walked by or came to visit throughout the day. I sometimes curled up on the floor and dozed off when a child, and oftentimes his or her mother as well, fell asleep in the haze of the afternoon heat.

I stayed until it got too dark to see anything inside the houses. And I was back again the next morning, before dawn.

The recordings and the observations I made during those hundreds of hours hanging out with caregivers and children allowed me to understand how Tayap was dying. In the book I wrote about the situation in the village in the late 1980s, I discussed how the transmission of Tayap to children had been irrevocably sundered. I predicted that the generation of children under ten years of age whom I had come to know would never learn Tayap, and I foresaw that unless some miracle were to happen, the Tayap language would soon disappear forever.

When I returned to Gapun in 2009 for my first long stay since the late 1980s, I naturally was curious to see whether the predictions I had made about the demise of Tayap had come to pass. The children whose language acquisition I had recorded in the mid-1980s were now grown-ups; many had children of their own. Had those kids somehow managed to acquire Tayap after I left the village? Was the language really dying, or had it turned out to be more tenacious than I had foreseen?

Unlike most researchers, who tend to stake their careers on always being right, I had high hopes that my predictions regarding Tayap had been utterly wrong. It would have given me enormous pleasure to realize that I had misjudged the situation in the village, and that tiny Tayap, instead of dying, on the contrary was flourishing. I even fantasized about the title of the book I would write announcing my mistake. I now forget what that title was, but I recall that it had something mawkish like "Resilience" in it, or, worse, "Phoenix."

Once I had established myself in the village again, I thought it would be an easy thing to discover whether young people spoke Tayap. Yet even after more than three months, I found that I was still unable to accurately judge whether young people commanded it.

Whenever I asked young people if they spoke Tayap, they all told me sure they did. The problem was, I never heard any of them doing so. Once in a while, I would hear a young person utter a few formulaic phrases in Tayap, like "Get out of my way" or "You're gonna piss" (because I will hit you). These phrases were usually delivered to mark a situation as funny, and they were often accompanied and followed by laughter. It also seemed to me that whenever villagers under age twenty-five mouthed even a short formulaic phrase in Tayap, their tone of voice shifted to suggest that they were quoting or imitating someone else, usually to mock them (a big man's Voice of Authority, for example).

Whenever I pressed the young people who told me that they spoke Tayap, and asked them to tell me what kind of things they said to one another in the language, they would list a few words like *mum* and *tamwai* ("sago jelly" and "sago pancake," respectively) and a few rudimentary formulaic phrases, such as the command to hand over some betel nut or tobacco.

TAYAP CONTINUES TO be heard throughout Gapun. Women and men over fifty use it habitually (even if they also continually switch between Tayap and Tok Pisin), and a few men and women in their midthirties and older also use Tayap frequently, including when speaking to their children. Even small children in the village understand the commands to go and fetch things, hit dogs, get out of the way, stop crying, and so on that adults are always hollering at them.

Since it was clear that Tayap was still used in Gapun in the late 2000s, and since it also was clear that young people all *understood* the language, for a long time I thought that perhaps the young people really were quite competent in Tayap, as they claimed to be. I fretted that I just never seemed to be in the right place at the right time to hear them actually speak it.

I began to wonder if the reason I wasn't hearing young people telling one another stories or asking each other questions in Tayap was because they spoke it mostly out of the earshot of older, more fluent speakers. Maybe they felt ashamed that they weren't speaking it flawlessly, I conjectured. Or perhaps Tayap, for them, had become tied to particular social events like same-sex gossip or hanging out in the rainforest—speech situations that happened only when young people were alone in groups and away from nosy and critical parents and elders.

To see whether any of this was, in fact, the case, I spent much of my time during that stay hanging out with young people between the ages of fourteen and twenty-five. I accompanied young men into the rainforest on frequent occasions, to go looking for birds to shoot with arrows or slingshots, and also when they went off together in groups to perform a variety of secret rituals that they say refresh their bodies and leave them feeling stronger and more attractive.

I also spent a lot of time hanging out with young women inside their maternity huts—those small, flimsy, hurriedly constructed little houses on stilts, set on the periphery of the village. During the entire period a woman is in a maternity hut, no man is supposed to visit her or even set eyes upon her or her newborn baby. Female visitors, though, drop by throughout the day, usually accompanied by their younger siblings and their own babies. They bring food, water, and gossip about the goings-on in the village from which the new mother is excluded.

It was not gender appropriate for me to sit in the maternity huts with new mothers and other young women, but the villagers regarded my enthusiasm for doing so as just a puzzling white-man eccentricity. Everyone in Gapun was convinced that I was going to get a fatal case of asthma from allowing myself to come in such close contact with the "heat" of women. When they give birth, women disgorge what to the villagers' sensibilities are unspeakable amounts of blood and uterine fluids. The women and their newborns throb with so much "heat" as a result of this gush of blood that they are a danger even to themselves: to protect themselves from harm, new mothers cannot touch the food they eat—they have to use small tongs or a spoon. Whenever I wondered aloud whether I might be coming down with a fever or a cold, a villager would always be on hand to ruefully shake his or her head and remind me how foolish I was to put myself at risk of bronchial collapse by sitting next to a woman who had recently given birth. Sure, I might take special white-people's medicine to protect against the ravages of vaginal heat, they told me (this is how they assumed I could survive the blasts at all), but sooner or later, they knew for certain, I would start spewing blood.

Despite their expectation that I would soon be coughing out both my lungs, women and men alike seemed to enjoy my visits in the maternity huts. Men enjoyed them because I took digital photos of the new babies. Only after I began showing these photos did I realize that before I came along, no adult man had ever seen a newborn baby. Men were anxious (could the new mothers' heat contaminate them even through an image?), but they were also mesmerized. "*Ye!*" they said, using the expression that signifies apprehension and alarm, crowding around my camera and pointing, "Look at that. *Ye*, their skin is really yellow." Women always welcomed me because I brought gossip and stories. They also liked looking at the photos of themselves and their babies. I usually also brought along some kerosene that could be put into a makeshift tin lamp, thus sparing the new mother and her baby pitch-black nights in a lonely, wind-rattled hut.

BECAUSE I SPENT so many hours in the company of young women in places like maternity huts, and of young men in places like the rainforest when they performed their secret ritual ministrations together, I came to see, over the months, that the young people in Gapun hardly ever used Tayap. All conversations between people younger than twenty-five, in all situations, were in Tok Pisin. Young people only used Tayap words that are common in the villagers' speech and that in many instances don't have Tok Pisin equivalents (for example, words for various birds and plants in the forest). And they do sometimes use short formulaic phrases to threaten their children, to provoke humor, or to "hide talk" from any nonvillager who might be in their company or within earshot. But that is all. Young people do not converse, narrate, gossip, argue, tell jokes, discuss romantic liaisons, or do anything else at all in Tayap.

I became curious to know if the young people's lack of Tayap was because they simply didn't command it. So to try to assess this, I began asking groups of friends, two to three at a time, to come into my house at night to narrate stories in Tayap. Because I knew by that point that young people didn't speak Tayap to one another or anyone else, I expected this task to be like pulling teeth.

Instead, to my great surprise, it was like slicing butter.

Not only were young villagers eager to narrate; it turned out that all but the very youngest of them were also *able* to narrate in Tayap. Many of the narratives were short, and most of them were scaffolded by the narrator's relatives and friends, who sat on the floor with them and helped the teller remember what things were called and figure out how verbs were inflected. But what emerged in the narrative sessions was that all young people in the village over age eighteen have some active competence in the vernacular, and some of them have excellent active competence—even though they *never* use it.

Several of the young villagers in their mid- to late twenties were highly proficient storytellers. They spoke relatively unhesitatingly, they had a broad vocabulary, they used a variety of tenses and verbs of motion (which are often irregular in Tayap and very tricky to inflect correctly) in the stories they told, and they also commanded other features of the grammar that showed unexpected mastery of Tayap. The truly curious thing about the speakers is that outside of these sessions, they never displayed their command of the language. I once asked Membo, a twenty-six-year-old woman, what she thought about her twenty-five-year-old husband Ormbes's competence in Tayap. Membo laughed dismissively. "Oh, he messes it all up," she told me, "He doesn't speak Tayap."

I later asked Ormbes to tell me a story in Tayap. He narrated an almost flawless tale of how he and his brother went hunting in the rainforest and speared a pig. Ormbes turned out to be one of the most fluent younger speakers in the village. That his wife, who not only had been married to him for ten years but also had grown up with him and had known him all her life, was convinced that her husband didn't speak Tayap, was remarkable—and telling.

I scoured the linguistic literature for a label to name people like Ormbes, and I came up empty. Ormbes isn't what's known as a passive bilingual because he is capable of relatively advanced language production. Nor is someone like Ormbes quite the same as what linguists who work with endangered languages call a semi-speaker. Semi-speakers are speakers of a dying language who have perfect passive competence and perfect communicative competence in that language. In other words, they understand everything that fluent speakers say to them, and they respond in culturally appropriate ways, using short bursts of the language. Semi-speakers' ability to get jokes, interject comments, and actively participate in conversations by contributing a few well-turned utterances here and there is deceptive, and it often masks the fact that they can't actually say very much. Linguists who work with endangered languages report cases in which their work with semi-speakers has caused extreme embarrassment to a whole community. The linguists have given such speakers language proficiency tests because they assumed that they were fluent speakers (having seen them conversing with fluent speakers, and because fluent speakers identified them as fluent speakers). When confronted with a language test, though—and to everybody's dismay—the people who everyone thought were fluent, in reality, could barely manage to compose a single grammatically correct sentence on their own.

Young people in Gapun like Ormbes aren't semi-speakers partly because they can construct grammatically correct sentences, and also because they don't ever actually converse in Tayap. They actively participate in conversations when older speakers speak Tayap, but their own contributions are always in Tok Pisin. With the exception of lexical items and a few formulaic phrases like "Give me betel nut," they never use Tayap at all.

Rather than calling the young people in Gapun who can narrate stories in Tayap passive bilinguals or semi-speakers, I've taken to calling them "passive active bilinguals." The convolutedness of that label seems fitting to describe speakers who possesses sufficient grammatical and communicative competence in their second language to use that language, but who never actually do use it because social and cultural factors make it unnecessary or undesirable to do so.

So what are those factors? Partly, they are the associations that the Tayap language has come to take on in the village: connotations of infantile stubborn willfulness, feminine hotheadedness, and the old, heathen ways of the ancestors.

But in addition to that, fluent speakers of Tayap, far from encouraging young people to speak the language, instead criticize them whenever they try to do so. The minute those older speakers hear a stumbled pronunciation or a wrong word, they pounce.

Once, I was sitting beside twenty-eight-year-old Mbonika as she wove a basket from reeds. I asked her what the Tayap word for the handle of a basket was, and she said "*nariŋ.*"

Overhearing this, Mbonika's fifty-year-old father intervened and corrected her. "It's not *nariŋ,*" he said crisply in Tok Pisin. "That's what they call it in Wongan. In Tayap it's called *merom.*"

Mbonika responded with irritation. "We don't know your language," she snapped at her father in Tok Pisin. "You all call it *nariŋ* and we follow you. If you'd taught us what it was called in Tayap, we'd know."

A few months later, Mbonika came to my house and delivered the most fluent story in Tayap of any young person in the village. I was astonished. I had seen Mbonika every single day for eight months, and I had hung out with her in a wide variety of situations. I had been actively listening for any indication that she spoke Tayap. I had never heard her say anything more complicated than "Leave that alone" or "Where's my net bag?" in the language.

After hearing her tell her story in impeccable Tayap, I asked Mbonika why she never spoke the language, even though she clearly knew it. "I'm ashamed," she told me, giggling shyly. "If I say something wrong and an old person hears me, I'll be ashamed. They'll make fun of me, they'll say, 'Oh, you all only speak Tok Pisin and don't know Tayap.' That kind of thing. So I'm ashamed to speak it."

Other young people told me the same thing. "They laugh at us," young people said, referring to villagers in their forties and older. "They'll say, 'Oh, he's someone raised in some other village.' Or 'Oh! A white-man child who doesn't know the village language.' They'll make fun of us. So it's hard to answer in the vernacular and we get mixed up."

Time and again, I saw that what the young people told me was true. Parents continue to blame their children for not speaking Tayap. They say in voices dripping with irony that their children have all turned white, and therefore they can speak only the language of white people—Tok Pisin. Young people, when mocked in this way, hit back. They say it's their parents' fault they don't speak Tayap: Drawing on ideas about the relationship between teaching and learning that they gleaned from sitting on hard school benches, repeating verbatim phrases that teachers ordered them to recite, young people insist that if their parents had taught them Tayap, they would be able to speak it.

The result of this mutual recrimination is that Tayap is edged ever closer to the grave.

So that, then, is what I eventually discovered became of the children I spent so much time with in the mid-1980s. All of them acquired some Tayap, and a few of them came to be passive active bilinguals, possessing good competence in Tayap but never putting it to any use. Perhaps as they get older, speakers like Mbonika and Orbmes will begin to use their Tayap in the village. But I predict that if they do so, they'll use it mostly to sourly chastise people younger than themselves for not speaking Tayap. And by then, it will be too late.

As I looked closely at young people's Tayap, I saw how the very idea of language death is misguided. A language never just dies; it isn't here one minute and gone the next. Instead, languages dissolve; they waste away. Looking at young people's Tayap is like watching ink fade or flesh wither: the language loses its suppleness and becomes etiolated and spare. It shrivels from blowzy fecundity to become a kind of stiff, desiccated husk.

In young people's Tayap, the first thing to go is the ability to construct intricate synthetic verbs like "She intends to carry him down on her shoulders." Next to disappear are the complicated ways of linking verbs and forming relative clauses and subordinate clauses (so no "the pig that I speared yesterday" or "we were eating when you came"). Verbs of motion—except "come" and "go"—melt away too.

As speakers get younger in age and less competent in their command of the language, Tayap's range of tenses disappears, and gender agreement gets wonky. The youngest and least fluent speakers lose the ability to inflect any verbs for their correct subjects and objects; they collapse all classes of verbs to a single paradigm, and they replace Tayap vocabulary with Tok Pisin words.

In their language, the mighty tree that once was Tayap has been whittled down to a skinny toothpick.

ONE EVENING, I sat in a men's house with some young men who were planning to hike for several hours through the rainforest the following day, to set fire to a grassland they all knew well. They did this because the sun had been shining brightly for a few weeks, and they felt like having an adventure. Setting fire to a grassland is always a communal undertaking. One group of men sets fire to the field, and another group fans out and walks towards the flames, to intercept and spear the pigs, cassowaries, bandicoots, and other animals that flee the conflagration.

The evening before they set fire to a grassland, men prepare a special dish—a soup made of coconut water, shredded coconut, and torn-up sago pancakes. They gather in a men's house, summon their ancestors by calling out their names, and ask them for help to kill many pigs. They feed the ancestral spirits some of the soup by throwing spoonfuls of it off the side of the house.

On this particular evening, the man who owned the grassland that was to be burned had brewed some white-soup alcohol for the young men, and about twelve of them sat in a little men's house drinking and laughing. Suddenly, a young man whom everybody called by his Christian name, Debid, announced in a booming voice in Tok Pisin that he had "some talk." He stood up drunkenly in the men's house and began speaking in solemn Tayap. "My talk is thus," he said, in mock seriousness. The young men sitting around Debid started to giggle.

"Banaŋ Maroka, Kruni Maroka, Ndair Andwari, Sando Saraki," Debid said, reciting the names of Gapun's founding ancestors. "*Epi yim okinaka*" ("Tomorrow, we will go and . . .")—here he threw a spoonful of the coconut soup off the side of the men's house with a ritual flourish—"*naw apukrunaka*" ("we will burn a grassland and . . .")—another spoonful of soup got tossed—"*mbor akrunaka*" ("we will eat pig and . . ."). Another spoonful went over the side of the house.

Debid then switched back to Tok Pisin. He said, "That's it, my little talk," and he plopped himself down on the floor, smiling broadly. The young men responded to Debid's speech with whoops of laughter.

I was sitting on the floor of the men's house with the young men. I couldn't help thinking that Debid's speech encapsulated the future of Tayap. Not only was the speech delivered in a simple and peeled form of the language: the whole thing consisted of only three unadorned verbs. But just as meaningful as its Spartan format was the tone in which the speech was delivered, and received. Debid's "little talk" was comic. He switched out of Tok Pisin into his ancestral language to be funny. Debid played Tayap for laughs.

And everyone laughed.

12: LIVING DANGEROUSLY

DEBID AND THE other young men sitting drinking with him had been small children or babies—several of them hadn't even been born—during my first long-term stay in Gapun, which started in 1986. I left the village in 1987, to return home to Sweden to write my PhD thesis, when Debid was just a shy, pigeon-toed three-year-old with big inquisitive eyes. I came back again four years later, in 1991.

The villagers welcomed me enthusiastically, and they immediately set about building me a new house to live in. The one they had constructed for me five years earlier had grown "cold," they said, and was irretrievably dilapidated. It took them three months to build the new one, which was bigger and about four feet higher off the ground than anyone else's. My new house loomed over the village like a kind of hovering mother ship that seemed either protective or menacing, depending on your point of view. I found it embarrassing. I protested many times when the structural posts started to be erected and it dawned on me what the villagers had in mind. They ignored me. My house was clearly meant to be a boastful, grandiose construction; a Gapun version of Nicolae Ceausescu's Palace of the Parliament or a Trump Tower. The villagers wanted to advertise to anyone who might happen by that their white man was back, and that they could house him in style.

Whenever a communal project like building a men's house (or building a house for the resident white man) is completed, villagers usually inaugurate the house by throwing an all-night *singsing*. *Singsing*s are celebratory events that everyone participates in, not least because there is always lots of food—most of it supplied by the owner of the newly completed house—as well as traditional singing and dancing. A *singsing* takes place in the center of the village. It starts right before dusk, and it continues all night until dawn.

During my previous stay in the village, I had participated in several *singsing*s. I dreaded them. They always made me feel like a bad anthropologist because they bored me. The songs, sung in a grating nasal falsetto by the men and women, are monotonous and repetitive. The lyrics are mostly the names of places that ancestral beings visited as they passed through the landscape surrounding the village. And the dancing consists of shuffling around in a circle waving some sago fronds, and occasionally giving a little hop.

I have colleagues back home who become electrified by stuff like this: they carefully plot the dance steps, they record the place names on detailed maps, and then they write earnest books full of arcane analyses and flowcharts with lots of arrows in tables with too-small print.

Those books, like the events themselves, put me to sleep.

In Gapun, I wasn't the only one who was less than enthusiastic about the prospect of sitting through an entire night of *singsing*. During previous *singsing*s, I noted that many of the young villagers made themselves scarce at some point during the night. They did what young people everywhere do: they took the opportunity of parental distraction to slip away into the darkness for amorous rendezvous.

Regardless of what I or anyone else thought about the *singsings*, though, it was clear that the older villagers loved them. Old Kruni in particular seemed insatiable. He was able to keep up a steady beat on an hourglass drum and sing for hours, and he was a nimble and tireless dancer.

On the occasion of inaugurating my new house, I had supplied fifty pounds of rice, six pounds of sugar, a few big tins of instant Nescafé, and a carton of tinned corned beef. Village men had hunted and killed a few pigs, sago was plentiful, and everyone had a full belly and was in a festive mood. I had volunteered my kerosene lantern as the source of light for the event, and villagers suspended it with a vine from a pole in the house where I had been staying since I had reappeared in the village. That house was six yards away from the merrymaking.

I stood watching the *singsing* in the dim kerosene glow for several hours, but by midnight, I was done. I had spent enough time in the village to know that no one would consider it hideously impolite for me to excuse myself for a little nap. I did just that, and I went up into the house I was going to move out of the next day. I crawled into my mosquito net, lay down on my mat, and settled in to try to sleep.

I had almost dozed off when a sharp crack hit the bamboo wall of the house. Like a small stone thrown hard. Then another one hit. And another. The adults dancing outside my house heard the shots, too, and several of them shouted into the darkness at unseen children, warning them to stop playing with slingshots and shooting stones among people at night.

I must have fallen asleep for a few minutes because the next thing I remember was a huge roar—an explosion—and a flash of white light. I sat up, alarmed. I quickly reached down to the foot of my mat and slipped on my shorts.

As I stretched my arm back towards my pillow to locate my glasses, my front door was kicked in.

Two men stormed up into my house. They ran straight towards me, in heavy boots that made the bark floor quake. They ripped open my mosquito net, shone a flashlight in my eyes, and one of them pushed the barrel of a sawed-off shotgun into my face.

The men were wearing black balaclavas to conceal their faces. The one with the gun screamed at me in English: "Give us the money! Give us the money!"

I felt more befuddled than frightened, because I couldn't comprehend what was happening. Where did these men come from? What money? I was in the middle of a New Guinea swamp, not on my way fresh out of a bank. And what happened to the villagers? A minute before, I could hear them singing and talking and laughing. Now everything had gone eerily quiet. Where were they? Didn't they realize what was going on?

I answered the masked man on the other end of the gun in English, a language I had never before used in Gapun. I told him to wait, to let me put on my glasses and find my flashlight because I needed to be able to see to be able to give him any money. He shouted "Hurry up!" and he punched me, bending my glasses and spraining the thumb on the hand I had raised to protect my face.

I stumbled over to the metal patrol box in which I kept my valuables. I had the equivalent of about thirty dollars with me for petrol to leave Gapun when I needed to go into town to buy supplies. I wanted to find it and give it to the intruders, to make them go away. But the men wouldn't let me locate my flashlight. The one with the gun kept screaming at me to hurry up, and his accomplice kept hitting me in the head.

It was at this point I realized that there were more than two men in my house. I heard muffled voices in the far corner and then clatter as the cassette tapes and notebooks that I stored on a shelf were pulled down and hurled onto the floor.

I lifted the lid of my patrol box, and the gunman's accomplice grabbed my tape recorder and dumped it into one of my cloth bags. Ever the intrepid researcher, I actually said, "I'll give you the money, but could you leave that?" How ridiculous that seems now. The reply I received was a loud command to "Shut up!" and a punch to the face that sent my glasses flying.

"Where's the money?!" the man with the gun shouted, again.

"I need my glasses," I told him. "I can't see to get the money if I don't have my glasses." He hit me again.

I rooted around blindly among the contents of the patrol box: scholarly articles about Papuan languages, blank cassette tapes, batteries, boxes of rubber bands, biscuits, bags of muesli, Maggi noodles, and other small items of food I hid from the villagers to eat surreptitiously on the rare occasions when no one invited me to their house for a meal, or brought me food. At last I found a little plastic bag and lifted it up.

"Here it is," I said, holding it out. But the bag contained spare parts for my tape recorder and not any money. I pulled it back.

"No, wait a minute," I said.

The man yanked the bag violently from my hand.

This kind of confusion must have gone on for about five minutes, by which time the men started to get nervous. They had clearly planned a quick heist, and hadn't really reckoned with a nearsighted simpleton who dithered around the inside of a patrol box. Outside the house, too, the villagers were beginning to stir. I could hear them moving around and speaking Tayap in quiet, urgent voices. Perhaps feeling like they were on the verge of losing control of the situation, the intruders pulled me up by the shoulders and pushed me out the door onto the veranda. One stood beside me gripping my arm; the one with the gun stood on my other side and pointed it at my head.

I have no idea what the masked men ultimately intended to do with me, because at that moment, there was a distraction.

Old Kruni's forty-year-old son, Kawri, ran past the house. Nobody knows why Kawri did this, but he was an impulsive, hot-tempered man with a big beard and a short fuse. Maybe he thought he could ambush the men and disarm them. Whatever he was thinking, he must have forgotten that he was wearing white shorts. Those stood out in the black night and made him an easy target. As Kawri sped by just below my veranda, the man gripping my arm turned his flashlight on him. And the man with the gun turned it past my head, aimed it, and fired.

Kawri grunted dully and fell to the ground.

As soon as the shot was fired, the men who had been ransacking my house panicked, and they jumped down off the veranda and scattered into the rainforest.

It was only at that moment I began to feel scared. I found myself alone and disoriented in the pitch-dark night. Everything had grown silent again. Even the omnipresent frogs had all stopped croaking. I could see or hear no one. I climbed down from the house and groped my way in the direction of Kawri.

A village woman appeared out of the darkness and pulled me down behind a *laulau* tree. She hissed at me to be quiet.

A few minutes passed, and then villagers began to emerge from the rainforest. They went to locate Kawri. His younger brother and his maternal uncle began weeping in the profoundly heart-wrenching tuneful way that villagers cry whenever they sense that somebody is near death or has died. They found Kawri lying on his stomach on the ground in the darkness, and they lifted him and carried him to his father Kruni's men's house, only twenty yards from the spot where everyone had been dancing and laughing just a few minutes previously.

I followed the quiet weeping, and found myself in the middle of a procession of villagers who were pouring up into the men's house.

Kawri lay heavily on the floor of the house, cradled by his uncle, and his wife. He was in great pain. He writhed and gasped throatily when water was poured onto the wounds that peppered his side and back. But there was little blood. My first thought upon not seeing much blood was hopeful: maybe Kawri hadn't been injured too seriously after all. I didn't register that what had struck him had been a cartridge full of buckshot, fired at close range. The buckshot was embedded deep inside his body.

Kawri died five minutes later.

Kawri's wife, Rosa, heavily pregnant with the couple's fourth child, caressed his head and berated him as tears streamed down her cheeks. "You didn't listen to my talk," she said hoarsely. "I told you to stay in the house and you didn't stay. Look what happened. You got hurt." Suddenly, she shook her two-year-old daughter, who was lying across her lap sucking at her breast. "Yapa," she said roughly, "your father is dead. You see his body laying here?! Is he gonna get up again?!"

Kawri's sister, Sake, reacted in a similarly irate way. Their mother, old Sombang, shouted from inside her house and Sake snapped crossly, "They shot Kawri. Sombang, did you hear that? They shot Kawri. He's dead. He's dead. He's laying here rotting."

This initial shock took a few minutes to wear off, and when it did, the crying began in earnest. Nobody pursued the men who had murdered Kawri and fled off into the rainforest. The villagers were completely consumed by grief. Person after person climbed the ladder of Kruni's men's house, flung themselves on top of Kawri's body, and sobbed uncontrollably.

I sat with the villagers throughout that night, in a daze, sobbing with them. I was devastated that my presence in the village had drawn homicidal criminals into Gapun, and that an innocent man had been slain.

I wondered where the armed men were, and I was terrified that they might come back.

KAWRI WAS BURIED the afternoon after the attack, even though many of his relatives who happened to be in neighboring villages that day didn't come to cry on his body. They were afraid. The morning after the shooting, a few men left Gapun armed with spears and axes. They went looking for the killers and to alert people in other villages about what had happened. But the news spread by those villagers had the effect of scaring people away from Kawri's funeral. Nobody wanted to come to Gapun and risk stumbling upon a gang of murderers anxious to find their way out of an unfamiliar rainforest.

After Kawri's burial, I returned to my wrecked house and surveyed the damage. It was ravaged. Papers were strewn everywhere across the floor, as were plates, notebooks, cassettes, clothes. The balaclava-masked men had torn open all my boxes and bags, and they had looted anything that looked valuable: my tape recorder, spare batteries, kerosene stove, camera, recording equipment, and so on. The utter pointlessness of the plunder made me weary. Most of what the men carried away with them was of no value to anyone but me. Which villager in the lower Sepik region would ever be interested in buying a Sennheiser microphone?

What the men hadn't taken was broken or damaged. My kerosene lamp was shattered, my table was smashed, my mosquito net torn, my bedding was black with mud from the men's big boots.

I walked around the house in a stupor, picking up the notebooks and the clothes, trying to determine how many cassettes were missing, arranging the loose pages of articles I collected as best I could. I swept the floor, examined the damage to my mosquito net, and tossed my bedding in a bucket to take to the water hole and wash later.

Then I sat down on the floor and thought about what I should do.

My instinct told me I should get out of Gapun as soon as I could. My presence in the village was clearly putting the villagers in danger. Plus, I was in danger. It was entirely possible that the cartridge that killed Kawri had been intended for me.

I should leave.

On the other hand, abandoning the villagers at this moment of trauma felt morally wrong. Although I wasn't exactly responsible for Kawri's death, I was implicated in it. If I hadn't come to Gapun, Kawri would still be alive. I couldn't just up and hightail it out when the going got rough, leaving the stunned villagers to pick up the pieces.

I should stay.

On the other hand, again, it was clear that I wasn't going to be able to do any more work. My tape recorder was gone, for one thing. And I was certain that the villagers, under the circumstances, would feel as little enthusiasm as I did for chatting about Tayap verb paradigms or ancestral myths. If I wasn't doing any work, what was the point of staying in Gapun? It wasn't as if I were there on holiday.

I should leave.

In the end, I made a decision to stay in the village for a few more weeks to share in the villagers' mourning—and also to give evidence when the policemen eventually arrived from the faraway Sepik River town of Angoram. Even though policemen rarely left the immediate vicinity of Angoram because they never had any petrol to go anywhere, I knew they would come to Gapun sooner or later. Villagers had sent messengers to tell them that the white man staying in their village had been held up and attacked, and one of their relatives had been fatally shot. That was the kind of crime that didn't occur every day. It was guaranteed to evoke a response.

THERE WAS, THOUGH, the problem of the vanished criminals. Where had the gang of men gone? The group of village men who had gone searching went down to the creek that flowed into the mangrove lagoon and discovered two canoes hidden behind some bushes. This indicated that the criminals hadn't managed to escape the area during the night. They were still at large somewhere in the rainforest.

The village men smashed the canoes to splinters with their axes.

In the meantime, I got some children to help me move what remained of my things out of the trashed house, up into my new elevated penthouse. I didn't like the new house at all. It was too big and far too high off the ground. Peering down on the other houses from my veranda made me think of the view from a prison watchtower. The house was an architectural miscarriage, as boastful buildings usually are. I spent as little time in it as possible.

Instead, I sat near Kruni in his men's house. Kruni was crumpled. His son's murder had aged him dramatically. His face looked papery and pale, and he seemed more stooped over than ever. He sat weeping quietly. Occasionally, he would suddenly raise his head and shout in a cracked voice in the direction of the rainforest: "He was your pig that you shot, ah?! Was he your pig? What did we do to you that you should come inside our village and shoot us with a gun?! Did we kill one of your people that you should come and shoot us like pigs?!"

Villagers wandered numbly from house to house recounting where they were when the men fired their gun. It emerged that the men were five in number. They had managed to sneak into the village under cover of darkness, and they had hidden on the outskirts of the dancing circle until I went up into my house. The stones that I heard hitting the wall of the house were the men shooting pebbles from a slingshot from their hiding place. They had intended to shatter the glass of the kerosene lamp that was illuminating the dancing area. When this failed, they jumped out, warned the startled villagers not to make a move, and fired two shots from their homemade shotgun. This was the explosion I heard and the white light I saw.

The terrified villagers did what they were ordered to do and remained silent. As soon as the men rushed up into my house, they bundled together their children and ran off with them into the rainforest to hide. No one in Gapun owned a gun, and all the villagers were too taken by surprise to think clearly about how, or even whether, to confront the men. When they heard the gunfire the third time, those who had hidden too far to perceive what preceded it said they thought that the men had shot me. It was only when the crying began and they heard Kawri's name being called out did they understand that the victim of the shooting had been him.

In the rainforest, there are no newspapers, no Internet, no independent sources of information. All there is is rumor. And a few days after Kawri's death, a rumor began to circulate that the criminals had located one another in the rainforest and regrouped. No one knew whether they had any more cartridges, but we all did know that they had a gun. People began speculating what the men would do. It had already been established that the intruders were from outside the area. Villagers wondered suspiciously how they could have found their way into the village. It was no easy task to get to Gapun by canoe, which was how the five men had come. You need to navigate through a vast mazelike mangrove lagoon, and you need to know the exact location of a particular breach in the seemingly impenetrable wall of mangrove trees that line the lagoon. That breach leads to a shallow creek that you paddle up for half an hour before you disembark at a path that cuts into the rainforest and that, eventually, takes you to the village.

Someone who knew how to get to Gapun had to have shown the men the way. Villagers began asking who.

As they spent the days quietly whispering among themselves trying to figure this out, I started hearing stories that someone had stumbled upon the men in the rainforest and had overheard them making a plan. Their plan was to ambush me when I went to the water hole to wash in the evening, or when I walked into the rainforest to go to the toilet—and to hold me hostage. With me in the men's grip, the villagers would have to provide them with canoes to leave, and to show them the way back to the mangrove lagoon so that they could escape.

I seriously doubted that anybody actually had heard the men forge such a plan. I reckoned that anyone who came near enough to overhear the men talking would surely have sounded the alarm and alerted the villagers as to their whereabouts, letting them take their revenge for Kawri's murder.

However, the fact that someone even thought of such a scheme meant that the men could too. And the more I pondered it, the idea of taking the white man hostage to secure a way out of the rainforest sounded like a pretty good plan to me. Here is where the villagers' belief that I already was dead weighed upon me heavily. I frankly didn't know (as I still to this day frankly don't know) whether they believe that, being already dead, I actually can be killed. That uncertainty has always made me uneasy, but in this case it frightened me. In my exhausted and paranoid state, I imagined a scene where the men succeeded in capturing me and held a gun to my head or a machete to my throat, demanding that the villagers give them a canoe. But the villagers, out of disbelief that I would die, or out of perverse curiosity to see whether I could, simply answered, "No."

Even if the villagers did provide them with a way out of the rainforest, I wondered what the men would do with me once they were out.

At that point, I decided to leave the village. Four days had passed since Kawri had been killed, and there was still no sign of any police. The food for the *singsing* had all been eaten, and everybody was too afraid to venture into the rainforest to go to their gardens to gather food or to process any sago flour. Accusations started to swell up and acrimony began to spread: Hadn't X gone to a Sepik River village a few days before the *singsing*? Who had he spoken to there? Why didn't Y tell others what he told Z, which was that he had seen some unknown men down by the creek right before dusk on the fatal night? Had Q cried on Kawri's body? No? Why not? Why had he made himself so scarce the day after the murder?

The atmosphere in Gapun was beginning to turn sour.

I spoke to Kruni and several of the other big men, telling them that I wanted to leave. I told them I would go to the police station in Wewak, the provincial capital, and file a report. I would see to it that police would come and do their best to arrest the men who killed Kawri.

They accepted this, and as the sun was setting, I packed a backpack full of what I had managed to salvage of my notebooks and cassette tapes. I abandoned the rest. As soon as it was dark, several young men guided me through the swamp, then down to the creek and a waiting canoe. Still fearing the fugitive criminals, we traveled without light of any kind, and without speaking. A journey that normally took an hour took more than two. In the canoe, we paddled silently for an hour, first through the creek leading to the mangrove lagoon, then through the lagoon until we arrived in the neighboring village of Wongan. From there, we walked for four hours along the beach, arriving in Watam village, where people had an outboard motor powerful enough to make the six-hour journey by sea to Wewak.

We left at dawn. I didn't think I would ever see Gapun again.

IN WEWAK, I filed the police report. Then I went to the airport and left Papua New Guinea. I flew to the Australian National University, where I was employed at the time as a post-doctoral researcher. There I lodged an insurance claim, explaining that Kawri was one of the villagers I had worked with, and that he was killed as a result of my presence in the village. The university's insurance company agreed to pay an indemnity settlement, and I arranged for the money to be sent to the nun who worked as a nurse at the Marienberg mission station on the Sepik River. This nun, a grizzled, no-nonsense old battle-ax from Switzerland called Sista Mariana, had lived at the mission station for decades. Nobody could remember a time when she had not been; she must have been 130 years old.

Sista Mariana was the closest I have ever come to a bona fide saint. She was the sole source of health care that anyone in the entire lower Sepik region had access to. Every six to eight months, she and several of her junior nurses would spend several weeks traveling by a motor-powered rowboat to every village in the region, vaccinating babies, dispensing pills, injecting antibiotics. Her decades of living in the area, and her regular travels throughout it, meant that Sista Mariana knew *everyone*. And everyone knew her.

I knew I could depend on her to get the money I sent into the right hands. I instructed her to give some of it to Kruni and the rest to Kawri's widow, Rosa, who was from a village located a day's journey on foot from Gapun.

Sista Mariana wrote to me saying that she had done as I had requested. Kruni received his share. She wasn't able to find Rosa, however, so she gave the money I sent for her to Rosa's brothers. She also told me that soon after I left, the police had unleashed their fury on villages throughout the lower Sepik. They invaded villages and beat up people savagely and indiscriminately. They shot pigs, destroyed betel palms, and threatened to burn down houses unless people revealed the identities and the where-abouts of the men who had attacked me and killed Kawri. These acts of brutality produced results: Sista Mariana reported that the police had arrested most of the men, and they were in jail awaiting trial.

A few months later, though, Sista Mariana died and my channel of communication about Gapun was severed. I was never called as a witness for any trial. All my attempts to contact the police to find out what was happening went unanswered.

LIKE MOST OF my anthropology colleagues of that time, I concluded that Papua New Guinea had become too dangerous to work in anymore. I made the decision in late 1991 to abandon my research there and not return. I was willing to sacrifice a lot for my profession, but I wasn't willing to sacrifice my life. Nor did I want to endanger the lives of any more villagers.

After that, I heard nothing from or about Gapun for fourteen years.

Then, in late 2005, out of the blue, at home in Sweden, I received a letter from Australia. The letter was from a linguist named Bill

Foley, a well-known expert on Papuan languages who until his retirement worked as a professor at the University of Sydney. I met Bill in 1987 when I swung through Australia on my way back from my first long-term field stay in Gapun. Until I left the Pacific region for good (or so I thought) in 1991, he and I met up for a drink whenever I was in Sydney.

In his letter, Foley told me that several years after I left Gapun, he started conducting research on the eponymous language spoken in the village of Watam—the village that I had trekked to the night I left Gapun. During the time he worked in Watam, Foley never visited Gapun. But in early 2005, a German research team that was collecting samples for DNA analysis in Papua New Guinea contracted him to guide the team around the lower Sepik River area, and to ask villagers to allow them to draw blood and poke swabs around in the mouths of their children.

One of the villages the team went to was Gapun.

When I lived in Gapun, I had spent a great deal of time explaining to the villagers that not all white people in the world know one another. They assumed they did. No, I would say, the countries are a lot bigger than Gapun and the surrounding villages. There are a lot of white people and we can't all know one another. It's impossible.

Bill Foley was the first white person who came into Gapun since I had left fourteen years previously. The first question the villagers asked him was whether he knew me.

"Sure I do," he answered cheerfully.

FOLEY AND THE German research team were in Gapun for only a few hours. They left the village to spend a few days in Watam, which, being on the coast, is a much more pleasant place to stay than is the foul sago swamp where Gapun lies. Two days later, a young Gapun villager turned up in Watam and presented Bill Foley with a letter addressed to me, written by gentle Monei.

In his letter to me, Foley enclosed the one from Monei.

It asked me to come back to Gapun.

I was surprised by the letter and I was moved. I was also curious to know what had happened to the villagers—and their language—since I had left. So I arranged to go back to Gapun the following summer for six weeks, to see whether it was feasible to return for a longer time.

During that trip, I finally discovered what had happened on the fatal night that led me to leave Gapun, I thought forever.

This is what happened.

Soon after I arrived in the village in 1991, a rumor began circulating throughout the lower Sepik area that I had brought 40,000 kina (at the time, about the same in US dollars, so $40,000) with me to Gapun.[1] How the rumor started is harder to know. Some villagers told me that two Gapun villagers spread it because they were resentful that I hadn't given them enough things. Those two villagers and their relatives claimed that it was started by someone in another village. I will never know for certain which of those versions is true. To this day, though, I wonder what in the world the people who believed the rumor imagined I would do with the equivalent of $40,000 in a swamp in the middle of the rainforest. I also wonder what the criminals with the gun would have done to me if I had succeeded in pulling out from my patrol box the thirty kina I thought they were after.

---

1. The value of Papua New Guinea's currency, called kina, has fluctuated significantly during the decades I have been visiting the country. The conversions to US dollars provided in the text represent the value of the kina at the time of the events discussed.

The five men involved in the crime were all petty criminals—
what are known as rascals (*ol raskol*) in Papua New Guinea. That
cute, urchin-sounding name is deceptive. Rascals are anything but
charming. They are disgruntled and violent young men, usually
armed with homemade shotguns and a grade-school education
that has made them malcontented with their lives for the same reason it made Gapun kids who attended Wongan Community School
disenchanted with theirs—grade school taught them that they lack
the cars, houses, clothes, and riches that they saw depicted in the
grimy Australian-donated schoolbooks they passed around in the
classroom. Gangs of rascals terrorize urban centers, regularly holding up stores and hijacking armed transport vehicles. They block
roads and bridges, robbing passengers on local buses and stealing
all their belongings, often gang-raping a few unfortunate women
in the process.

Since the late 1980s, impromptu gangs of young men have
also been active in rural parts of the country like the lower Sepik
region, attacking village trade stores and anyone who seems to
have some money, shooting anyone who gets in their way. Outside
Port Moresby, the nation's capital city, rascals largely operate with
impunity, partly because there are no policemen to stop them or
capture them, and also because even if there are policemen, many
of them, when off duty, are rascals themselves.

Enticed by the rumor of 40,000 kina lying unprotected in an
isolated village, the five men from different Sepik villages who had
loose connections to one another from previous crimes decided
to get together and for what they thought would be easy pickings.
None of them had ever been to Gapun before. As the villagers
realized in the days after the crime, somebody who knew the way

had to have shown them the route. They were convinced they had figured out who that person was, and they confided his name to me in hushed whispers.

A few days after I left Gapun amid the trauma that followed Kawri's murder, a village man came upon one of the five rascals wandering around in the rainforest, weak with hunger and desperate to get out. The village man tied him up and brought him back to Kruni's men's house, where a lively discussion ensued about whether Kawri's brothers should spear him to death. Fearing that the police would punish them if they took the law into their own hands, the villagers decided to spare the man's life. They put him in a canoe and took him to Watam to await the police.

When the police finally arrived several days later, they took the man into custody. But Sista Mariana was right: they also terrorized the villagers in Watam. Upon arriving in Gapun, they wreaked havoc *there* as well. They beat up young men, they ransacked houses, and they threatened to arrest random villagers unless they revealed the names of the villagers who had helped the five men find their way into Gapun. Those who could fled into the rainforest, and the police left after a few hours with some chickens they shot, out of petty malice, but little else.

Two of the five men were never found by the police. All three men who were arrested were eventually sentenced to two years in prison. Today, they all still live in the area, and villagers occasionally run into them when they travel along the Sepik River. Even though a murder in Papua New Guinea normally demands a large compensation payment to be considered settled, none of Kawri's killers has ever paid anyone in Gapun so much as a cent in compensation for their crime.

By the end of my six-week stay in Gapun, I decided that the area seemed safe enough for me to come back for another long-term stay, and so I returned just over two years later, in 2009, intending to stay in the village for ten months. As it happened, though, that trip, too, ended up being cut short by several weeks because I began to hear rumors that on the day of my departure, I was again going to be robbed by rascals, who would hold me up as the villagers carried my belongings through the rainforest towards the canoe that would take me away. On my way through the rainforest, it began to be whispered, rascals would *ensapim* me, "hands-up-im" me—that is, ambush and rob me.

I was decidedly unwilling to lose all the recordings and field notes I had made during the nine months I had been living in the village. And even though I had been in Gapun far too long to be taken in by most of the rumors that villagers entertained one another by reporting or inventing, I was wary of the villagers who, I had been told, had dreamed up the Saraki-has-40,000-kina-on-him lie. The people who purportedly spread that rumor, as well as the man who villagers told me was the one who showed the rascals how to get to Gapun, were all close relatives of Kawri—of all people.

When I first heard that Kawri's relatives supposedly had been involved in the attack that left him dead, I refused to believe it. But throughout my stay in Gapun in 2009, those same relatives persisted in conveying a continual series of low-level threats to get me to pay them more than twenty times the income of the entire village as compensation for Kawri's death. The money that I had sent via Sista Mariana didn't count. They disavowed all knowledge of any money that Kruni (who died in about 1993) might have received. And the money that Sista Mariana claimed she gave to Kawri's widow's brothers was not their concern. They knew nothing about that money, they said. In any case, it should have been given to them, not dispensed to unfamiliar men in another village.

There is a certain logic to claims that I should compensate Kawri's relatives for his death. In Gapun, as in many other Papua New Guinean societies, whether a person intended for something to happen, or was responsible for it happening, is often not a matter of any particular importance. This is partly because people are imagined to be constantly acted on by forces outside themselves: I can steal my mother's brother's newly purchased batteries and say, when I am discovered, that "something" (*wanpela samting*) made me commit the theft even though I didn't want to do it. That something might be a random spirit or somebody else's avariciousness and envy that magically moved me to act in ways that are contrary to my own self-interest. I am an instrument or a conduit of action rather than its source. I will still be responsible for compensating my mother's brother for the theft, not so much because I committed it but because a "heavy" arose as a result of the batteries being taken. Even if I had nothing to do with the theft, if everyone is convinced that I took the batteries, then I will still need to cough up some compensation because, as villagers say, "the heavy came up in my name" (*hevi i kamap long nem bilong mi*).

Clearly, the "heavy" of Kawri's death came up in my name. I was therefore expected to pay.

But just because I understood the logic behind such demands, it didn't mean I needed to accept them. Especially not when it was obvious to me that the villagers who made the demands were blackmailing me: pay up, they hinted darkly, or else. I also realized that they were choosing very selectively from their cultural repertoire: In a case of cold-blooded murder, the person who is called upon to pay the bulk of compensation is, unsurprisingly, the murderer. That person can claim that he was an instrument of someone else's malice and that he isn't responsible for his actions. But he still has to pay. If I had not been a white man with presumably easy access to untold amounts of money, the demands that Kawri's relatives made of me would never have arisen. They would have gone after the men who killed Kawri.

In one recklessly heated discussion with one of Kawri's maternal relatives over this issue, I pointed this out. I had already paid compensation, I reminded the man, but none of his murderers had ever paid anything. Why didn't he go to the men who had been convicted of shooting Kawri and order them pay him the money he was demanding from me? You know who they are, I told him. Go tell them to give you money. Did I shoot Kawri? I asked him, having long ago mastered the villagers' style of asking rhetorical questions to which the answer is obvious. Did I pull the trigger of the gun that killed him?

The tenacity with which these villagers pursued their demands for compensation eventually led to me change my mind about their involvement in the attack. I have no doubt that whatever they may have imagined to be in store for me had gone very wrong, and that Kawri's death was a tragic mistake. But the more overt the threats became, the more convinced I was that several of Kawri's relatives had indeed started the rumor that drew the rascals into Gapun. Their insistence that I compensate them for Kawri's death was possibly a way for them to deal with the guilt they no doubt felt about the hideously botched outcome of their scheme.

And that, I felt, made them dangerous.

So when I started hearing the rumors about a plan for rascals to ambush me on my last day in the village, I decided to head those rascals off at the proverbial pass. I used the satellite telephone I had brought with me (marvelous invention, those), and a substantial chunk of my bank-account savings, to surreptitiously charter a helicopter to airlift me out of the village two weeks before I was scheduled to depart. The villagers had razed their old village and remade it to resemble a big airstrip; fine, I thought, I would bring them an aircraft.

On the morning I had arranged to be airlifted out of Gapun, I told villagers that during the night I had received a call informing me that my government was pulling its citizens out of Papua New Guinea because of some impending danger to those citizens that it had been made aware of. I needed to leave right away. I felt bad about that deception, but I didn't know what else to do. If I had told anybody the real reason for wanting to escape, I would have been heard as making an open accusation against Kawri's relatives, a move that would have escalated a bad situation into a truly perilous one. I knew that orchestrating a caper like being rescued by a helicopter would only reinforce the villagers' conviction that I had access to power and vast resources that I declined to reveal. I knew they would ask themselves things like: If my government could send a helicopter to airlift me out of the village, why couldn't it send them a submarine?

At that point, though, I didn't care. With the possibility hanging over my head that nine months of research might be violently ripped away from me only to then be unceremoniously dumped in a swamp when the men who stole it realized its utter worthlessness to them, I concluded that the risk of pouring yeast into the villagers' already well-fermented ideas about my celestial connections was of less urgency than the risk of not getting out of Gapun safely. I would deal with the fallout from my hasty departure when I returned later, I reasoned, after I had deposited all my field notes and recordings in a secure place, far away from the village.

And so, on that agreed-upon morning, the prearranged helicopter swooped down from the sky and plucked me out of Gapun, to the villagers' perplexed surprise.

I RETURNED THE following year, in 2010, making sure to purchase a gigantic two-hundred-pound bag of betel nut in town to bring with me. Villagers told me that they had been bewildered and dismayed by my sudden departure, and they appreciated that I acknowledged their umbrage by presenting them with the betel nut, which they interpreted as *kup*, a peace offering like what Moses sent to Samek to diffuse the tension that arose when the young men started obeying his exhortations to chop down all the village trees. Villagers happily distributed the extravagant quantities of betel nut that I had brought, and they seemed to forgive me. The helicopter had disconcerted them, clearly, but it also impressed them. To my relief, the relatives of Kawri's who had been menacing me quieted down. From that point onwards, the threats subsided.

The danger, though, ultimately didn't.

13: WHO KILLED MONEI?

A FEW MONTHS after I had reestablished myself in Gapun as a result of Monei's letter inviting me back—during the nine months I spent in the village before being airlifted out—Monei died. The illness that killed him started almost imperceptibly. One evening, Monei rubbed his temples and complained to his wife that he had a headache. Three weeks later, he stopped walking. Then he stopped eating, and two weeks after that, he was dead.

I'm not a doctor, but to my untrained eyes, it looked to me like Monei died of a fatal case of cerebral malaria. To the villagers' much more keenly trained eyes, though, it was obvious that Monei was murdered.

But who killed Monei?

Villagers in Gapun live in a world of magic, where people possess spells to do everything from making the girl you desire fall desperately in love with you to darkening the eyes and blocking the noses of your hunting dogs so that they won't ever find wild boars. In such an enchanted world, death is never accidental; it is always a deliberate act. Every single man, woman, and child is eventually murdered. You can be old and feeble, or young and strong and in the prime of life. You can be a newborn baby—it doesn't matter. When you die, somebody is responsible.

The ones responsible for everyone's death are sorcerers. This is true even in those relatively infrequent cases when somebody actually kills someone, like what happened to Kawri. Villagers believe that even physical homicides are the result of magic. The fatality is caused not by the offensive weapon: the knife, ax, machete or dart—or, in Kawri's case, the gun—but by the fact that the knife, ax, gun, or whatever had been bewitched. If it hadn't been bewitched, the victim would be injured by the assault but would eventually recover. If the victim dies, though, a sorcerer is responsible.

Sorcerers are men who have acquired dark knowledge of how to bewitch people and murder them. They kill in several ways. Most gruesome, known throughout Papua New Guinea as *sanguma*, involves being waylaid in the rainforest, and disemboweled. The sorcerer fills the victim's empty abdominal cavity up with leaves, stiches it up, and then he sends the poor person back to the village like a stuffed turkey. There she or he will continue living, sort of, in a zombielike state. But on a day marked by the sorcerer, the victim will keel over like a puppet from which the puppeteer's hand has been removed, and expire.

Much more common than *sanguma* is death by way of being shot by a bewitched object: small pieces of wire bent into nasty-looking hooks, the root of a ginger plant spit on with a hex, small stones, the chalky powder that, when chewed with betel nut, makes one's mouth turn bright red. These objects are magically injected into the body and lodge in the soft organs, causing the victim to waste away and die. People know the objects that make them sick and kill them because they have seen the objects removed from their own bodies, and from other people's bodies, by men who know special spells or prayers that they use to remove them.

Who are these malevolent men who sooner or later end up murdering everyone, including one another (since even sorcerers eventually die)? No one knows exactly who the homicidal witchmen are. People strongly suspect they know, and they certainly spend a lot of time trying to discover the identity of the sorcerer involved whenever somebody falls seriously ill—because they think that by sending the right man money and pigs, they can persuade him to "cool" the magic and allow the victim to get better and continue living. But to talk too openly about any of that would be a foolhardy act. It would make the sorcerers aware of you. Their antennae would quiver, and their perception would start to throb. They'd sense you, which is something you'd rather avoid. Better to stay under their radar for as long as you can.

Problem is, no one can do that for very long because sorcerers (all of whom villagers believe live in the neighboring village of Sanae) are attuned to people's feelings of anger and dissatisfaction. When a person gets angry because someone went into that person's garden and stole some bananas, or because someone swore at him or her, or hit the person in the heat of a drunken brawl about nothing—that anger, villagers say, can set into action a chain of events that will often alert a sorcerer in Sanae, and it will result in the sickness and perhaps even the death of someone, whether the person who got angry wants that to happen or not. It is as if the cosmos itself is attuned to the emotions of each individual in Gapun, connecting all to one another, and to sorcerers, in a kind of supernaturally sentient spiderweb. Pluck on one string on the web, they all vibrate.

The fact that everyone in the village is connected like this means that substitutions for who gets punished for what people do to others are possible. If my sister's son steals some betel nut from a grumpy old man, *I* may get sick and die. If I shout at someone I think has bewitched my hunting dogs, my grandmother may suddenly keel over. If my sister accuses her neighbor of having an affair with her husband, my two-year-old toddler might be targeted.

People in Gapun die, they say, because of other people's "wrongs."

This understanding that I (or my baby, my mother, my sibling, my uncle, and so on) may get sick or die because of what *you* did helped pave the way for the entry of Catholicism into Gapun, because when villagers began hearing about Christianity after World War II, the idea that Jesus died for the sins of other people made perfect sense.

"How else *could* anyone die?" villagers wondered ingenuously.

But the idea that you get sick and will die because of what someone else does also means that the number of things for which other people can be blamed is truly vast.

WHEN MONEI FIRST started feeling sick, he thought he might have malaria. Living in a mosquito-infested swamp, any villager who manages to survive malaria beyond the first year of life lives with the illness chronically. It breaks out occasionally, and villagers suffer for days with headaches, body aches, and bouts of intense fever followed by just as intense episodes of feeling freezing cold (the villagers' name in Tok Pisin for malaria is *kol sik*, the "cold sickness").

Monei recognized his symptoms, and he asked his daughter-in-law Maria for some medicine. Maria had once attended a two-day course about malaria at the Marienberg mission station. At the conclusion of the course, she had been given a large plastic bottle full of chloroquine pills. She returned to the village with the bottle, but she never dispensed any of the pills because she was a choleric woman who decided, for no particular reason other than orneriness, that the medicine was hers. She refused to give it to anyone who asked. "I don't have any medicine," she lied crossly to villagers who came to her when they fell ill—and eventually, they all stopped asking. Monei, though, remembered that the bottle of pills was shoved somewhere up into the sago-palm-frond ceiling of Maria's house.

Maria couldn't deny her father-in-law the medicine, and she found the bottle and extracted seven pills, which she gave him and which he swallowed, one after the other.

The pills apparently helped, but only temporarily. A few days later, Monei called me over to his veranda when I returned from my evening wash at the water hole. He wanted to know if I had been asking for him during the day. I told him yes, I had asked a child whether he was at home, and the child had told me that he was away in his garden.

Monei told me that when he went to his garden, "Something did something to me. It must be a bad spirit—I got dizzy and fainted."

I stood there thinking, "I wonder what it was?" But Monei's question to me had already provided the answer. His wife, Sopak, who was sitting in a corner of the veranda ripping the spines off the fan-sized tobacco leaves that Monei had brought back from his garden after he recovered, filled in the blanks: it was because of *me* that Monei became dizzy and fainted.

In the village, to call someone's name is to potentially weaken them, to suck some energy from them. To persist in calling someone's name is a provocation. With a disregard for the truth that was one of her most charming, and most infuriating, personality traits, Sopak announced, "Don came looking for you, and he kept asking and asking where you were. That's why you fainted."

Sopak had not actually been in the village at the time that any of this happened, nor had she been with Monei in his garden; she was away at a creek, fishing. But she wasn't getting any nibbles, and she felt that something was wrong. She later came to believe that both her own lack of luck fishing and Monei's fainting spell in his garden were caused by me persistently asking where Monei was.

I was going to protest that I had asked only a single time about Monei's whereabouts; it was untrue that I had "kept asking and asking." But I knew that Sopak had made up her mind, so I bit my tongue and changed the topic, asking the couple instead what they thought of the word an old man had just given me for "rainbow."

PERSISTENTLY CALLING A person's name may weaken him or her momentarily and cause that person to be unable to find food in the rainforest, but (luckily for me) it can't make the person sick. When Monei's health continued to decline, other explanations began to be sought. The last thing anyone considered was that Monei might have an illness that could be cured by a doctor. He had, after all, already taken medicine. That it hadn't worked could only be explained by its power to heal having been chilled by "something in the village."

Finding that "something" is what now began to occupy increasing numbers of villagers.

A week after concluding that I had caused Monei to faint in his garden, Monei asked one of his sons to cut him a long branch off a tree so that he could use it like a staff to support himself when he walked. He told me that he couldn't control his legs anymore when he stood up—they moved in different directions. He wasn't in any pain, he said, but he was dizzy all the time.

And so the village prayer group was called upon to pray over him.

MONEI'S SESSION WITH the prayer group occurred under the weak yellow glimmer of a flashlight, its batteries dying, that had been suspended from the roof by a vine. It began as prayer sessions always begin, with one of the three village men who led the group explaining to Papa God why they had gathered, and exhorting God to show mercy on their spiritual brother (in this case, Monei), cover him with His mercy, and take away his pain. This is always followed by talk about how sorcerers don't believe in God, and how they are evil men who shoot people with hooked wires, ginger roots, and little bundles of magic to make them sick. Papa God is called upon to remove these objects from the victim's body.

Within ten minutes, all three of the men started speaking in tongues. Each man had a different ecstatic style: one whispered almost inaudibly to himself; one alternated between praying loudly and then suddenly hissing in creepy, slithering dark tones that made me think of Hannibal Lecter in *The Silence of the Lambs*. The third barked things like "*Aut*, Devil, *aut!*" ("Out, Devil, out!") and "*Yu Pawa God!*" ("You're a Power God!"), which seemed to me to make God sound like one of the Power Rangers.

The prayer group prayed over Monei for almost an hour, but nothing emerged from his innards. This might have been a good sign, or it could mean something very bad. It maybe meant that Monei's illness was not caused by a sorcerer, which would be good. But it could also have indicated that the enchanted objects were embedded so deeply in Monei's organs that extracting them would be next to impossible. That would be dire.

When I spoke to him the next day, Monei had decided to be optimistic: he thought that his illness was a punishment from God because a number of men had stopped attending the Sunday-morning Mass. I told Monei that I thought it was pretty mean of God to punish him—if God was disgruntled about people not attending Mass, why didn't He punish the ones who had stopped going?

"I know," Monei said disarmingly. "I'm mad about that too. Why didn't He make them sick instead?"

Whatever the source of Monei's illness, the prayer session hadn't helped. In fact, Monei complained that he felt worse after the praying than he did before.

At this point, multiple explanations for Monei's illness started to pour in: Monei was sick because he harbored a desire to marry an old widow in the village as his second wife, thereby angering both God and his wife, Sopak. Monei secretly used magic chants to thwart men's work in their gardens. Monei's son Moses had been cross with some Sanae men because he thought he heard them whispering about how they were going to kill his wife, peevish Maria, through sorcery. Monei's son Rafael had cut down a tree on top of the mountain and enraged the spirit of the mountain. Monei had uttered the secret names of the mountain in some context (perhaps, it was implied, to inquisitive, nosy me).

Having unsuccessfully tried medicine and then prayer, Monei's children now began sending money to Sanae, hoping that it would reach the sorcerer responsible for Monei's condition. It so happened that Monei's children were flush with cash at that moment. A funerary feast that celebrated the end of mourning for a woman who had died several months previously had been held in Sanae a couple of weeks earlier, and to feed all the guests who had come to that feast, Sanae villagers had come to Gapun and bought several pigs, some of them, as it happened, from Monei's sons and daughters. They had earned 750 kina from the sale of their pigs, a handsome sum in a village where the average yearly income is about one hundred kina (about thirty-five US dollars).

Now, though, this money began being sent back to Sanae. Some of it was used to "shake hands" (*sekhanim*) with the Sanae men who the villagers suspected might be behind Monei's illness. Moses asked the men whom he had been cross with because he had overheard them talking about killing his wife, Maria, to come to Gapun, and he bought rice, coffee, and sugar from his wife's village to treat the men to a sumptuous meal, in addition to giving one man fifty-six kina in cash.

Another one of Monei's sons, Kosai, gave twenty-five kina to a Sanae man who said he knew who had ensorcelled Monei, and who promised him to pass the money on to the correct sorcerer.

Monei's son Rafael gave one hundred kina to two Gapun villagers who volunteered to take the money to Sanae and discreetly see who would take it. And so on.

But Monei just kept getting worse.

And so a "glass man" was called upon to identify the sorcerer who was making Monei sick.

"GLASS MEN" (*ol grasman*) are men of local renown who claim to be able to see into the realm of sorcerers and death by putting on a pair of magic spectacles. Or by peering into a specially prepared mirror. Glass men who work with a mirror are the more popular ones because mirrors permit an audience. Before the glass man arrived in Gapun, the villagers prepared me by excitedly explaining that the mirror the glass man looked into would be transformed into a television screen that would show them who shot Monei with the enchanted objects that were making him sick.

The villagers had seen a television screen a few times before because a group of young men from a coastal village had lugged a fourteen-inch television set into Gapun, together with a generator. They spent several entire nights screening DVDs of Hollywood action movies and locally produced Papua New Guinea music videos, which are extremely low-budget films of popular bands playing their unique tinny combination of oompah-pah and Hawaiian ukulele music, with voices distorted by some kind of filter that makes it sound as though all the singers are underwater.

The glass man whom Monei's family sent word for was from Sanae, which meant, everyone hoped, that he would have privileged access to the sorcerers in that village and would thus be able to see them clearly and identify them positively. As soon as this man arrived in the late afternoon, the villagers surprised me by seeking me out at the other end of the village. They wanted to borrow the large eighteen- by twenty-four-inch mirror that I used for shaving each morning, to substitute for the round compact mirror that the glass man had revealed to them that he used. That tiny mirror, they unanimously concluded, wouldn't do at all. They wanted to make sure they would get a good view of the upcoming action.

Like the prayer group, glass men do their business only at night. This one set up shop in a large house near Monei's at about 9:00 pm. The house quickly became packed with villagers of all ages. They jostled with one another for choice seats near the peg where the glass man would hang up my mirror.

By the feeble light of my kerosene lantern, the glass man extracted from his basket a little notebook, a small carved mask that must have been some kind of magic talisman, and two small plastic Coke bottles.

The bottles contained "nature oil," which is oil imbued with power by ancestral spirits and would turn my ordinary mirror into a cosmic portal. The glass man blew on his hands, took a capful of the oil, and poured it in patches onto my mirror. He rubbed the oil over the mirror, smoothing it out with a shirt. He tweaked the smears on the mirror by rubbing and smudging. When he was satisfied with the pattern, he hung the mirror on the peg for everyone to see.

Then he took up a powerful flashlight, which he turned on and shone directly into the mirror.

The live-action televised sorcerer extravaganza that the villagers were expecting to view didn't materialize. I sat in the dark squeezed in between eager villagers, and having gotten caught up in the enthusiastic hype that had preceded the glass man's arrival, I realized that I was actually hoping to have some kind of mystical experience. Instead, I found myself staring at a tray-sized mirror smeared with grease, onto which a bright beam of light was being shone.

The glass man stood in front of the mirror and helpfully drew attention to certain images that he saw there, pointing and making comments like "See, there's a woman" and "There's a man standing there."

Looking around at the villagers turning their heads and squinting as they tried to view the mirror from different angles, I could see that they were just as perplexed as I was.

The next morning, the general consensus was that the glass man was a fraud. Most people hadn't seen anything. A few, however, did see something. After I finally left the house at about midnight to go to bed, a couple of villagers claimed to have glimpsed a white man in the mirror. They debated whether the white man was me, or whether it was one of their ancestors (who, being dead, would also be white).

The significance of that vision became clear later.

By now, everyone was seriously concerned about Monei. He had stopped communicating and he ate nothing. He was emaciated, his breath smelled foul, and his eyes were glazed over and were half open, as was his mouth. His front teeth were protruding, like someone who is dying or dead. He looked like the mummy of Rameses II.

Several days after the glass man left Gapun, a bill arrived. Hand delivered by a visitor from Sanae, the invoice was to Monei's sons for the glass man's services. He had already received thirty kina to come to the village, but he apparently decided to charge more. The bill was itemized.

It read: "Saving a life, 150 kina" (about $50).

Monei's sons were outraged. His son Rafael came to me with the bill and asked me what I thought of it. I was outraged too. Surely, they weren't going to pay it?

They didn't want to, Rafael said, they thought it was an affront. The glass man hadn't saved their father's life. Monei hadn't improved; if anything, he was worse off than before the glass man's visit. But if they didn't pay, then Monei would have yet another Sanae man angry with him, and that would surely make things even worse.

The problem was, Rafael confided, that he and his siblings had no more money; all the money they had earned from selling their pigs to the Sanae men was gone—it had all been sent back to the Sanae men.

Maybe I could help them with this little worry?

As MONEI CONTINUED to wither and faded ever closer to death, a final possible cause of his illness—one that implicated me—was proposed, this time by "Big Belly" Onjani, the local carbon cowboy from Sanae.

Onjani hadn't been seen in Gapun since his unsuccessful attempt, several months earlier, to get the villagers to sign away their land to him so that he might make money by selling the villagers' air. He must have sensed defeat at the end of his "awareness" in the men's house because he never returned to collect the form. The whole issue ended up fizzling out, as so much talk about development in the village invariably does.

Onjani arrived in Gapun one afternoon and announced that he had been pondering Monei's illness. He concluded that Monei was not ill because a sorcerer from his village had penetrated him with a bewitched object; he was sick because the spirit of old Kruni was angry.

Kruni had died during the nearly fifteen-year period in which I had stopped going to Gapun because of Kawri's murder. When I returned in 2006, I learned that after Kruni's death, his children had never mounted a funerary feast for him. Funerary feasts were a crucial part of mourning, and they normally took place a few months to a year after someone died. During the period of mourning, the person closest to the deceased (a husband whose wife dies, a wife for her husband, a mother for her child) would stay inside their house, in an area separated from everyone else by a sago-palm-frond partition.

The person in mourning is regarded as dangerous because the spirit of the deceased is said to "stick to" his or her skin. People in mourning weren't allowed to leave the house except to go to the toilet at night. They weren't permitted to make food, or eat with their bare hands, because they are dangerous even to themselves—like women after childbirth, mourners in seclusion had to use small chopstick-like tongs to eat with. They covered their heads, they let their hair (and, if they were men, their beards) grow, and they were not permitted to wash for the entire duration of the mourning period.

Depending on how diligent a deceased person's relatives were in acquiring the pigs and growing the garden produce that were required for the funerary feast that announces the end of the mourning period—when the mourner was finally let out of the house, bathed, and could get on with his or her life—staying sedentary and unwashed could last a very long time. I was in the village in the mid-1980s, the last time this tradition was practiced in Gapun. I visited several people who sat miserably in mourning, and I can attest that they could get extremely cranky and very rank.

By the time Kruni died in his early seventies in about 1993, villagers had more or less abandoned the lengthy seclusion period that mourners had to undergo, and they had also begun postponing the funerary feast that marked the end of mourning—partly because they no longer had to worry about having a smelly, impatient mourner marking time in the corner of their houses. Kruni's feast kept getting put off, and by 2006, it still hadn't taken place.

This was a serious affront to Kruni's spirit because in addition to marking the end of a mourner's seclusion, the feasts also celebrated the status of the deceased—the more important the person, the bigger and more impressive the feast. Kruni had been the single most commanding presence in Gapun from at least the 1970s until his death: he had been elected the village *komiti* (the "headman") many times; he had been a key figure in getting the government to establish the primary school in the neighboring village of Wongan; he had been a keen Catholic and was instrumental in persuading various priests in Marienberg to visit Gapun occasionally to baptize babies and marry couples. And having, himself, been initiated into the ancestral cult of the *tambaran* before World War II, Kruni had also been a rich repository of traditional knowledge. To have neglected to honor Kruni's life with a funerary feast was a scandal.

Villagers understood this, of course, and one of the first little worries I was presented with upon my arrival in the village in 2006 was a request for help with financing Kruni's funerary feast. Rice needed to be bought, and coffee, and sugar, and tins of corned beef, and, ideally, even beer. I gave 900 kina, a substantial sum, dividing it equally between three senior men, all of whom were related to Kruni and all of whom represented different kin factions in the village.

Despite my contribution, the feast still never materialized.

The following year, in 2007, one of the men I had given money to was bitten by a death adder. He had buried the money somewhere in the rainforest for safekeeping, and villagers told me how—as the man lay frothing at the mouth and writhing in burning agony from the venom of the death adder—in what must have been a wildly tragicomic scene, they desperately tried to get the man to tell them where he had buried the money. He expired before he could divulge.

One of the two other men I had given money to was Monei. His 300 kina went to a man who visited Gapun a single time, heard that Monei had a substantial amount of money in his possession, and persuaded him that he would take the money to a town and change it into gold. This is a modern-day "Jack and the Beanstalk" story, except that in this version, Jack didn't even get any beans. The man left with Monei's money and was never heard from again.

Onjani had concluded that Kruni's ghost was angry that no funerary feast had been mounted for him. Two facts pointed in this direction. The first was Monei's fainting spell in his garden—the one that his wife, Sopak, decided had been caused by me "asking and asking" about him one day. Monei's garden was near Kruni's old garden, and that proximity was now recalled and made meaningful.

The reason this became meaningful was because just outside my house had lain the ruins of a men's house that had been erected for Kruni. After the men built my house, they cleared away the skeletal old posts that remained of that men's house. But when they took down the massive center post that stretched the length of the house and held up the roof, it rolled away from them and came to rest at the base of my house. This, it was realized, transferred some of the power of Kruni's men's house to my humble abode, and it made me a kind of conduit for Kruni's ghost. The men all knew that I was unhappy because they had not spent the money I had given them for Kruni's funerary feast. (The third man I had given 300 kina to was one of Kruni's sons, who used it to buy presents for himself.) Onjani concluded that my dissatisfaction, amplified by Kruni's ghost's wrath, resulted in Monei being brought to the brink of death.

When Onjani told me this, I couldn't help but reflect on the fact that my largesse in contributing a considerable sum of money to villagers for a good cause had resulted, in their eyes, in the death of one respected senior man and the impending death of another.

In Gapun, it is truly the case that no good deed goes unpunished.

Luckily, Big Belly had a solution to this lamentable situation that, needless to say, involved a large meal he would partake of.

The following day, Onjani led the village men in breaking a coconut at Monei's feet, summoning Kruni's spirit, and asking the ghost not to be angry at Monei. The men then walked to my house in a single-file procession. They circled the perimeter of the house, dripping coconut water as they did so, and then they climbed up into the house, and walked around inside, dripping coconut water onto the floor to "cool" the house and sever its links to Kruni's old men's house.

One of the few pigs that Monei's children still had left was killed, and I contributed a large tin of Nescafé, a pound of sugar, and ten pounds of rice. Women prepared copious basins of boiled pork and rice, and they boiled huge pots of water for the coffee, sending everything to a men's house in the middle of the village. Before any of this banquet could be consumed, however, Onjani instructed villagers to publicly apologize to me for not having used the money I gave them to mount a funerary feast for Kruni. I was then required to make a little speech about how I wasn't angry about any of this, and to call on Kruni and ask him not to be angry either.

At that point, a glass of water with some leaves of a croton plant was taken around, and Onjani instructed all the men, women, and children present to dip their finger in the water. This was to cool the anger that anyone still felt. When this was done, everyone filed past me in silence and shook my hand. I was then instructed to carry the glass of water to Monei's house, where Monei's wife, Sopak, and several of his relatives sat caring for him. When we arrived in the house, Onjani told everyone to shake hands with one another to show that everyone was in agreement and there was no anger. I was told to feed Monei some of the water with a spoon.

Monei was lifted to a sitting position by one of his nephews, and I tried to gently pour a few drops of water past his protruding teeth and swollen tongue. I was then instructed to use the leaves in the glass to splash water around the house, which I did. Then I put the glass of water on a wooden stool near Monei, and with that, the ceremony was over.

Satisfied that Kruni's spirit had been pacified and my irritation had subsided, Big Belly patted his paunch and announced eagerly that we should all go back to the men's house and dig into the food that surely was getting cold just sitting there, waiting to be eaten.

MONEI DIDN'T IMPROVE, and he was finally taken to the Marienberg health-care station on the Sepik River. Having done everything they could think of to persuade sorcerers to defuse their witchcraft, and to get ancestral spirits to chill their anger, Monei's children now made the decision to take him to Marienberg.

This progression of events is typical. Villagers hesitate to take sick people to the health-care station partly because it is so far away—it is more than eight hours from Gapun, a journey that involves paddling hard in a dugout canoe. But mostly, they hesitate because they associate the station with death. Almost inevitably, sick villagers who are taken to Marienberg come back dead. That high fatality rate has partly to do with the fact that the health-care station has very little medicine and no facilities to conduct medical tests like X-rays or perform surgery. But mostly, people die in Marienberg because when villagers do finally seek medical help, if they seek it at all, it is already too late.

As Monei was fastened to a makeshift bier and hoisted onto his sons' shoulders to be carried for an hour down the road through the rainforest to the canoe that his sons would paddle to Marienberg, it was obvious that he was dying. His unseeing eyes were covered with a pearly membrane, his blistered tongue was hanging out of his open mouth, and all around him, like a haze, was the sickly sweet magnolia-scented smell of death.

Monei's corpse was carried back to the village a few days later on the same bier on which he had left. His body was laid out in his son Rafael's house, which quickly became filled with weeping villagers. They spent the night caressing Monei's body and sobbing loud laments over it, crying that Monei had left them, beseeching him to wake up and talk to them, bewailing that the place where he always sat on his veranda was empty now.

In the morning, Monei was carried to the village graveyard and, like all the other villagers, he was buried in an unmarked grave. His wife, Sopak, who was old and who respected the traditional ways, went into seclusion for a month, after which time her sons upbraided her for acting like a heathen and told her to stop hiding herself.

When the dust cleared, of all the possible causes of Monei's death, the one the villagers settled on was that a sorcerer from Sanae had tried to shoot Moses's splenetic wife, Maria, with a bewitched object to kill her because she was always cross about something, but he had fired his magic projectile sloppily. It hit poor Monei instead.

And so it came to pass that Monei, like all the other villagers, and like Jesus Himself, died for someone else's "wrongs."

14: LUKE WRITES A LETTER

Sunrises and sunsets are a hurried business in a tropical rainforest. Just before 6:00 a.m., the thick, feltlike blackness of night fades to milky gray, and fifteen minutes later, the sun has suddenly leapt up into the sky and begun radiating light, and heat. In the evening, pretty much exactly twelve hours later, the sun doesn't so much set as it dashes off, as if it is late for an appointment and needs to squeeze itself below the horizon as quickly as it can.

Once the sun disappears, the village becomes pitch-dark. Villagers move around by the dim light of the moon, when there is one, and with flashlights, which most adults own, even if bulbs are often burned out or batteries are flat.

In their houses, villagers either sit by a small fire that has been used to prepare the evening meal (women try to finish making food before nightfall, while they can still see what they are cooking), or they move outside onto their verandas, where they sit beside a big metal bowl with burning embers inside. Those embers emit a faint glow, but mainly they are on hand to light the villagers' ubiquitous rolled-newspaper cigarettes.

When I was in the village and brought kerosene, most villagers took advantage of that by constructing small makeshift lamps out of old tins with a piece of rope stuck in as a wick. They used the weak yellow flicker that my kerosene provided to light up the night. When I was not in Gapun, some people turned on cheap Chinese-manufactured battery-powered LED lanterns that an enterprising villager purchased in a town and brought back to Gapun to sell at a profit. That light cast by those lanterns is blue and cold and garish. The lanterns last only a few days because the batteries drain quickly, and batteries are a scarce commodity in the rainforest.

The early evening is a time for socializing. Some men construct open-air shelters in front of their houses, and in the evenings, they sit there and wait for other men to come park themselves on the floor next to the bowl with burning embers, to smoke and chew betel nut, tell stories and share gossip. Women sail through the village carrying nursing infants and trailed by lines of children, who follow their mothers up the notched poles that lead into houses, arrange themselves on the floor, and amuse themselves while the women sit, smoke, chew betel nut, and chat.

My evening routine mirrored that of the villagers. Before it gets dark, villagers try to wash off the day's sweat and grime by dunking themselves in the chest-deep swamp water off a long "bridge" just outside the village, or by going to a water hole and washing there. I avoided the bridge because it is a random collection of slippery, poorly secured poles that villagers have no trouble navigating with their broad bare feet and seemingly prehensile toes, but that I unfailingly fell off. I went to a water hole used by young men at the far end of the village. I drew the water with a half coconut shell attached to a pole, lifted it over my head, let it pour over me, and pretended that it was a shower.

When I got back to my house, a child usually appeared shortly before dusk to summon me to his or her mother's house to eat whatever the woman had prepared for dinner. I went and sat talking to whoever had invited me, then I took my leave and made my rounds. Sometimes, I had a goal—to visit a particular person, either because I wanted to ask them something, because I hadn't seen them for a while, or simply because I enjoyed their company. But often, I would wander around and end up talking to whoever was sitting on their veranda or in their open-air shelter looking like they wouldn't mind a little visit.

This evening socializing ends by about nine o'clock on most nights, by which time it will have been dark for almost three hours. By nine thirty, most adults will have lifted up their children—who often fall asleep at some point strewn about on the floor—and crawled inside their mosquito nets to go to sleep. Men usually sleep with the boys in the family who are over five years old; women sleep together with their daughters and young children. Bedtime is the time when mothers sometimes suddenly discover that they are missing a child who "conked out" (*katop*), as the villagers say, on the floor of the house they visited, unseen in the darkness. "Eh, where's Kama?" a voice will rise up from inside a house, calling the name of the speaker's five-year-old daughter. "She was with me when I was down at Wandi's, wasn't she? Where is she? Kama-oooooo!" The mother calls out her missing child's name across the village until she is located and either woken up and sent home waving a lit ember in front of her to help her see in the dark, or pulled inside a mosquito net to spend the night in the house where she slumbered.

By 9:30 p.m., I was usually done for the day too. I would go up into my house and close my door behind me. Closing my door was a sign. The only times I closed it were when I sat transcribing audiotapes with somebody, when I worked with an old person on the details of the Tayap language, or when I wanted to sit writing field notes at night before I went to bed. Otherwise, the door was always open, just like it was at the other village houses that even had doors. As the stars shone brighter and the Milky Way fizzed up and illuminated the black night sky, the village quieted down. The only sounds left were the pulsating buzz of crickets, the barking of dogs, the shrill squealing of flying foxes, the smattering chorus of frogs that one never, ever saw, and the occasional crying baby. In this nocturnal stillness, I was relatively certain that I could sit by my lantern light and write up the events of the day without having to worry that anybody would bother me with the kinds of requests that otherwise constantly punctuated my days.

Sometimes, though, very late at night, there would be a discreet knock on my bamboo door. When this happened, I would brace myself because I knew that whoever was standing on the other side of that door was about to ask me for something out of the ordinary.

TWO WEEKS AFTER Monei was buried, I heard a series of short, dull thumps late at night on my door.

When I opened the door, Monei's youngest child, nineteen-year-old, Luke, stood outside with his winsome James Dean smile. Luke had recently gotten a haircut by his brother, who functioned as the village barber because he was the only villager who owned a pair of scissors. The brother had given him a flattop with short back and sides—the kind of haircut that was de rigueur during colonial times for "cook boys" and mission students. The new haircut made Luke look old-fashioned and innocent. He was wearing a robin's-egg-blue polo shirt buttoned up to the neck. He looked dapper and fresh, like he was dressed up for church.

I invited Luke in, shut the door behind us, and went and sat down in my blue plastic chair. He followed me and sat down in the identical chair opposite me. Closing the notebook I had been writing in and setting it to one side, I smiled at Luke and asked him my standard opening question: "What's your worry?"

Luke said he wanted to know when I was leaving. I thought he meant when was I next leaving to go to Madang, the town I traveled to about once every six weeks to get supplies. I told him I didn't know. But something about the way he asked the question made me pause after I answered him and say, "Do you mean when am I going to Madang?"

He said no, he meant when was I going back to my country.

This surprised me. The answer to that question was common knowledge. As soon as I had arrived in Gapun several months earlier, I informed everyone how long I intended to stay, and I repeated the timing frequently, whenever anybody asked. I was sure that Luke knew when I was going back to Sweden, so my brain started racing: Why did he want a private late-night session with me to ask me that? Did he want to come with me? Was he going to ask me to buy him a ticket and take him with me?

I tensed up, wondering how I would tell him that taking him with me when I left was beyond my means and out of the question. I told him what I had been saying to everyone all along: that I would be leaving in December, four months away, but that the exact date of departure was uncertain as of yet.

Luke nodded. If he wrote a letter, he asked, would I take it back to Sweden with me?

I thought with relief, "Phew! Luke wants a pen pal." During the previous few weeks, villagers like Saragum had been talking about this phenomenon, which they had heard about from young men in coastal villages where a cruise ship with tourists came ashore briefly once every six months. Apparently, some of those young men had asked tourists for their address so that they could become "pen friends" (*pen pren*), and the tourists had obliged. This sparked excitement that a new road to change had been discovered.

"Yes, sure," I told him, "I'll take a letter back with me."

Luke smiled.

The conversation seemed over. But Luke made no move to go. This made me feel uncomfortable, like there was something more he wanted to say. So I asked him, "Who do you want to send a letter to?"

His answer froze my blood.

"Papa," he said. "I want to send it to Monei."

WHEN THE VILLAGERS revealed to me on the night of that violent thunderstorm in 1985 that in their eyes I was a dead person who had come back to life, it was unsettling. At the time, I had no comprehension of the beliefs they held that could have led them to identify me as a resurrected villager, plus I was a bit afraid about what the role might entail. How did they think one of their own dead should act? What did they expect me to do?

As it turned out, my status as a dead villager returned to life did not affect my relations with the villagers in any dramatic way. If anything, their belief that I was one of them in an altered state seemed to predispose them to accept me into their village with a graciousness and warmth that I still find remarkable.

Over the years, partly by asking discreet questions but mostly by overhearing villagers talk to one another, I pieced together an understanding of why they think I am a resurrected villager—and how they think the world beyond Papua New Guinea looks, and what their place in that world is.

Imagine if extraterrestrial aliens suddenly appeared out of nowhere. Imagine that they looked humanoid but spoke in strange languages that nobody had ever heard. That they had different hair, and a different kind of skin—that they had pouches in their epidermis from which they could extract mysterious objects (Papua New Guineans, who had never seen shirts or trousers before, thought that these garments were part of the skin of the first Europeans they saw). Imagine that they arrived on fantastic vessels that one had never even imagined existed. That they possessed contraptions that did astonishing things, and that could cause death and destruction if the aliens became displeased or angry.

Such was the situation that Papua New Guineans found themselves in when they first encountered white European explorers and colonialists. Those first encounters happened at various times throughout the country, starting in the mid-1800s and ending only in the 1930s. Gapuners heard about the existence of white people in the first decade of the 1900s. The first villager to encounter one, a man named Ndair, traveled to a coastal village expressly to see the alien creatures. He took with him four large yams, which he exchanged for a steel adze.

Once villagers confirmed with their own eyes that white people were not just a rumor or a figment of someone's imagination, they began to ask themselves: "What are these beings?" "Why have they come?" "Why have they come *now*?"

And "What can they give us?"

Those four questions are at the core of the mystery that villagers in Gapun are still trying to solve.

At first, they turned to traditional myths for explanations. Villagers have a myth of two brothers, Arena and Andena. The brothers live in fraternal solidarity until a woman enters the picture: Arena, the older brother, marries her, and she betrays him by turning around and seducing the younger brother, Andena. The older brother learns of his wife's unfaithfulness and plots to kill Andena in revenge. One day, Arena asks Andena to help him dig a hole that will support the massive main post of a men's house that he wants to construct. He bids his younger brother to go down into the hole to dig more deeply, and Andena descends and keeps digging. Once Andena is at the bottom of the hole, the older brother lifts the mighty house post and plunges it straight down, thinking that Andena will be crushed. Andena, however, was the cleverer brother. Sensing his older brother's scheme, he managed to dig an escape tunnel. When he looked up and saw the post plummeting towards his skull, he stepped into the tunnel. He later emerged in another part of the rainforest, far away from his brother.

The myth continues, following the exploits of the inventive younger brother. It tells of how he at one point made two kinds of human beings: dark ones, out of wood, and light ones, made out of the pink pith of sago palms. Eventually, the jealous older brother realizes that Andena had not been killed, and he goes looking for him. The myth ends with the two brothers reuniting and leaving Papua New Guinea forever in an enchanted canoe. With them they take pale creatures that Andean had fashioned out of sago-palm pith. The dark ones they leave behind, along with Arena's adulterous wife.

The two brothers sail off across the sea and are never heard from again.

The old men in Gapun who knew this myth reasoned that the two brothers sailed to the countries. And obviously, the men all agreed, white people are descended from the pink beings that Andena had molded in Papua New Guinea. They surmised, furthermore, that Andena had brought his skills to the countries and invented the factories that manufactured all the money, airplanes, subway tunnels, outboard motors, clothes, and other goods that white people have access to. Then the villagers began filling in the blanks: Somehow they concluded that eventually Andena felt sorry for his native Papua New Guinea and wanted to return there to "fix" (*stretim*) the poor dark creatures he had left behind. He was prevented from doing this, however, by Australians, who blocked his return. They didn't want Papua New Guineans to have the same knowledge, power, and skin that they had.

As villagers became converted to Christianity, myths like these made even more sense. Arena and Andena, clearly, were Cain and Abel, two brothers in the Bible who fought with each other. The Virgin Mary was Njarí, a mythological ancestor who arrived long ago in the area to discover that pregnant women were all murdered by being split open to allow the babies they carried to be born. Njarí gave them vaginas so that they could give birth without dying. She also made a few anatomical switches, taking the breasts that had formerly adorned men's bodies away from them and slapping them on women instead. In return, she gave men the women's beards.

Random remarks fed the villagers' search for answers. In the late 1950s, a priest who visited Gapun a single time mentioned in passing that his country of origin, Belgium, was *namba wan kantri*. This is an ambiguous phrase in Tok Pisin that can mean either "the best country" or "the first country." Villagers chose the latter interpretation, and the idea that "Beljum" is the place where Earth meets Heaven persists to this day and is firmly established in Gapun.

If Beljum is the place where Earth meets Heaven, villagers tell one another that Papua New Guinea is the "last country," the one farthest from the celestial center of power, glory, and manufactured goods. As far as I was ever able to tell from the way villagers talk about the world, they all—and I really do mean all of them, including the ones who have been to school and who have seen maps and maybe even globes—imagine the world to be arranged in a kind of mystic arc, starting from under the ground of Papua New Guinea, the last country, progressively curving upwards towards Beljum, which borders on Heaven, and ending in Rome, the country where the Pope lives with Jesus and his mother, Mary, and her husband, God. (Mary's earthly spouse, Joseph, is absent from the villagers' discussions about the afterlife.) People from the countries travel freely to Rome and Heaven in airplanes, which gives them access to the glory of God. Translated, this means: "access to filthy lucre."

Most Papua New Guineans can currently get to Rome only by dying. There are a few exceptions, the most important being the country's first and multiple-recurring prime minister, Sir Michael Somare. Villagers agree that Somare is one of the few Papua New Guineans to have been granted access to white people's secrets. He has been to Rome, he has met the Pope, he has been given powerful books that make money appear. He won't ever die (and indeed, there might be something to that belief, given that at age eighty-two, Somare has already lived longer than the vast majority of Papua New Guineans). Villagers say that he will just get older and older until he becomes decrepit, then he will take some medicine and become young again. Like, in other words, Cher.

When Papua New Guineans die, some who have committed a major sin (such as self-inducing an abortion) end up at the base of a sago palm in the forest, where they get rained on all the time. But a Sanae man accepts fifty kina from family members of deceased villagers to "register" them and help them move on. When they do move on, they join all the other dead villagers who have gone to the countries, where their skin has turned white. In the countries, villagers are provided with shoes and socks. They occupy fancy houses with water and electricity, where all they do to obtain food, fresh clothes, or anything else is push a button. They go to school. Once they have perfected their English in school, they find work (the man in Sanae who communicates directly with the dead has informed villagers that most of their deceased relatives are employed as nurses or accountants), and they worry about their families back in the village. They want to send them money. Sometimes, they come back to Papua New Guinea in the guise of tourists, to catch a glimpse of family members. But they are also contactable through letters (the villagers' interest in obtaining a "pen friend" is not an innocent hobby; they want a direct line to the goods), and also, these days, by mobile phones, if one can only manage to discover their phone number.

Beliefs like these, kooky as they may seem, are not unique to Gapun. The whole island of New Guinea has become famous for its "millenarian" or "cargo" cults; words that refer to the idea that if believers perform certain actions in the proper way, the heavens will open, Jesus will descend back to Earth, and a millennium of plenty will ensue. Called by various names—the Vailala Madness, the Mambu cult, and the Paliau movement, among others—cargo cults have existed throughout the country since the arrival of white people, and they are still going strong today.

One of more recent of the several cults that swept through Gapun after the Second World War centered on a Sepik River man named Lambet who appeared in the village one afternoon in the early 1990s and proclaimed that God had sent him. Villagers built him a house and they followed his teaching, which involved praying all afternoon and most nights. During these prayer sessions, some villagers would begin speaking in tongues and collapse and shake in noisy religious ecstasy. This continued for several months. Unfortunately for Lambet, though, on the day he had appointed for the dead to return from the grave, white-skinned and laden with money, the one-year-old boy of a woman who was also the mother of seven girls died. Lambet announced that he would raise the child from the dead. He stopped the mother and everyone else from crying, insisting that their tears would "block the road" needed for the boy's soul to return to his body.

For an entire night, Lambet and the villagers prayed over the boy's body, asking God, Jesus, and Mary to resurrect him. By sunrise, it was clear that the boy would not be returning. At that point, the husband of one of the boy's sisters flew into a violent rage and kicked Lambet in the head. Lambet was carried to a neighboring village, and from there he was taken by canoe up the Sepik River. Eventually, he made it to a hospital in the provincial capital of Wewak, where he was treated for a broken jaw. He returned to Gapun to collect his belongings a few weeks later, and from there, he went to the city of Lae, where he promptly died.

Luke's request for me to deliver a letter to his dead father turned my blood cold not just because it reminded me so nakedly of the villagers' conviction that I am dead. It also confronted me with an ethical dilemma.

If I said "No, I'm sorry, but I can't deliver a letter to Monei because I don't actually ever travel to Heaven," I knew that Luke would regard this answer as a refusal. He would hear: "Don, who is dead, is going to where my equally dead papa is, but he won't take my letter to him."

If I said "Yes, of course I'll take it," I would be confirming Luke's belief that I am dead and commute between Heaven and Papua New Guinea.

Caught between those two equally impossible alternatives, I responded to Luke's request the only way I could think of. I heard myself squeak: "I'll do my best."

I didn't know what else I could add to that. But Luke sat opposite me and flashed his endearing toothy smile, clearly expecting me to elaborate. What could I possibly say? That I had already penciled in cocktails with his father's ghost when I got back to Sweden and would deliver the letter then? I was at a loss. Grasping at straws, I talked about a cassowary egg that someone had given to me to look after until it hatched. I talked about how I thought of Monei whenever I passed his house on my way to and from my evening wash at the water hole, because he usually sat on his veranda and we would always have a chat. I talked about how it sure had been raining a lot lately. I practically started singing Luke a song and doing acrobatic tricks to avoid having to come up with anything more to say about what I would do with the letter to a dead soul I had somehow just acquiesced to dispatching.

Finally, I forced a yawn and said it was late and I was tired and that unlike Luke and the other villagers, I didn't sleep during the day. And besides, I needed to use the toilet. I paused for a minute in case there was anything else he wanted to tell me. He just stared at me and smiled. "OK," I thought, "enough of this." I got up and moved towards the door. Luke told me that he had asked me what he had come to ask me. He followed me to the door and down the pole, bidding me good night as we parted and I headed off to my spider-infested little privy in the forest that I didn't have to visit at all.

SINCE LAMBET LEFT Gapun with a broken jaw almost thirty years ago, there has been one more bout of full-blown cargo activity in the village. In 1994, Monei's son (and Luke's twenty-year-older brother) Rafael was bitten on the foot by a death adder on his way back through the swamp from a trip to another village. Realizing what had happened, Rafael made a promise to God that if he didn't die, he would do God's work. He declined all traditional help, such as asking old men to spit on him while intoning magical chants, instead telling his family, as he lost consciousness, to pray for him to recover. They managed to get him to the Marienberg Catholic mission health-care station within a day, and he recovered.

Rafael had an out-of-body experience on his way to Marienberg: he appeared before a massive door, and he spoke to a tall white man sitting in a chair in front of the door, who told him that his time had not yet arrived to enter—and that he had to go back. He recounted that, while recovering in the mission station, he saw two white men and three white women arrive in a canoe. They carried briefcases that contained presents to give him, but they ended up speaking only to Rafael's father, Monei, assuring him that Rafael would be all right. Then they got into their canoe and left again.

Monei, who had taken his son to Marienberg and was by his side the entire time caring for him, said he never saw, let alone spoke to, five white people. But Rafael insisted that they had been there.

Villagers know from frequent tragic experience that being bitten by a death adder usually means certain, painful death. Rafael's recovery was miraculous, and he capitalized on that miracle. He was bitten on a Thursday, and by the following Sunday, he was recovered and attending Mass in the mission station's church. He informed anybody who would listen that his body was dead for three days, and at the end of the third day, he rose again.

The parallels with a certain son of God couldn't be clearer.

Upon his return to Gapun, Rafael gathered together the surprised villagers and took them off into the rainforest to do a "penance." They spent a week in the bush without food, only drinking water to sustain themselves. They spent the days and nights praying. In their exhausted and famished state, they heard Rafael speaking to them in the voice of a prophet. When they returned from the rainforest, the villagers collectively began to travel to neighboring villages to spread the Gospel of Rafael. The message was that traditional artifacts were Satanic and must be destroyed so that change might come. Gapuners made their rounds to all the surrounding villages, but few people listened to them.

After about two months, the villagers stopped touring and returned home. The cult of Rafael burned out as men began to accuse him of using his newfound status as a prophet to try to sleep with their wives.

Today, Rafael remains the village prayer leader and the contact person for the Catholic mission in Marienberg. He plays a leading role in organizing church events such as the confirmation of young people, every decade or so that this occurs, and the nightly reciting of the Rosary during October, the month of Mama Maria, aka the Virgin Mary. His role as prayer leader gives Rafael a certain status in the village and provides him with opportunities, which he clearly covets, to boss people around. But he roundly resents the fact that his fifteen minutes (or, in his case, two months) of fame is long past. He often finds occasion to remind villagers that he was killed by a death adder and returned to life, and he is quick to mention that his encounter with the afterworld gives him access to powers that had best not be provoked. He speaks darkly of possessing "prayer points" (*ol pre poin*) which are prayers that can shoot people like arrows. And hinting that he has Mama Maria's ear, he is not above muttering in the direction of people who have angered him, "All I have to do is make an offering, and someone's gonna die."

Even though there has been no overt cargo activity in Gapun for almost twenty years, the millenarian ideas that animate the villagers' view of the world course constantly just beneath the surface of their lives like powerful undersea currents. Hardly a month goes by when someone doesn't announce news about a "road" somewhere that will open the tap to the cargo. Throughout the years I have been going to Gapun, I have recorded a truly depressing number of schemes that guileless villagers have fallen for, always perpetrated by men from other places who convince them that if they pay to "become a member" (*kamap memba*) of a bank, an NGO, a company, a land-rights deal, a carbon trade agreement, or whatever, then they will receive untold amounts of money and goods at some indeterminate point in the not-too-distant, but somehow never quite arriving, future.

. . .

LUKE BROUGHT ME his letter to his father a month and a half later. It was handwritten on three separate sheets of mildewed lined paper, and it had clearly been composed over a period of time. Two of the pages were written with a blue Bic pen that I had given him when he asked for one to write letters to his numerous girlfriends; the third page, which he had authored as a kind of addendum, was written in fading black ink.

I asked Luke if he wanted me to type the letter up for him on my computer and print it out, like I did with the love letters—or if I should just deliver what he gave me. I should type it out and print it, he told me. "Great," I thought, and I reminded him of the deal I had made with him and other young villagers, that anything I typed up and printed out for them I could use in my work and publish. That was fine with him, he said.

Here, then, with Luke's permission, is his letter to his deceased father, in its entirety. I have translated it into English but have retained the original's spacing, underlining and punctuation. With the exception the phrase *Tayap Num*, which is Tayap for "Gapun village," and the almost-English phrase "Your's faithfull," the letter was written in Tok Pisin:

> Tayap Num
> Angoram District
> Weweak East Sepik
> Province

Dear Papa!!
Number = 1)!! We in the family are really worrying about you you were sick and we thought you would get better, but

no, you left us and died and are gone. You went to a place of happiness and we are in a place of hardship. Who will take your place. Who will teach us. like you did.

Number (2)
Papa when you were alive you used to see all the fights that would happen to us. The community has broken with us. Papa what is our worry? When you answer our letter you have to write down your mobile number. And now that you are a spirit you see the kind of trouble that has happened to us.

Papa you are in a place of happiness
We are in a place of hardship

Papa you have to write down your mobile number you have made us worry Ah!
Papa this is Luke I'm writing this letter to you with our family's worries!! That's all

Your's faithfull

Number (4)[1]
Papa a really big thing the family doesn't know I'm writing this letter in secret to you with the big worry of family members. Papa you have to send some money to us the amount is K30,000 Kina [about $20,000 dollars]. The money should go to your children papa you have to send it with Don Saraki

---

1. There was no "Number (3)" in Luke's letter. It went from "Number (2)" straight to "Number (4)."

You have to send exactly that amount

And papa you have to send me a flashlight like the one
Don has

That's all

Your faithfull Papa

<u>Number 5!!</u>

Papa the whole community inside Gapun. They all say to
me that I'm a boy who writes love letters to girls. And they
know that I'm a boy who tells Don his worries. And I know
that my worry will be delivered and I'll be happy afterwards
when I see that they've all wasted their time talking about
me. True true I've found the road.

Number 6!!

Papa true true you have to send that amount of money
to us · the amount is K30,000 Kina.

1) And you have to send a flashlight to me

2) Pap you have to send a satellite mobile phone, two of
   them

Papa will you send these things? The community will see a
big change happening in the family.

Your's faithfull papa
Love my father

Luke's letter is a moving microcosm of everything that makes
the Gapun villagers such sincere and poignant critics of the gro-
tesque inequalities that mar our world. The sweetness of Luke's
lament that his father has gone to a place of happiness, whereas he

and everyone else in the village remains in a place of hardship, is a pungent commentary on the way the villagers see their lives in relation to the countries, where Monei has gone.

But Luke's lament is not just an innocent observation, or a poetic reflection on the evanescence of life—it is a call for responsibility. Precisely because Monei has gone to a place of happiness (and by now presumably has secured employment as an accountant and lives in a house where everything is provided for him at the push of a button), he has to share, and the letter gets right to the point: Luke wants his father to deliver the goods. He throws in some presents for himself: the flashlight and the satellite mobile phones like I had. But the main point of writing to Monei in the afterlife is to ask for more money than the whole village would ever have seen (let alone earned) during Monei's entire lifetime.

This is the essence of what cargo beliefs are: peel away the histrionic trappings, and what you see at their core is a rock-hard realization that white people have too much stuff. And because they have so much, they have an obligation to share.

In this sense, Luke's letter was addressed as much to me as to his father. Maybe that's why he didn't mind that I read it, and why he agreed so readily that I could share it with others.

I read Luke's letter as an entreaty to white-skinned people everywhere, I see it as an appeal. I think it is a guileless call to acknowledge the privilege that white skin has acquired, and a gentle request that white people recognize the vast inequalities that we have begotten around the world. Most of all, it seems to me that Luke's letter is a heartfelt plea to begin to redress those inequalities by giving something back.

15: GOING TO HELL

BEFORE SIGMUND FREUD irrevocably changed our own understanding of dreams by saying that they reveal half-forgotten whispers of our childhood, most people in most places saw dreams as omens, or as messages from the spirit realm. Dreams pointed to the future, not, as in Freud's model, to the past. And so they remain in Gapun, where dreams are avidly discussed and interpreted as signs of future occurrences, not as traces of bygone events.

It was by talking about dreams—or, really, about an out-of-body experience, which in Gapun is pretty much the same thing as a dream (people leave their bodies when they dream, and travel)—that I discovered what villagers think about Hell.

All villagers are acquainted with Hell. Hell is the antithesis of Heaven. It is the place where sinners, as opposed to believers, are supposed to go when they give up their ghost. The occasional priests who came to Gapun threatened villagers with Hell, warning them that it is a place of damnation where they will end up for eternity if they swear, engage in polygamy, don't go to church, attempt an abortion, and so on. Some priests who traveled to

Gapun in the past brought pictures of this unsavory place, which they disingenuously passed around, knowing that villagers did not perceive the difference between drawings and photographs, and knowing, therefore, that the villagers believed that someone had actually visited Hell and returned with photographs of tortured souls toasting in agony.

Some villagers have even seen Satan. Old Kruni spoke occasionally of a "moving picture" he had watched at some point in the 1960s or '70s at the mission station in Marienberg. In the movie, Satan appeared. "He was decorated," I once overheard Kruni telling a group of adolescent boys. "Really nice decorations on his body. But he had wings like a flying fox. And he had two horns. And a spear, a big fork. Man, to plunge into people. Moving pictures don't lie," he continued. "Things are there and they photograph them."

ONE EVENING I was sitting with Erapo, a woman who, at age thirty-five, was one of the youngest people in the village to speak absolutely fluent Tayap in conversations with others. I liked Erapo because she was tough like my neighbor Ndamor. The oldest child in a family of four girls and four exceptionally belligerent boys, Erapo had been keeping other people in line her entire life. She had divorced her husband when he insisted on taking a second wife. She sent him packing to the village on the Sepik River from whence he came, keeping her seven children with her in Gapun.

Erapo had invited me to her house for an evening meal of sago jelly and boiled bandicoot, and after we had finished eating, we sat talking. She told me about a dream that she had had several days previously, in which she had seen me speaking in Tayap, saying that I was a child of Gapun. In her dream, I told her that when people die, there is medicine they take to turn white. In the same dream, she watched with fascination as a white sago pancake lay on a plate and started drawing breaths.

"*Fwhhh, fwhhh, fwhhh*," she said, imitating the spooky breathing pancake.

As Erapo was telling me her dream, her younger brother, Kak, came up into her house and sat down on the floor with us. Before we could discuss the possible meaning of Erapo's curious dream, Kak announced that he wanted to tell me about something that had happened to him the previous year. He had been meaning to come and tell me about it, he said, and seeing me sitting and chatting with his sister about dreams, he decided it was a good time to talk.

"But it wasn't a dream," Kak began.

"It was when they ensorcelled me the first time, last year. I was really sick, I had stopped eating. I went to Watam to get Apusi's father [a man who called himself Albet Profet and who claimed to be able to see, by praying, the identity of the sorcerer who had made someone sick], and he prayed over me—and he saw who it was who had ensorcelled me. After he prayed, I fell asleep.

"Only I don't think I fell asleep," Kak said. "I must have died. I left my body and I came up to a big road. There was a big house on it."

I asked Kak, "What kind of house?"

"A white man's house," he said impatiently, as though that should have been obvious. Kak was, after all, dead.

"I was standing there. I was dead. And a man, a really young man, was running, a white man. I saw him, it wasn't a dream. I had died. I left my body and went out. I went and saw this white man running in my direction. I started following him. We went and saw a big door that was there. It's the door that when you die, the door opens and you go in, one-way.

"And so I saw a woman coming too. A young woman. She was coming and I asked the man, 'Do you want me to follow that woman?'"

"Was she white?" I asked.

"She was white. There was no more black business," Kak said, laughing at my seeming naïveté. "She was white. So the man sees her and he says, 'Yeah, you can follow her.' OK, I started following the woman.

"And she says to me, 'Let's go see Hell.'"

THIS WHITE WOMAN was later revealed to be Kak's niece, Yakera, who had died several years previously after having been bitten by a large tarantula-like spider (whose venom had been made lethal through sorcery). She took Kak to see Hell by way of a detour. First, they went back to the house he had seen. And at this point, I entered the picture.

"We went up into the house," Kak said. "And inside this house, there were mountains of shoes. There was nothing else, just lots of shoes. The house was full of shoes."

"What kind of shoes?" I asked.

"The ones you had when you were here last time," Kak said to me. "Think of them."

Erapo, who clearly had heard her brother's story before, interrupted and said, "The kind you wore when you slipped and fell off the bridge going across Kawiengimin."

"*Which* of the times I slipped and fell off the bridge going across Kawiengimin?" I thought caustically. I slipped and fell off the damned half-submerged poles the villagers called bridges every time I set foot on them.

"The ones that are black-and-white?" I said, describing the pair of cheap knockoff Converse high-top sneakers that I had bought before I came because the water runs out of them quickly.

"That's the ones," Kak said. "And so the woman and I went around in the house and saw all these shoes. And she said to me, 'You see all these shoes? Before Don went to the village, he took these shoes and he used them in the village.' She told me this."

Kak looked at me expectantly.

I didn't know what to say. I wanted to protest that I had exactly four pairs of footwear in Gapun: a pair of sandals, a pair of rubber Wellington boots that I put on whenever I went out in the rainforest at night to pee because I didn't want to be bitten on the ankle in the middle of the night by a death adder, and two pairs of cheap canvas sneakers. That was four more pairs of footwear than any villager owned, granted, except the one young man who owned a single soccer shoe, which he proudly sported on his left foot whenever he played soccer. But owning four pairs of shoes hardly made me Imelda Marcos.

Kak paused to let his information about the shoes sink in, except that it didn't because I still haven't the faintest idea what it might mean. That the sneakers were a symbol of Kak's belief that I have endless supplies of cargo in my home in Heaven is clear enough. But why that cargo should manifest in mountains of fake Converse sneakers is a question I fear I would need Sigmund Freud himself to help me figure out decisively.

LEAVING ME TO stew in the story of my shoes, Kak continued his Dante-esque tour of the afterworld.

"We left the house, and I told the woman I was hungry. She said, 'Let's go.' When we were walking, I saw a little boy—Pita's boy," Kak said, using the Christian name of his cousin Kosai. "His boy who had just died, Njab. I saw him. When I went down from the house and looked outside, I saw him. Ah, I saw him. He came towards me, and I saw that he had changed. His skin was white."

"How did you recognize him?" I asked.

"His face was the same," Kak said. "But his skin was white. He went through the door that was opened. Ah, I saw through the door.

"*Tru*," Kak said, using the Tok Pisin word for "true" and the rising intonation that expresses wonder. "They talk about going to Heaven. Those countries, I'm telling you, there's another kind of light. And they look completely different from here. They're cities."

"You saw them?"

"I saw them through the door. When the kid went through, the big door opened. When it opened, I looked through it. I saw what was on the other side. When he went through, the door closed."

At that point Kak, said that he repeated to the young woman that he was hungry.

"She said, 'OK, let's go.' We went to another house, and it was full of food. The food was all already cooked. It was just there, waiting to be eaten. There was food like we make here in the village: taro and bananas and sweet-potato soup. But it was full of white men's food too: rice and tinned fish and tinned meat, coffee . . .

"I went in and said, 'I'm gonna eat,'" Kak said he told the woman.

"But she got cross," he continued. "'You can't eat that food. You haven't died yet. You're going to go back.' She said that to me. We had an argument. 'I'm hungry, I want to eat,' She said, 'No. You haven't died, you're going back. But before you go—let's go to Hell.'"

And so Kak went to Hell.

"I WAS THINKING," Kak said quietly. "People talk about 'Heaven' and 'Hell.' I know this. It's like if you swear too much, priests say, 'You swear, or you want to kill somebody, you're gonna go into hellfire.' They say that. And if you're a good person, you'll go to Heaven. That's what they say. OK, when the woman said, 'Come on, let's go see Hell,' we went inside Hell. And you know what?"

"What?" I said.

"Hell isn't fire. The priests all lie to us, saying that it's fire. Hell isn't fire. Hell is here. We're in Hell here.

"I saw the people inside Hell," Kak continued. "They were sweeping out toilets. I asked them, 'What are you doing?' They said, "We're sweeping out toilets. We're waiting for Jesus.'"

"What color was their skin?" I asked Kak, even though I already knew the answer.

"Black," he said flatly. "They had really black skin. And they were in a bad way. It's a place of hard work. It's the place where we are now.

"This," Kak said, "is Hell. Here. I woke up in my mosquito net. The woman sent me back to Hell."

16: WHAT ACTUALLY DIES WHEN A LANGUAGE DIES?

I HAVE COMPILED a dictionary of the Tayap language, but it has gaps. One entire area that is missing is the language's extensive lexicon for plants and trees. I am not a botanist, and even though at one point I actually schlepped specialist books with titles like *Handbook of the Flora of Papua New Guinea* into Gapun, I wasn't able, for the most part, to distinguish between—let alone identify or describe—the numerous vines, bushes, roots, trees, and grasses that exist in the villagers' rainforest. Walking through the forest, villagers would often point in the distance and mention the name of whatever tree or vine they happened to notice. I usually had no idea what they were pointing at—to an untrained eye, vegetation in a rainforest looks an awful lot alike. After telling me the name of whatever it was they had pointed at, villagers would often then add that the thing they had drawn my attention to was similar to another kind of plant they had gestured towards on some previous occasion, but "not too much" (*i no tumas*).

This is the equivalent of taking a Gapun villager who perhaps has never seen an automobile to a busy Los Angeles freeway interchange, waving in its general direction, and saying, "We call that one a Honda. It's like a Toyota, but not too much."

Needless to say, the information imparted on those rainforest promenades was almost invariably lost on me. Even when I was sure that I was looking at the same tree or vine or bush that someone was pointing at, I was usually unable to distinguish it in any meaningful way from most other trees, vines, or bushes growing around it.

My ineptness in this regard means that unless a trained botanist hastens to Gapun in the not-too-distant future and sits down with some old people, Tayap's unique nomenclature for rainforest flora will be lost forever. According to linguists who write about language death, such a loss will be a tragedy of practically cosmic proportions. One reason that linguists habitually cite for being concerned about language death is that small indigenous languages like Tayap are fragile treasure troves of knowledge about nature, climatic cycles, and the harmonious balance in ecological relationships. It is often suggested that such knowledge is precious and irreplaceable. It is lost at our collective peril. Local knowledge about the healing properties of different indigenous plants might help scientists find cures for diseases, linguists conjecture; it might help us think more holistically about environmental sustainability and well-being more generally. It might provide us with insights into nature and the natural world that can benefit all mankind.

LANGUAGE DEATH IS an emotional issue for linguists. In recent years, there has been a spate of publications reporting on language loss, and lamenting it. There is something self-serving about such lamentations since language, after all, is a linguist's bread and butter. Fewer languages mean fewer job opportunities (even if, granted, the overwhelming majority of linguists work on English or some other world language, most professional linguists wouldn't know an endangered language if it bit them).

Regardless of that, no one could dispute that the disappearance of a human language is cause for mourning. When a language dies, something unique, delicate, trellised, and ancient has been irrevocably lost. Languages are disappearing these days at an unprecedented rate: linguists estimate that 90 percent of the world's approximately six thousand languages are endangered. That figure, which might seem hyperbolic and unbelievable at first, becomes more comprehensible when you realize that most people in the world speak one (or more) of the one hundred largest languages. Those big languages are spoken by 96 percent of the world's population. This means that 4 percent of the world's population speaks the overwhelming majority of the world's languages. And those languages—thousands of them, many of them undocumented—are believed to be in danger of vanishing within the next one hundred years.

Tayap is, of course, one of those languages; it will certainly be gone within the next one hundred years. My own work will ensure that the language doesn't go down like the proverbial tree in the forest that no one hears. But when Tayap is extinguished, when the last prune-like old speaker of the language finally takes her leave and turns off the lights, what, exactly, will be lost?

LINGUISTS WHO WRITE books about language death usually include a chapter that asks some version of the question: "Why should we care?" And they offer a number of reasons why we should. These include the idea that linguistic diversity is better than uniformity; that languages express identity; that languages reveal particular knowledge about the world; and that languages are the repositories of a people's history.

All those reasons are good ones; they are all indisputably true and genuinely compelling. But they are bird's-eye views. They represent the assessment of experts who are privy to a vast panorama. The perspective of people who have lost or are losing their language will inevitably be quite different. People in Gapun can't be expected to care, and they don't care, that the little language they speak constitutes a singular contribution to the total linguistic diversity in the world. And they still have their identity, even if their local language is dissolving. They are still Gapuners—who else, after all, could they be? They are all still born in the rainforest surrounding their village; they grow up wading through the swamps where their parents pound and leach sago; they know exactly who owns the grasslands and the vast tracts of rainforest where they hunt—and the gardens where they grow food. It is true that the loss of the traditional stories that used to be known by old men like Kruni and Raya will make Gapuners more vulnerable to the claims of other nearby villages, should those villagers ever assert ownership rights over areas of Gapun's traditional land. But disputes about land will not make villagers any less, or any other, than Gapuners.

When it comes to particular knowledge about the world, and history, much of what once was specific to Gapun disappeared long before Tayap began to wane. Like a gigantic, implacable bulldozer, the twentieth century crushed the life out of everything that people in Gapun—and most everywhere else in Papua New Guinea—had ever believed or accomplished. Labor recruiters in the early decades of the century started a process of cultural reconfiguration when they took young men away and shipped them off to work as plantation laborers on faraway islands, sending them back several years later, with impressive stories and a new language. World War II caused the villagers to flee from their homes into the rainforest, where they lived in misery for at least a year, and where the population of the village was decimated by a dysentery outbreak that was probably brought by Japanese soldiers. As soon as the war ended, Catholic missionaries popped up, converting villagers to Christianity, and convincing them that their ancestral ways needed to be abandoned because they were Satanic. Cargo cults amplified this Christian message, exhorting villagers to destroy what was left of their traditional sacred objects, to stop passing on traditional stories to children, and to prepare for the second coming of Christ, who would change their black skin to white and reward them with the Glory of God, i.e., money, outboard motors, and corrugated-iron houses. A school appeared for a short time, teaching village children literacy skills that they put to use writing love missives, and letters to overseas mail-order catalogues that promise magic chants for fast cash and riches. Government officials turned up urging villagers to plant cash crops that few buyers ever came to buy. NGO representatives exhorted villagers to cut down all their trees. Corrupt politicians came with eager promises of development, and left sniggering counting the money they successfully swindled from the ingenuous villagers.

Throughout the twentieth century, and continuing today, villagers have been exploited, deceived, lied to, humiliated, cheated, and robbed by practically every outside person, entity, or organization with whom they have had contact. They haven't just been passive pawns in this process—they have actively and enthusiastically sought those contacts, and they have wanted to change. But Karl Marx's famous observation that "Men make their own history, but they do not make it as they please; they do not make it under self-selected circumstances" has a particular poignancy in Gapun's case because the history that villagers have made has effectively reached back retroactively and erased much of their collective life. It has left them bereft of their culture, ignorant of their traditions, impaired in their ability to control violence—and it will ultimately render them speechless in their ancestral tongue.

In a situation like this, what actually dies when a language dies is the last remnant of an utterly broken culture. Because the forces that flattened that culture, and broke it, are far beyond the control of the fifty or so remaining speakers of Tayap, it strikes me as insensitive and even patronizing for us to lament that villagers are abandoning their language. Yes, it is almost unbearably sad that this unique expression of how the human mind works will no longer be around to enrich the treasure chest of humanity. And who knows? Maybe one of those indistinguishable plants that villagers pointed out to me in the rainforest holds the cure to cancer.

But that is just too bad.

Rather than lament the loss of Tayap, which under the circumstances is akin to bemoaning the loss of a bald man's comb, we should perhaps instead be delighted and impressed by the fact that the villagers continue to live at all—and to thrive. They continue to plan, and act; they continue to swear and laugh and love and hope. Big men like Kruni and Monei liked to complain that villagers these days have "grown down"—they have grown weaker, slower, and more stupid than their ancestors, to the point that they are actually, physically shrinking. Maybe they're right. Villagers have certainly been worn down by the weight of a century of change that saw them giving up everything and getting virtually nothing in return. But even if the villagers are diminished, they are still proud and irascible—and they are still going strong in their swampy rainforest home. Their society is becoming increasingly violent and dysfunctional, and who knows, maybe it will implode or tear itself apart in the not-too-distant future.

But surely we can also say the same thing about our society, and about ourselves.

WHEN I LIVED in Gapun in the mid-1980s, old Raya told me stories of how, in the time of his grandfather, the rainforest was full of different kinds of supernatural beings. These ranged from powerful spirits called *emari*, who commonly took the form of giant crocodiles, to mischievous elflike dwarves who lived in the crowns of trees. People of Raya's grandfather's generation used to occasionally encounter these beings in the rainforest, and they deferred to them and paid them respect by talking to them in Tayap and leaving them small offerings of betel nut or tobacco whenever they sensed that the beings were nearby.

When Raya was a young boy, he once saw one of the elves. On a walk through the rainforest, he and a friend spied a small figure who whistled in an eerie way, and who had decorated his septum and his ears with lengths of knotted string. Thinking they had happened upon a young boy like themselves, Raya and his friend chased after him—until he ran straight up a tree. At that point, the two boys realized with a start that the creature they had been running after wasn't a human being at all. They turned around and hightailed it back to the village as fast as their eight-year-old legs could carry them.

Raya laughed nostalgically when he remembered that encounter, and then he grew serious. Nobody ever sees forest beings these days, he told me in a quiet, puzzled tone. He guessed that this must be because they have retreated; they've either moved ever deeper into the rainforest, or they've paddled away over the sea. Raya surmised that the departure of the forest beings was due to the arrival of white men in Papua New Guinea. Perceiving that villagers were no longer interested in them and were no longer paying them any attention or respect, the crocodile spirits and the tree-dwelling dwarves must have packed up their belongings, and left.

Whenever I remember Raya's story about the departure of the supernatural life that used to throb in the heart of the villagers' rainforest, I find myself thinking about Tayap.

And sometimes, I think that maybe at the end of the day the villagers of Gapun haven't abandoned Tayap at all. Maybe Tayap—worn down by decades of disinterest, weary of neglect, and disconsolate at what the future seems to hold in store . . . maybe Tayap, instead, in the end, has abandoned them.

17: THE END

THIS HAS BEEN a book about endings: of traditional ways of living, of old men's lives, of the pre–"modern living" layout of an entire village, of exuberant creative obscenity, of a tiny Papuan language that has been spoken for generations by a feisty group of people in the middle of a rainforest.

At the end of this book about endings, I conclude with another kind of end: the end of my visits to Gapun.

I have enjoyed many hours of enjoyment and conviviality in Gapun, but I also had to leave the village several times earlier than I wanted to because of violence or the imminent threat of violence. The attack by rascals that left Kawri dead resulted in me abandoning my research in Papua New Guinea and not returning for almost fifteen years. The rumors that I would be robbed of everything I had at the end of my second long-term stay in 2009 led me to enlist a helicopter to pluck me out of the village like a raisin from a bun.

I went back to Gapun after having been whisked away by the helicopter. The following year, I came and went without incident, staying in the village for one month. Four years later, in 2014, I returned for what I thought would be a six-month stay. That stay, alas, also ended up being cut short because of violence.

The reason for the violence this time had nothing to do with me. It was a dispute between Gapuners and men from the sorcerer-laden village of Sanae. The dispute was ostensibly because two young villagers were accused of raping the daughter of a Sanae man and a Gapun mother. The real reason, however, I am convinced, was because the girl's father had been growing marijuana on village land, and village women had complained that he was bringing strange men from faraway places into the rainforest to sample and buy the dope. The presence of those unknown, stoned men in their forest, Gapun women said, was making them feel unsafe. I believe that this man, sensing that his livelihood was under threat, got his relatives—one of whom was widely feared as a mentally unstable murderer—to band together to intimidate villagers and teach them not to mess with him.

So one morning at dawn, sixteen men from Sanae, armed to the teeth with spears, bush knives, big bows and arrows, axes, and, most worrisomely, "wire catapults" (the slingshots that shoot barbed steel darts fletched with cassowary feathers), poured into Gapun.

The men came with the intention of killing the two young men who had been accused of rape, and burning down their houses. One of those houses happened to be right next to mine, and if it had gone up in flames, mine would have too.

I witnessed this invasion through eyes still sandy with sleep, and as I stood watching the ambush and hearing villagers' panicked screams, faded scenes from childhood Westerns drifted through my consciousness: scenes where Hollywood "Indians" smeared in war paint ride into an enemy village on horseback, set fire to teepees, and shoot all the panicked, fleeing inhabitants in the back with well-aimed arrows.

As a young boy in a movie theater, I remembered a scene like that as exciting.

As an adult man in real life, I can attest, it is absolutely, grippingly terrifying.

The two men who were the targets of the Sanae men's wrath had somehow managed to hear them approaching and had sped off into the rainforest just in time. Finding them gone, the Sanae men began wreaking havoc. They shot random village pigs with their spears, and they threatened the families of the men. They destroyed everything in the house next to mine, and they repeatedly set it on fire. Luckily, the flames they lit were determinedly doused by their female relatives who lived in Gapun—and who gathered in the house to try to calm the invaders down. The village men did nothing at first, but after a few hours of quietly swallowing the Sanae men's intimidations, they revolted. They grabbed their own spears and bush knives, and, whooping in indignation and rage, they routed the invaders, who fled back into the rainforest.

With that action, the ante of the conflict had been upped. In the days that followed, persistent rumors said that the Sanae men would soon be back, this time carrying guns.

Having twenty years earlier witnessed the carnage that a single gun in the hands of a criminal can wreak in the rainforest, I decided not to wait this one out. I used my satellite telephone to call the man in a village five hours away who brought me to Gapun in his outboard-motor-powered rowboat, and I left.

THE VIOLENCE THAT continues to wrack the area around Gapun is extreme, but it is not really an exception or an aberration. It is symptomatic of the more general condition of anger and escalating conflict that exists today throughout the entire country.

Since its independence from Australia in 1975, Papua New Guinea has steadily contracted as a functioning state. Services and support for rural populations, which make up the vast bulk of the country, has dried to a trickle. The country is formally a democracy, but the politicians whom people vote for because they promise to give them things like outboard motors or money, in fact provide them with nothing. They are too busy "filling up their own banks," as jaded villagers put it wearily. Transparency International, a nonprofit NGO based in Berlin that uses expert assessments and opinion surveys to determine the levels of corruption, agrees. In 2017, it ranked Papua New Guinea as one of the most corrupt countries in the world, noting it near the bottom of its list: number 135 among 180 countries listed.

In the area around Gapun, in addition to having had no school to speak of since the mid-1990s (and none at all since 2009), there is also no functioning hospital within several hundred miles. The nearest so-called aid post, which is in the village of Watam—a four-hour journey from Gapun by foot and then dugout canoe—most often has no medicine at all; its stock for the most part consists solely of lubricated condoms, which have two uses in this area: villagers rub the lubrication on their skin as a way of trying to alleviate ringworm, and they tie the condoms together to provide a sling for their homemade slingshots they use to kill small birds, which they then roast over a fire and eat as snacks.

There are no roads in the area around Gapun, and very little money enters the village. For a while during the mid- to late 2000s, the villagers earned some money selling cocoa beans to buyers who would occasionally come to the village and underpay them. But that market collapsed in 2011 when the region was hit by a parasite called the cocoa pod borer. And when cocoa collapsed, there was nothing. Now the only people from outside the area who come to Gapun are con men like the wannabe politician Onjani and "glass men" who claim to be able to identify sorcerers by staring at mirrors smeared with oil.

My educated guess, at least for the part of the country I know best, is that in the years to come, the situation will get increasingly worse. If present trends continue, dissatisfaction among the kinds of young men most likely to become criminal rascals will intensify, which means that more and more of them actually will become rascals. The people living in rural areas will remain beyond the reach of even the most basic educational or health services. The rural population is growing (partly because of Christian opposition to traditional postpartum taboos) and as it continues to increase, conflicts about land will intensify and doubtless become violent. The complete absence of any functioning police force or court system except in the country's few towns will mean that outside those towns, anarchy can reign. The young rascals with the most smuggled-in guns (and there is a brisk trade, these days, in guns, smuggled into Papua New Guinea from across the border in the Indonesian province of West Papua) will win.

All this suggests that the future of Papua New Guinea may have more in common with a place like Somalia than it does with Australia or the European countries that Gapun villagers fantasize they one day will find the road to become like.

IN THIS CONTEXT of steadily escalating violence, this book marks the end of my work in Gapun. During my last trip to the village, I grew tired of "sleeping like a pig," as the villagers like to say: I grew tired of falling asleep from exhaustion with one ear cocked and one eye open, ready to flee into the bush at the slightest sign that the village was under attack. I grew tired of the isolation, weary of worrying that the blast of a gun might rip through and light up the thick tropical night, sick of thinking that I might lose all my work and that I might not be able to get out of the village, or that I might be killed.

I reckon my karmic dance card for reckless adventure, close calls, near-death experiences, and exotic illnesses is full, several times over, after my years in the village. (I've had malaria five times and dengue fever twice; I've hosted whole populations of intestinal parasites; I've had countless gaping tropical sores; and once my entire body was covered for three weeks by an itchy red fungus that looked like and felt like—and, worst of all, smelled like—athlete's foot.) I also feel that now that I have completed my grammar of the Tayap language, and written this book, the obligations I have towards the villagers to document their language and their lives are finally, after three decades, more or less fulfilled—to my satisfaction, at least.

I doubt that they would agree. But since I genuinely am not in a position of opening the heavens and calling forth the change that villagers all so ardently desire, I admit insufficiency. I concede defeat.

Working in an isolated village in the middle of a tropical rainforest swamp is never dull, but it is not easy. It is not like being a character in *Avatar*, nor is it the titillating macho adventure promoted by television personalities who have adopted furry mammalian names like Wolf or Bear. University-based researchers like me do not enter a place like Gapun together with an eight-person film crew and a chartered airplane scheduled to fly everyone away after a few days of play-roughing it. We go alone, with very limited resources; we incur debts; and we stay for a long time.

I've now stayed for long enough.

The end.

POSTSCRIPT: AFTER THE END

AT THE BEGINNING of this book, I mentioned Margaret Mead, the ur-mother of modern anthropology. Mead is still one of the few anthropologists known outside the discipline to a wider public. And like mothers everywhere, over the years Mead has evoked the whole gamut of emotions from her descendants, ranging from adulation to abuse.

In the 1940s and '50s, Mead was adored as a celebrity who dispensed sought-after advice on everything from the vicissitudes of the Soviet character to whether women should engage in premarital sex. By the 1980s, her star had dimmed, and she began to be criticized and dismissed. One prominent anthropologist named Derek Freeman went so far as to mount a personal crusade in which he attempted to commit symbolic matricide, insisting that Mead was a deluded charlatan, that she ingenuously believed lies that people who were having a laugh at her expense told her, and that, generally speaking, she got everything wrong.

Mead survived that determined attempt to discredit her and her legacy, and now that the dust kicked up by the famous Mead–Freeman controversy has settled, it has become clear that Mead will endure.

One reason she will endure is because the questions that Margaret Mead asked, and the way she asked them, will never become dated or irrelevant.

Mead believed that people have a responsibility to engage with others who are very different from themselves. Everyone has that responsibility, but the ones who have more of it than others are people who live in countries like the United States and western Europe. These are the places of privilege from which the active agents of change have emerged—active agents who have purposefully and irrevocably transformed the lives of people in faraway places, through colonialism; by converting them to Christianity; by drawing them into the capitalist world by conscripting them as servants, as factory workers, as plantation laborers; by imposing borders that separate them where none existed before; by engulfing them into previously unimagined and demeaning racial hierarchies in which they find themselves on the bottom, with white people looming over and braying orders at them from the top.

Margaret Mead was not opposed to many of those sorts of changes. She didn't expect or want the people she worked with in Samoa or New Guinea or Bali to remain preserved in aspic, and she recognized that non-Western people, confronted with the possibilities that new phenomena like paid labor or Christianity presented, often embraced them willingly.

What she called upon her audience in the United States to do was to learn something about the people whose lives Americans inexorably were changing, and to use that knowledge to reflect critically on American culture, and on Western culture more generally, to decenter it from being considered as the be-all and end-all measure of all human life, and all human value.

A few years before Margaret Mead embarked on her first fieldwork in Samoa in 1925, Sigmund Freud gave a series of lectures in which he declared that there had been three great revolutions in the history of mankind's understanding of itself. The first was the Copernican revolution, which debunked the notion that the earth that humans inhabited was the center of the universe. The second was the Darwinian revolution, which dislodged humanity from its privileged position as a special creation of God. The third revolution, according to Freud (who was not, himself, of modest disposition) was his own, psychoanalytic revolution. His discovery of the unconscious and its role in our lives, he said, showed that man was not even master in his own house, and that the importance we have always placed on reason is misguided since we all are riven with repressed forces that continually wreak havoc from within.

To Freud's cheerfully self-gratifying list, I would add a fourth revolution: the revolution wrought by Margaret Mead and her anthropologist colleagues of the early twentieth century. That revolution hinged on the shockingly novel idea that all cultures, however outlandish they may seem from a Western perspective, have value and dignity. And that the difference between "them" and "us" can teach us all something valuable about human variation, human potentiality, and our place in a world where many different viewpoints, perspectives, customs, behaviors, and understandings all coexist and, ideally, can flourish.

THE IDEA THAT people who are different from us can teach us something can be a controversial proposition, however. Many people whose lives are invoked to teach us lessons about our place in the world respond to being called upon to do so with indignation. They do not feel that their role in life is to teach other, usually more privileged, people anything at all. And they resent—rightly, in my view—the idea that their lives should be displayed like a tattered classroom chart, or dissected like a high school bull-frog, for the edification of earnest Western liberal humanists who feel better about themselves if they convince themselves that they know more about the world.

There is also the question of whether we actually ever do learn anything, no matter how well taught, or dearly bought, the lesson might be. As the dark, cold clouds that seem disconcertingly similar to the ones that enveloped Europe in the 1930s appear again on the horizon and edge ever more menacingly into our lives today, one might begin to despair about whether knowledge about anything, these days, is of any use at all.

BECAUSE OF THE patronizing implications of proposing that Gapuners might serve as our uplifting instructors, and also because I lack Margaret Mead's breezy confidence that learning about exotic cultures is enough to have a noticeable impact on the forces that structure our world, I will not conclude this book by offering any self-assured Meadean advice about what Gapun villagers might teach us.

On the other hand, though, I wouldn't have written a book about the villagers if I didn't think that their lives had value, and are worth thinking about. Furthermore, I wholeheartedly agree with Margaret Mead that privileged people have a responsibility to engage with the lives of people who are less privileged than themselves, even if that engagement restricts itself simply to knowing that those other people exist somewhere else in the world, and that they have their own viewpoints about their existence—viewpoints that may confound, complicate, and challenge our own.

Rather than try to formulate what the villagers in Gapun can teach us, let me instead mention some of the things that I came to learn from them.

THE FIRST THING I learned from villagers is banal, but it still bears repeating, and it is this: despite the fact that they live in a backwater swamp in the middle of a faraway New Guinean rainforest, and despite the fact that their day-to-day lives are exceedingly different from my own, and from that of anyone I know in the United States or Europe, villagers are, in fact, at the end of the day, not all that different from us.

One of the main things that I wondered about when I first went to Papua New Guinea was the banalities of life—for example, what people talked about when they were just chatting. Reading anthropology books, it is easy to get the impression that non-Western people like Gapuners never just sit around and shoot the breeze. Instead, steeped in ritual and weighted down with tradition, all they do is declaim. In anthropological studies written up until sometime in the 1960s, they do so, to boot, in pedantically literal translations, which have the effect of making them sound like Elizabethan actors onstage: "I do not desire that thou shouldst take a new woman," one famous anthropologist quotes a Trobriand Islands woman from Papua telling her lover. "Just thou and I."[1]

Reading studies like those as a young anthropology student, I never quite believed that living people, anywhere on the

---

1. Bronislaw Malinowski, *The Sexual Life of Savages* (Boston: Beacon Press, 1987), page 287.

planet, actually spent their days perorating like King Lear or Lady Macbeth, and I was curious to know exactly what people in a place like Gapun said to one another when they woke up in the morning; when they sat socializing with their spouses, or their friends; and when they spoke to their children.

It turns out that while many of the topics of conversation, inevitably, are different (people in the United States and Europe complain to their spouses, over breakfast of cereal or eggs or croissants and coffee, about the injustices foisted upon them in their workplaces; people in Gapun complain to their spouses, over breakfast of boiled mangrove slugs on sago jelly, about the possibly ensorcelled hooks they think a visiting sorcerer may have implanted in their bodies), many are the same: speculation about who is having an affair with whom, displeasure at a neighbor's possibly critical remark, rumblings about a relative's stinginess, worry about a sick friend, laughter at a minor mishap, plans for the day to come. And the tenor and cadences of the conversations are similar. Conversations are colloquial; confidences are exchanged in simple, everyday language. No Shakespearean flourishes, no Prosperian declamations.

Senses of humor are also similar, or at least recognizable. Villagers love slapstick comedy. Favorite stories are about people who become so startled by an unexpected noise or by the unanticipated sudden encounter in the rainforest with a snake, a wild pig, or a cassowary, that they fall to the ground and *pispis pekpek wantaim* (urinate and defecate on themselves). Stories involving these elements are retold constantly as entertainment. One story that involved an old Sanae woman who became so terror-stricken by an earthquake that she rolled on the ground and *pispis pekpek wantaim* has been recycled countless times during my stays in the village. Each time it is recounted, listeners scream, laughing so hard that they have to hold their sides.

This penchant for slapstick makes me certain that villagers would absolutely love Charlie Chaplin. And they would undoubtedly be as entertained by the actor Jerry Lewis as much as the French apparently are.

Topics of anger and conflict are similar too. Extramarital affairs are a dependable source of strife, as is laziness on the part of a spouse and recalcitrance on the part of one's children. Sound familiar? Theft occurs frequently and gives rise to numerous conflicts.

Another recurring topic of anger concerns animal poo. Every morning, one of the first things that village women do when they wake up is patrol the grounds around their house with a shovel that is poised to scrape away the feces that the pigs that wander throughout the village deposit on the women's "premises." A continual source of rancor is that not all women own pigs. This means that any pig that has dared to defecate in the yard of such a woman during the night presses the Gapun equivalent to an alarm clock, one that sounds off and wakes up everybody who is still managing to sleep.

"I don't own pigs that I should have to shovel up pig shit-o!" the alarm bell screams, shrilly bringing whatever dreams one had retreated into during the cool dawn minutes to an abrupt and undignified end.

"You women who own pigs, come over here and shovel up the shit in my yard-o! I'm sick of shoveling pig shit! Come on, where are you?! I don't see you shoveling up the shit of your pigs! Get over here now and shovel shit-o!"

Having lived in Manhattan, where strangers monitor the toileting behavior of dogs walked by their owners with eyes as sharp as a hawk's—and with a hawk's shriek, too, that they loudly emit to publicly shame any owner who neglects to bend down, hand scrunched inside a little black plastic baggie, and carefully collect up off the sidewalk each and every one of his or her pet's freshly laid turds—I can attest that anger about having to deal with the droppings left by other people's animals is a widely shared, and quite possibly universal, human trait.

AMIDST SUCH SCENES of familiarity, there were also, needless to say, instances of hearty incommensurability.

The villagers' caregiving practices gave me pause at first: the blithe handing over of butcher knives to grasping babies; the continual ordering to fetch this, do that; the violent threats. Over time, though, I came to see that the style of caregiving practiced by Gapun mothers resulted in exceptionally capable and competent young children. And once children begin to speak and show their *save* by acting independently, adults treat them much the same way they treat other adults. They don't hide talk about anything from them, they joke with them, they beg them for betel nut (children always seem to have a secret stash hidden in the corners of the little net bags they all carry), and they rely on them for gossip. Because small children come and go freely in all the village houses, they are valued as spies who are privy to a great deal of information that adults can't easily access. The early distracting routines, in which babies are turned out to face the village and directed to look at nonexistent pigs, teach children that they can't trust what anyone says. Instead, they understand that they have to work things out for themselves. Those skills come in useful, and much of the information that villagers possess about one another has its source in the intelligence taken in by tiny, sharply tuned eyes and stealthily pricked little ears.

An important difference between common Western-style care-giving and the villagers' way of interacting with their children is that the overwhelming majority of village parents don't ever "pun-ish" their children. They shout at them and threaten them, and mothers sometimes whack a noncompliant child with her wooden cooking tongs, or throw the tongs across the room in a usually well-aimed shot at the child. But the only result that such an action inevitably has is that the child screams and runs down out of the house and off into the rainforest. The mother will shout darkly "*Yu bai kam!*" ("You'll be back!") after the fleeing child, but the result of her actions is that she is left to either find another child willing to carry out the intended task, or she has to do it herself. When the child who ran away does return, often several hours later, the matter has invariably been dropped and is forgotten.

The only people in the village I have ever observed beating a child—that is, holding the child by an arm and hitting him or her repeatedly with a straw broom, a stick, or, in one particularly egregious case, a bicycle chain that the child's father had acquired somewhere—were all men like Rafael who strongly identified as good Catholics, and who also spent a few years attending the primary school that used to exist in the neighboring village of Wongan.

In my darkest moments, I sometimes think that the only prac-tical knowledge that Christianity and Western education has given the villagers of Gapun is proficiency in how to beat their children.

Oh, that, and proficiency in a language that has come to replace their ancestral tongue.

THIS ALL LEADS me to what is perhaps the most important lesson I learned from the villagers: there is no such thing as that cherished fetish of Western fantasy, namely the "untouched savage." The island of New Guinea, along with the Amazon basin, is the only place on Earth where we still occasionally are informed in breathless headlines that some new "undiscovered tribe" has been found.

I'm never sure what we are expected to feel when we read such stories. Excitement? Triumph? Sorrow?

There is rarely ever a follow-up story to the ones about "first contact," usually because it always turns out that the supposedly undiscovered tribe had, in fact, been in contact with missionaries, plantation workers, and trade-store proprietors for many years prior to their purported discovery. Sometimes, the tribe turns out to be a group of people who grew tired of being made sick and degraded by settler colonialists, and who retreated deeper into the rainforest to escape them—only to be flushed out again by gonzo "explorers" and nosy journalists hungry for a headline.

What the bogus stories about undiscovered tribes tell us is that the farthest reaches of the globe are not "untouched" at all. On the contrary, every nook and cranny of humanity, at this point, has been brutally fondled and painfully probed by the sticky fingers of colonialism and capitalist exploitation. The result is often everything other than happy. Gapun is far from the only indigenous society that has seen its traditional culture wither and its ancestral language rendered mute. Places like Gapun exist everywhere, and they are becoming more numerous with every passing year.

I LEARNED FROM villagers that we all are linked to one another, in circuitous and frequently perplexing ways, but linked together nonetheless. Villagers identified me—no, they *recognized* me—as a member of a community that extends far beyond the limits of their swampy rainforest home. They marshaled ideas about Heaven, about the afterlife, and about change—ideas that my Western culture had introduced to them—to draw me into that community, to hold me accountable, and to make me responsible.

If the lives of the villagers of Gapun have anything to teach us at all, it is perhaps that there are people in faraway places in the world who enthusiastically and ingenuously insist on a kind of mutuality, a kind of sameness, and an affirmation of community that many of us, on the contrary, prefer to disavow or deny. Those people call upon us to reexamine that disavowal and overcome that denial. They enjoin us to stop only taking from them, to stop encouraging and facilitating the dissolution of their cultures and their languages and then withdrawing and abandoning them, leaving them to stagger through the wreckage, and to wonder in bewilderment what in the world it was they gave it all up for.

A NOTE ABOUT THE NAMES IN THIS BOOK

ANTHROPOLOGICAL WORK LIKE this book is not fiction. "The people are real, the cases are real," to steal an opening line from a popular American television show in which an acerbic, tight-faced old woman, Judge Judy, listens to small claims court cases and passes judgment on them, but only after she has first belittled and ridiculed some of—or more often all—the people who seem to provoke her to apoplexy merely by daring to show up and stand before her in her television courtroom.

Despite anthropology not being fiction, one of the complaints that anthropologists frequently hear about their work from historians is that the detailed descriptions of people and activities that we provide are often little better than fiction. What we write is useless as history, they say, because these days anthropologists usually change the names of the people, and sometimes even the names of the places, they write about.

The reason for giving people and places pseudonyms is, of course. to protect their identities; it is an expression of concern, an assumption of ethical responsibility. Whether such disguise always is necessary is debatable. What is certain, though, is that the practice does constitute a serious deficiency in terms of reliability, and what historians say is true: the use of pseudonyms in anthropological writing makes it of very limited value to them or anyone else who might want to use it in the future to understand the past.

In my first book about Gapun, I didn't change any names because I saw that work as a documentation of village life in the 1980s that might be valuable one day to the villagers themselves. No villager has ever read the book (or, indeed, any other book), and who knows, maybe no one from Gapun ever will read it. But to give the villagers pseudonyms would have bewildered and insulted them since the one thing they have looked in my book to see has been their names, and that has always been satisfying to them. "It's in the book," they say meaningfully, pointing to their name, undoubtedly imbuing its appearance with a cosmological significance that I would rather not think about.

This book is a more honest take on my life in Gapun than that last one. Because some of what I write about individual villagers is not especially flattering, I have decided that it is necessary, this time, to change the names of many of the villagers I mention. Some names I have not changed. The names of most people I discuss in the first book and who are now deceased, for example, are not pseudonyms. But I have changed many of the young people's names, and if I say anything uncomplimentary about anybody, then that person's name is also probably a pseudonym.

This sleight of hand may vex a future historian of the lower Sepik River area of Papua New Guinea, but if that improbable scholar or anybody else really thinks it is crucial to know the identities of the villagers and the details of the events I write about here, they can contact me—or, when I am no longer around, they are welcome to find the archive into which I, in my dotage, hopefully, will have deposited my field notes and all my recordings and transcripts from the village, and they can search through them.

ACKNOWLEDGMENTS

THIS BOOK IS based on research made possible by generous grants over the years by the Swedish Agency for Research Cooperation with Developing Countries, the Swedish Council for Research in the Humanities and Social Sciences, Australian National University, the National Endowment for the Humanities, the Wenner-Gren Foundation for Anthropological Research, the John Simon Guggenheim Memorial Foundation, and the Swedish Research Council. I thank the University of Chicago and Uppsala University for providing me with research leave that has allowed me to stay in Papua New Guinea for extended periods of time during my most recent visits. I am also grateful to The Bergman Estate on Fårö for a weeklong residency, during which I put the finishing touches on the manuscript, in Ingmar Bergman's house, humbly seated at the great auteur's writing desk.

The book was written during two stints I spent as a visiting professor at Divine Word University in Madang, Papua New Guinea. I am indebted to John Burton for facilitating those visits, and also to everyone else who made my stay in Madang pleasant and productive: John Mackerell, Pam Norman, Cecilia Nembou,

Fidelma Takaili, Iwona Kolodziejczyk, Gert van den Berg, Patricia Paraide, David Lloyd, Edwina Jangi, Barbara Tseraha, Sr. Miriam Dlugosz, and Frs. Philip Gibbs, Patrick Gesch, and Garrett Roche.

My agent, Doug Stewart, was enthusiastic from the moment I approached him about this project. His supportive advice and extensive editorial suggestions at a crucial stage were invaluable. My sharp-eyed editor at Algonquin, Kathy Pories, gently but firmly shepherded me through the process of transforming my manuscript into a book. What could have been a painful experience was instead an enjoyable and educational one. Robin Cruise's superb copyediting filtered my prose through a fine-meshed net of linguistic acuity.

Several chapters in various stages of completion have been presented at Monash University, University of Cambridge, Divine Word University, Uppsala University, Stockholm University, Chinese University of Hong Kong, and University of Gävle. I thank everyone who commented on the text on those occasions for all the helpful feedback I received.

Ana Deumert, Emily Martin, and Sharon Rider read the entire first draft and gave me encouragement and generous, incisive, and thoughtful criticism. Christopher Stroud and Jonas Tillberg read and commented on each chapter as it was written, and then they reread it when it was rewritten again. And again, ad nauseam. I am eternally grateful to both.

The people to whom I owe the largest debt are the villagers of Gapun—past, present, and future. They are with me every day of my life.

Hammars, Fårö, Sweden
August 21, 2018

DEDICATION

I DEDICATE THIS book to Kaŋirase Mbanu, my neighbor Ndamor's bossy little four-year-old boy. I came to love Kaŋirase during my last trip to Gapun. He was the boy who was my "security guard," walking around with me at night, shining my flashlight into his eyes, and who cheekily told me "Open your hole" when I lied to him to get him to come out from underneath my house. (I renamed him in the chapters where he appears with the easier-to-read pseudonym Amani.)

Kaŋirase was such an effective and beguiling *sukuriti* that when I left the village, I told him that I would put him in my big metal patrol box and take him home with me, giving him a biscuit to eat during the journey.

He was all for it, he said. But he wanted two biscuits.

THIS BOOK IS for you, Kaŋirase *bilong mi, tarangu*, with heartfelt hopes that your future will be brighter and more promising than anything I, after thirty years working in Papua New Guinea, am right now able to discern or imagine.